ATLAS OF ALABAMA

NEAL G. LINEBACK
Director and Editor

CHARLES T. TRAYLOR
Cartographic Director

THE UNIVERSITY OF ALABAMA PRESS
University, Alabama

PHOTO CREDITS

Alabama Bureau of Publicity and Information (ABPI)

Alabama Department of Conservation and Natural Resources (ADCNR)

Alabama Development Office (ADO)

Alabama Forestry Commission (AFC)

Alabama Highway Department (AHD)

David Blakeman

Delta Air Lines, Inc. (DAL)

Geological Survey of Alabama (GSA)

Rodney Huey

Humble Oil & Refining Company (HORC)

Andy Russell

United States Air Force (USAF)

Larry Walker

Copyright © 1973 by
THE UNIVERSITY OF ALABAMA PRESS
ISBN 0–8173–9000–6
Library of Congress Catalog Card Number 72–11148
Manufactured in the United States of America

DEDICATED TO

STAFF

Neal G. Lineback
Director and Editor

Charles T. Traylor
Cartographic Director

Jo Ann Bonham
Cartographer

Clay P. Davis
Cartographer

Richard Brough
Design Consultant

H. Don Hays
Associate Director, Editorial Staff

Frank D. Huttlinger
Editorial Staff

Walter F. Koch
Editorial Staff

Sara C. Spiller
Secretary

Shirley M. Baird
Varitypist

CONTRIBUTORS

DR. SIDNEY C. BELL
Department of Agricultural Economics and Rural Sociology
Auburn University

COLONEL BILL R. BLALOCK
Army ROTC
The University of Alabama

MISS JO ANN BONHAM, Cartographer
Department of Geology and Geography
The University of Alabama

MR. JAMES J. BRITTON
Alabama State Chamber of Commerce
Montgomery, Alabama

DR. NICHOLAS E. D'ANDREA
Department of Geology and Geography
Troy State University

MRS. CLAY P. DAVIS, Cartographer
Department of Geology and Geography
The University of Alabama

MR. W. B. DeVALL
Department of Forestry
Auburn University

DR. JAMES F. DOSTER
Department of History
The University of Alabama

DR. PATRICK FERGUSON
Department of Education
The University of Alabama

DR. MARY FISH
Department of Economics
The University of Alabama

DR. WILLIAM O. GUNTHER
Department of Economics
The University of Alabama

MR. W. KNOX HAGOOD
Department of Broadcast and Film Communication
The University of Alabama

MR. H. DONALD HAYS
Department of Geology and Geography
The University of Alabama

DR. SELWYN HOLLINGSWORTH
Department of Sociology
The University of Alabama

DR. W. GARY HOOKS
Department of Geology and Geography
The University of Alabama

MR. REUEL HUFFMAN, III
Center for Business and Economic Research
The University of Alabama

DR. TRAVIS H. HUGHES
Department of Geology and Geography
The University of Alabama

PREFACE

The dictionary defines an atlas as "a volume of maps," but such a description of the *ATLAS OF ALABAMA* would be incomplete. This atlas is designed to be much more than a collection of descriptive maps of Alabama. The desire of the Atlas Committee was that this work objectively describe the physical, cultural, and economic characteristics of the State in a manner that would involve the most effective use of maps, graphs and text. It is hoped that this work will serve a dual purpose by providing a ready reference source of geographical information for the people of Alabama and by depicting the State of Alabama in an objective, impartial way to readers beyond its borders.

The geographical inventory that is here provided is essential to understanding relationships which exist between *man* and the *land*. While most people recognize geographic differences between two areas, many fail to realize how the role or function of one affects that of the other. Maps provide the tools which enable the reader to obtain an "overall view" by permitting a visual comprehension of geographic distributions and interrelationships.

"Where?" and "why?" were the two main questions which confronted the director, contributors and editors of the book. To know one without the other affords only an incomplete understanding of the geography of Alabama. For this reason every effort was made to explain the location factors for the various phenomena shown on the maps. In order to accomplish this end, each subject was divided into a graphics (maps) and a text section, the first showing where the phenomenon occurred and the latter telling why.

It is hoped that this atlas represents only a beginning, and that periodic updating and additions will occur in the future. Obviously, much of the census information will be dated even before publication, but that detracts little from the value of an atlas. It is all here—"under one roof"—so to speak, representing a major geographic study of Alabama at this point in time.

A work such as the *ATLAS OF ALABAMA* represents the coordination of the efforts of many people involved in the research, writing, editing, cartography, photography, and publishing. A particularly critical aspect of an atlas is the cartography. My heartfelt thanks go out to Charles Tim Traylor and his cartographic staff, who worked so diligently and proficiently toward making this publication a credit to the University, the State and the geographic discipline. Many thanks also go to the editors, the design consultant, and the many contributors who worked under such rigid deadlines. I owe a deep debt of gratitude to members of the administration of The University of Alabama and the Department of Geology and Geography for their moral support and their firm belief that a state atlas is a prerequisite for both constructive state growth and public support of that growth.

Neal G. Lineback, Director
The ATLAS OF ALABAMA Project

CONTENTS

Contributors	iv
Preface	vi
Reference Map	viii
Introduction	x

PHYSICAL LANDSCAPE

Geology	2
Physiography and Topography	5
Soils	8
Water Resources	10
Weather and Climate	12
Natural Vegetation	15

CULTURAL AND SOCIAL PATTERNS

Early Explorations	18
Early Boundaries and Surveys	20
Early Population In-Migration	22
The War Between the States	24
Population Growth, Density and Distribution	26
Urbanization	31
Black Population	33
Age Structure	36
Education	38
Births and Deaths	40
Physical Health Facilities	42
Higher Education	44
Military	46
Politics	48
Religions	50

ECONOMIC CHARACTERISTICS

Incomes	52
Tax Base	56
Agricultural Regions	58
Historical Changes in Agricultural Land Use	60
Farm Size and Land in Farms	62
Agricultural Value and Employment	64
Major Crops	66
Livestock	70
Agricultural Land Values and Expenditures	72
Mineral Production	74
Commercial Fishing	78
Forestry	80
Manufacturing	84
Manufacturing Types	86
Construction	96
Transportation, Communication, and Utilities	98
Major State and Federal Highways	101
Railways and Railway Traffic	103
Commercial Water Traffic	104
Airports and Air Traffic	107
Telephones	108
Radio and Television	110
Electrical Power Production and Transmission	113
Petroleum and Natural Gas Transmission	116
Business and Commerce	118
Wholesale Trade	120
Retail Trade	122
Selected Services	124
Summary of Business and Commerce	126
Outdoor Recreation	128
Tourism	130
Prospects for the Future	134

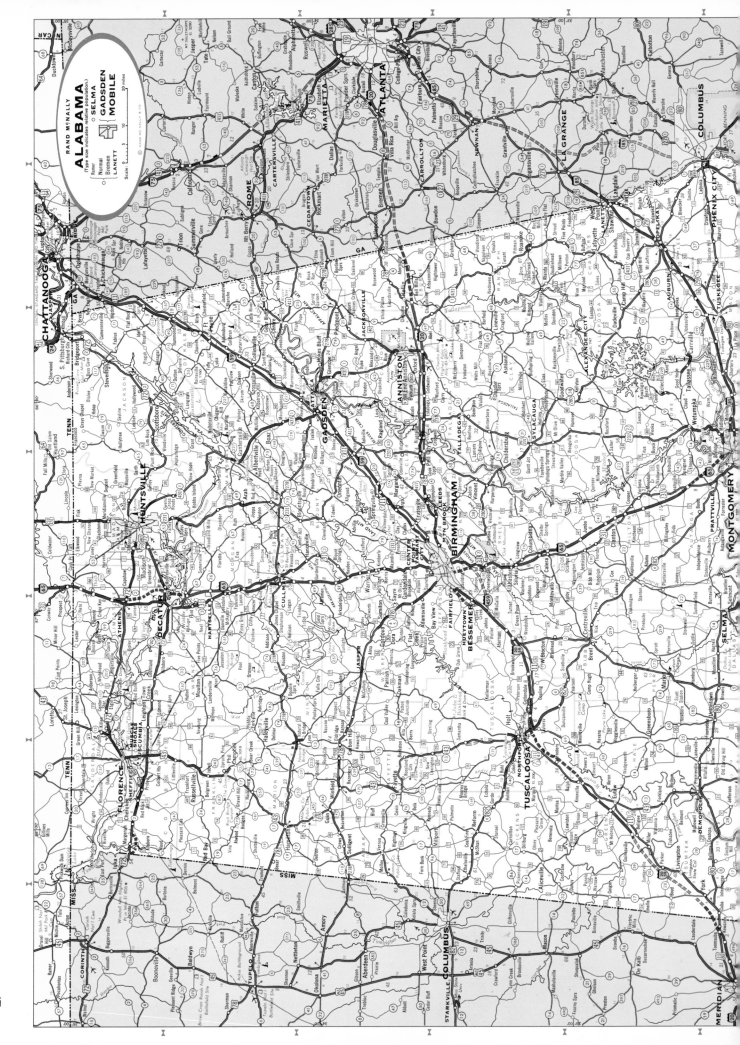

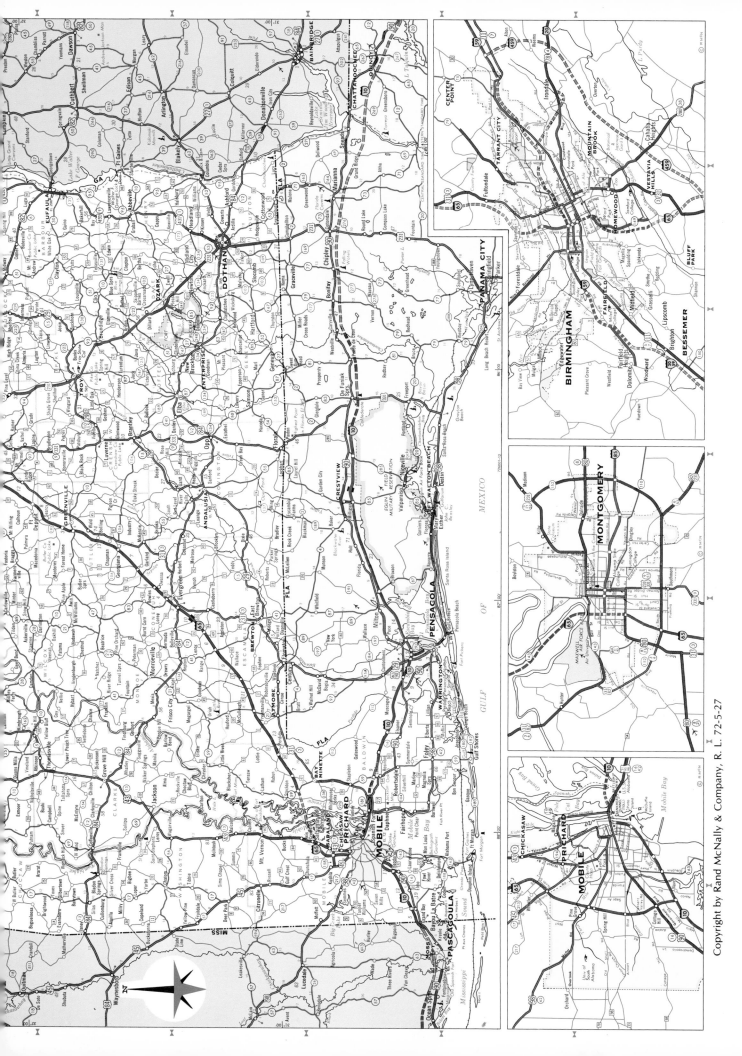

ix

INTRODUCTION

In many respects the State of Alabama is unique. Situated at the junction of the Appalachian Mountain System and the Gulf Coastal Plain, there is a diversity of landforms, soil types and, to a much lesser degree, climatic zones. This geographic diversity is exhibited by a variety of landscapes from the Appalachian Highlands in the north to the sandy beaches and salt marshes along the Gulf of Mexico.

The State also exhibits interesting cultural differences from one section to another. These are partly due to the manner in which the different soil resources were utilized during the agricultural settlement of the 19th Century. Early settlement patterns in Alabama were, in large part, a reflection of the availability of tillable crop lands and access to navigable waterways. The plantation system of agriculture on rich limey soils of the Tennessee River Valley and the Black Belt contrasted sharply with that of the small family farms in the intervening hilly region.

In modern times, we see an increasing need to utilize our natural and human resources in a more responsible and productive manner. Rapid industrial growth, accompanied by a dramatic population shift to urban areas, makes us acutely aware of the need for exercising some control over the changes which are taking place. As industrialization continues and the blight of urban decay presents critical social problems, we must change our resource and economic priorities to find both realistic and humanistic solutions to these problems.

The educational system of the State must train personnel and develop methods to meet this challenge. The assets of our State, when properly presented, will serve to attract industry, but we must develop a planning capability so that the mistakes of the past will not be repeated and a better future will be assured. The University of Alabama is vitally concerned with its responsibility in this respect.

Based on this recognized need for resource planning for economic development, proper use of the environment, and the general good of the public, the Department of Geology and Geography at The University of Alabama has provided the faculty leadership which is responsible for the creation of this significant geographic atlas of Alabama.

Through the generosity of the Ireland Foundation of Birmingham, Alabama, the considerable financial cost of producing this document has been accommodated. Our thanks go out to them for this expression of confidence. The University of Alabama was enthusiastic in its support of actual printing costs under the direction of The University of Alabama Press. Appreciation is expressed to the University's Office for Development which assisted in seeking financial support. To the Editorial Committee and the Cartographic Branch of the Department of Geology and Geography, and to more than fifty text contributors, I express the collective thanks of the University.

Douglas E. Jones, Dean
College of Arts and Sciences

ATLAS OF ALABAMA

THE PHYSICAL ENVIRONMENT

Appalachian Plateau

GEOLOGY

Rocks and their distribution determine the configuration of the land, the nature of ridges, the position of mountains, and the location of valleys. Rocks hold the key to our mineral wealth and control the quality of soils—and soils have unlocked the door of our agricultural abundance. Geology serves as a literal, figurative, and economic foundation of Alabama.

Methodical and intensive research by geologists from Alabama and other areas is gradually revealing the geologic history which produced our bedrock foundation. This history is extremely complex, and yet it is being pieced together like a giant jigsaw puzzle from which most of the pieces are missing. The history involves hundreds of millions of years now past, in which life existed on land, and in seas which regressed and transgressed as mountains were born and destroyed. Our picture of the present land distribution is an instantaneous, stop-action view of change, as the engraving hand of erosion passes into a future of constant modification.

The earth is at least four and one-half billion years old. Accurate information about most of the earth's geologic history is hidden, at best obscure and, in truth, unknown. Evidence of the events which occurred and the episodes which incurred change throughout seven-eighths of geologic history (the Pre-Cambrian eras) has been erased by recurring waves of geologic activity.

That part of the story which can be best substantiated begins in Cambrian time (about 600,000,000 years ago). Early in the Cambrian Period, most of the eastern United States, including Alabama, was beneath a broad, shallow sea which bordered on a mountainous, barren, and desolate landmass to the west. Turbulent streams, created by heavy rainfalls, rapidly eroded the land, since there

was no carpet of vegetation to retain the soil. Sediment from this denuded land was deposited as gravel, sand, and clay upon a sea floor of unknown rock type. As the landmass eroded, the sea advanced westward. Because the climate was warm and equable, the sea was hospitable and teemed with many diverse, but now extinct, forms of invertebrate life. These conditions prevailed for about a hundred million years (until middle Ordovician) as great thicknesses of limestone and dolomite accumulated. Thus, writing their own stone epitaphs, the animals became entombed in the carbonate rocks which are used in our cement industries, as building stone and road material, and serve as flux in the fiery furnaces of our steel mills.

During middle Ordovician time, volcanic islands appeared in eastern Alabama and the volcanic ash was incorporated in the sea floor sediment. Gradually, under the influence of strong compressive forces pushing from the southeast, much of the eastern United States emerged from beneath the sea. The older rocks were tilted and eroded to a fairly level surface before the sea reinvaded portions of Alabama during Silurian time. Deposited in the Silurian seas were sandstone and shale, derived from adjacent lands. Also deposited in the Silurian sequence were two beds of iron ore which some 500,000,000 years later served as the basis of Birmingham's steel industry.

The contact of the Silurian rocks and the erosional surface upon which they rest represents an unconformity in Alabama, or a "time gap" from which millions of years in earth history have been torn from the recorded log of time. Data from other areas indicate that life flourished in the Silurian seas and fish were present,

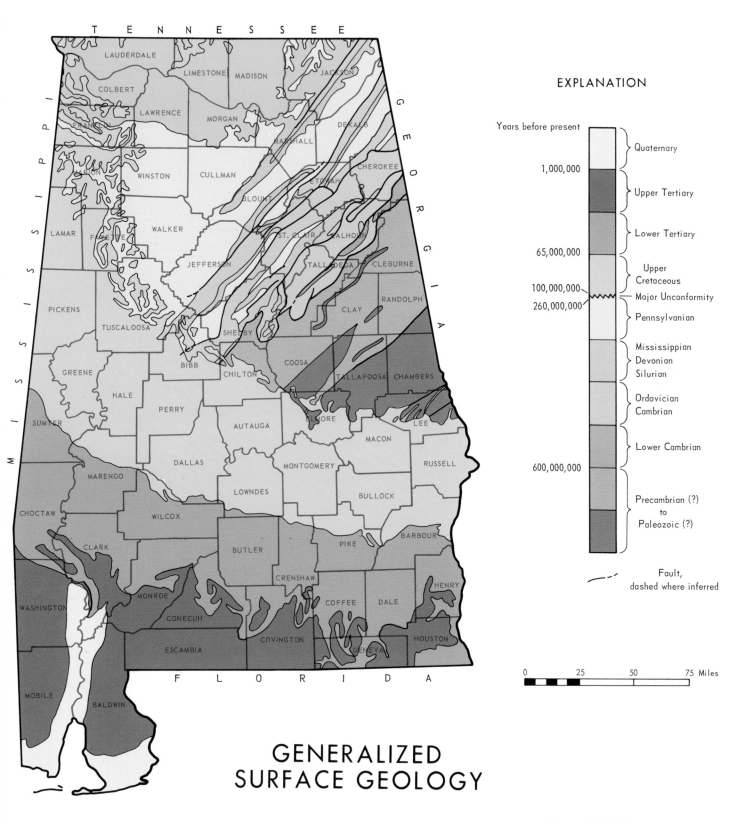

GENERALIZED
SURFACE GEOLOGY

EXPLANATION

Years before present

	Quaternary
1,000,000	Upper Tertiary
	Lower Tertiary
65,000,000	Upper Cretaceous
100,000,000	Major Unconformity
260,000,000	Pennsylvanian
	Mississippian Devonian Silurian
	Ordovician Cambrian
	Lower Cambrian
600,000,000	Precambrian (?) to Paleozoic (?)

Fault, dashed where inferred

0   25   50   75 Miles

Source: U. S. Geological Survey

3

but not abundant. Plant life was developing, and the first animals (perhaps scorpions) had invaded land.

Uplift occurred again in Devonian time (The Age of Fishes) as a result of continued compressive forces from the southeast. The Devonian system is composed of thin limestone, sandstone, and shale beds unconformably resting on Silurian and older rocks. Shale and limestone were deposited on the Devonian erosional surface from warm, shallow, intermittent seas during early Mississippian time. In places the Mississippian limestones are quite fossiliferous, indicating the presence of abundant marine life in the hospitable seas. During the late Mississippian began one of the greatest of all geologic events, The Appalachian Revolution, an orogeny or mountain building event which would literally change the face of the earth.

Compressive forces, again pushing from the southeast, coupled perhaps with vertical uplift, created a large mountain range, centered to the east of Alabama. Forces within the interior of these mountains were so great that the previously deposited sedimentary rocks were broken, deformed, crushed, sheared, and transformed into metamorphic rocks. Sedimentary rocks were converted to quartzite, marble, slate, schist, and gneiss. Igneous (fire-formed) rocks were changed into amphibolite and gneiss. Granite was formed in the hotter regions, either by direct metamorphism or by melting and recrystallization of the melt. Deposits of gold, copper, iron, mica, beryl, and feldspar were formed. Molten rock provided fuel for countless volcanic eruptions, creating lava cascades, or spewing into the air as ash and cinders which rained into regressing seas. The mountains rose higher and higher until, by Pennsylvanian time, they occupied the entire eastern coast of the present United States and equaled the majesty of the modern Alps.

As the mountains were formed, weathering agents decomposed them and streams carried the sediment to a sea in central and western Alabama. Here the material was deposited as shale, sandstone, and conglomerate. The deposits filled the sea, but a sagging earth's crust allowed the sea to return, only to be filled again and again. With each cyclic recession, the shoreline of the sea was flanked by swamps and inhabited by exotic, luxuriant vegetation and monstrous insects. When these plants and animals died, their bodies were submerged beneath the waters of the stagnant swamps, to be buried and converted to coal—one of our most important sources of natural fuel.

The mountain building forces had not yet diminished in intensity. Unmetamorphosed, lower Paleozoic rocks and the Pennsylvanian coal-bearing beds of the Coosa and Cahaba Valleys were bent, contorted, tilted, and folded into anticlines and synclines on the western side of the mountains. These rocks were then broken by thrust faults, and great slices of crustal material were stacked one on top of the other; while farther to the west, the relatively flat-lying Pennsylvanian rocks were little affected by the compressive forces.

As orogenic forces waned, the slow, everpresent, persistent hand of erosion obliterated the mountain chain during the next two hundred million years.

The land was again submerged in Upper Cretaceous time to receive deposits of sand, gravel, clay, chalk, and some volcanic ash. Roaming the shores and swimming in the waters of the Cretaceous sea were the last of the great dinosaurs—both the large and terrible, and the dainty and petite. The seas returned again in Tertiary time to unconformably deposit more sand, gravel, clay, and limestone; then retreated to their present position in the Gulf of Mexico.

A geologic map of Alabama demonstrates the glory and scars of this noble history. The Piedmont of Alabama is underlain by igneous and metamorphic rocks. These rocks, roots of the ancient Appalachian Mountains, are exposed in tribute to the stately grandeur of an aged mountain chain and to the inconceivable forces of its creation.

Folded and contorted sedimentary rock slices from the Paleozoic Era (pink and blue bands on the map), interlaced with thrust faults (heavy black lines), form the Valley and Ridge Province. Weaker, more easily weathered rocks, such as shale, limestone, and dolomite, have been incised to form valleys. Chert and sandstone support long ridges (called hogbacks), which stand boldly in defiance of their erosional fate.

In northern Alabama the relatively horizontal clastic rocks of Pennsylvanian time (blue area on the map) resist degradation as broad, flat-topped hills of the Cumberland Plateau Province.

And finally, as if in vain effort to veil their disfigured ancestors, the Cretaceous and Tertiary rocks of the Coastal Plain Province (green and tan bands) dip gently toward the now-subdued waters of the Gulf of Mexico.

Travis H. Hughes

PHYSIOGRAPHY AND TOPOGRAPHY

The diversity of landscape in Alabama can be directly related to two principal factors: the type and structure of the underlying geologic formations, and the geomorphic processes which later have modified these formations. Based on similarities in geologic and geomorphic features, Alabama can be divided into four major physiographic regions or provinces. These provinces include: the Coastal Plain, the Piedmont, the Valley and Ridge, and the Appalachian Plateau. The physical characteristics of each province have been significant in their effects on prior settlement and industrial development patterns in Alabama and will play a critical role in planning for future urban and industrial expansion.

The Coastal Plain. The Coastal Plain is underlain by relatively unconsolidated Mesozoic and Cenozoic sediments which dip gently towards the Gulf of Mexico. Although the entire surface may be considered a youthful to mature area of undulating low relief, several resistant formations have formed low lines of hills called cuestas. These cuestas are separated by lowland areas, and the alternating low hills and valleys are called a belted plain. Elevations vary from sea level at the coast to approximately 200 to 300 feet in the northwestern margin of the plain.

Prominent topographic subdivisions within the Coastal Plain include, from north to south: the Fall Line Hills, Black Belt, Ripley Cuesta, Flatwoods, Red Hills, Buhrstone Cuesta, Jackson Prairie, and the Southern Pine Hills. One of the most important subdivisions is the Black Belt, a continuous low valley across central Alabama. The Black Belt, underlain with chalk of Cretaceous age, has a rich soil and has historically been the Cotton Belt of Alabama.

Although no major rivers originate in the Alabama portion of the Coastal Plain, many large rivers including the Tombigbee, Black Warrior, Alabama, and Chattahoochee cross the region and serve as important transportation arteries. The completion of the Tennessee-Tombigbee canal system would provide water transportation from south Alabama into the rich industrial areas along the Tennessee River in north Alabama and east Tennessee.

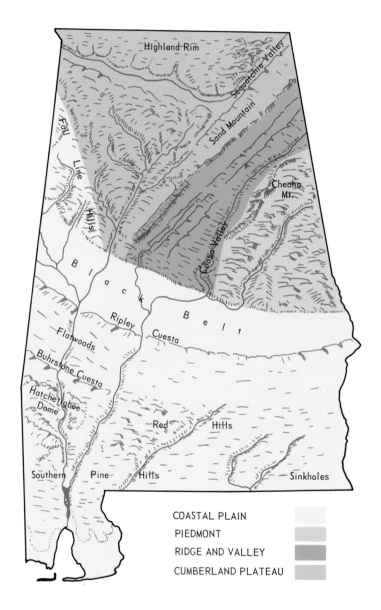

COASTAL PLAIN	
PIEDMONT	
RIDGE AND VALLEY	
CUMBERLAND PLATEAU	

PHYSIOGRAPHY

0   25   50   75 Miles

Source: Adopted from Erwin Raisz

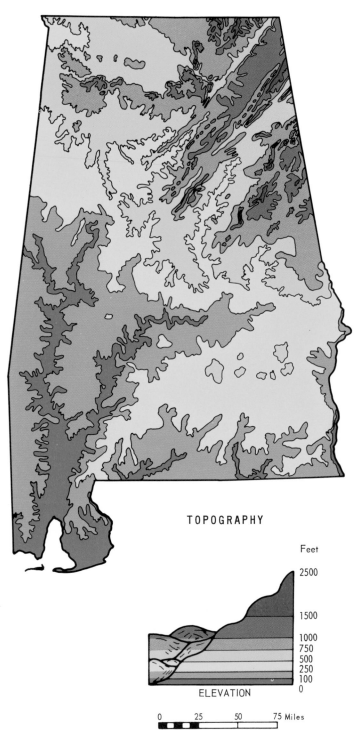

TOPOGRAPHY

	Feet
	2500
	1500
	1000
	750
	500
	250
	100
ELEVATION	0

0   25   50   75 Miles

Source: Geological Survey of Alabama

The Piedmont. The Piedmont region, in east central Alabama, is a maturely dissected peneplain surface that is underlain by igneous and metamorphic rocks of Precambrian and Paleozoic ages. Most of the Piedmont can be described as a region of rolling hills of moderate relief with the major streams occupying valleys from 100 to 200 feet below the upland surface. Several mountains, including Mount Cheaha, the highest elevation in Alabama at 2407 feet above sea level, rise considerably above the general upland surface, and are probably remnants or monadnocks from the original peneplain or older land surface.

Major drainage within the region is collected by the Coosa and Tallapoosa river systems. Because of rocky, narrow channels these rivers have not served as important transportation routes. Several hydroelectric facilities, however, have been erected along some of the rivers.

The southern margin of the province marks the contact between the crystalline rocks of the Piedmont and the sedimentary rocks of the Coastal Plain, and this boundary has been called the Fall Line.

The Valley and Ridge. The Valley and Ridge province in Alabama consists of a series of parallel ridges and valleys with a conspicuous northeast-southwest trend. Differential erosion of the underlying Paleozoic sediments has produced a striking correlation of topographic form and geologic unit. The ridges are underlain by sandstones and cherts, whereas the valleys are primarily developed upon carbonates and shales. Most of the major mountains or ridges are formed by the erosion of large folds, and mountain crests are remarkably uniform except where broken by water gaps or fault valleys. Some of the major mountains in this province include: Red Mountain, Red Ridge, Shades Mountain, Oak Mountain, Lookout Mountain, Chandler Mountain, and Blount Mountain. Elevations of 1200 feet are found as far south as Birmingham.

The southeastern portion of the Valley and Ridge province is a wide lowland area of approximately 500 to 600 feet above sea level which is drained by the Coosa River. This region, the Coosa Valley, has been considered to have been a peneplain.

Little River Canyon

In general the drainage in the Valley and Ridge is longitudinal; and most of the major rivers, such as the Coosa and the Cahaba, follow zones of weak rock. Predominant drainage in most of the central part of this region is carried by small streams which are tributaries of the large rivers on the northwestern and southeastern boundaries of the province.

The Appalachian Plateau. The Appalachian Plateau, which includes most of northern and northwestern Alabama, is underlain by horizontal sediments of upper Paleozoic age. The plateau, which is called the Cumberland Plateau in Alabama, Tennessee, and Kentucky, consists of an undulating, submature to mature surface that has been intricately dissected by young valleys. Elevations range from 700 feet in the south to approximately 1000 feet in the north where the floodplain of the Tennessee River forms a large break in the plateau surface. North of the Tennessee River the plateau continues into Tennessee as the Highland Rim.

The monotonous plateau topography is broken in the east by a long, narrow anticline which extends into Alabama from east central Tennessee. This anticline, the Sequatchie, is breached in the northeastern part of Alabama, and is followed by the Tennessee River from Chattanooga to Guntersville where the river leaves the anticlinal valley and turns sharply to the northwest across northern Alabama. South of Guntersville the Sequatchie anticline continues as a low line of hills into Jefferson County where the structural trend disappears into the basin of the Black Warrior coal-field.

The major drainage in the Cumberland Plateau is to the south through the basin of the Black Warrior and its tributaries. Through the construction of a rather elaborate lock system, the Black Warrior is navigable to near Birmingham; and this river serves as an important transportation route for many bulk mineral products such as coal and iron ore.

W. Gary Hooks

SOILS

Parent material, surface slope, climate, biological activity, and time all contribute to soil formation and character, and all are important in producing soil variations. Mature soils with a well-developed topsoil and subsoil are formed upon well-drained moderate slopes which make them well-suited for agriculture.

Alabama, located in the humid subtropics, has soils which are transitional between those of the cool climate regions and the tropics. Podzolization, a soil-forming process of the humid cool climates, and laterization, a soil-forming process of the lowland humid tropics, are represented by the Red and Yellow Podzolic soils and the Reddish-Brown Lateritic soils respectively. Soils developed under both processes are placed under the Ultisol order of the present Soil Conservation Service classification system. Some soil groups of this system are noted hereafter in parentheses.

In Alabama, the most extensive great soil group is the Red and Yellow Podzolic (Hapludult and Paleudult groups). These soils are formed in a humid climate with a short or no dry period during the year, and have a layer, or "horizon," of clay accumulation which is low in organic material. The descriptive name, Red and Yellow Podzolic, was applied because accumulated iron compounds in the subsurface horizons produce red to yellow coloration. The topsoil shows the effect of podzolization because much of the clay and soluble compounds have been leached or washed out of the topsoil, which is often left with a thin surface organic accumulation above an acid friable horizon high in silica and of low fertility. In some places in the State, the topsoil has been removed by accelerated erosion and the heavier clay-enriched red to yellow subsoil is exposed at the surface.

The red to yellow color of the subsurface horizons is the most evident effect of the laterization process. High temperatures and heavy rainfall of the lowland humid tropics, through time, will produce red, strongly-leached soils high in iron and aluminum, low in silica, and of low fertility. However, this has not occurred to such a degree in the southeastern United States. The Reddish-Brown Lateritic soils in Alabama (Rhodudult group) have dark red subsurface horizons of clay accumulation and, where not eroded, have a light brown or yellowish topsoil.

Other soil groups in the State, primarily reflecting the soil-forming factors of slope and parent material, include Grumusols, Rendzinas, Sols Bruns Acides, Humic Gley, Alluvial soils, Regosols, and Lithosols. Historically, the most important of these are the Grumusol and Rendzina soils common in the fertile Black Belt, which takes its name from the dark soils of that region. Grumusols (Vertisol order, Chromudert group) are clay soils with a brown surface horizon which develops vertical cracks when dry, and when wet become very plastic and tenaceous. Rendzinas (Mollisol order, Rendoll group) are soils with a nearly black, friable, organic, and base-rich surface horizon and a subsurface horizon high in calcium carbonate but without accumulated clay. The intrazonal Sols Brun Acides (Inceptisol order, Dystrochrept group), formed in crystalline clay mineral materials, have light-colored surface horizons and subsurface horizons that have been leached. Soils of the last four categories—Humic Gley, Alluvial, Regosol, and Lithosol—lack pedogenic horizons and are termed azonal (Entisols). Humic Gley soils are seasonally wet and poorly drained; Alluvial soils are buried before pedogenic horizons form; Regosols are formed on recent materials such as coastal sands; and Lithosols overlie bedrock on rocky, steep slopes and are common in the Appalachian Highlands.

The classification system adopted by the U.S. Soil Conservation Service in 1965 employed new terminology and aimed at a more precise classification based primarily upon quantitatively measurable properties obtained from soil samples. A generalized soil map of the United States employing this new system appears in *The National Atlas*. The accompanying map of Alabama illustrates the general distribution of representative soil series, which is approximately equivalent to the genus category in biological classification, with the great soil groups, such as Red and Yellow Podzolic, and Reddish-Brown Lateritic, equivalent to the class category.

Eugene M. Wilson

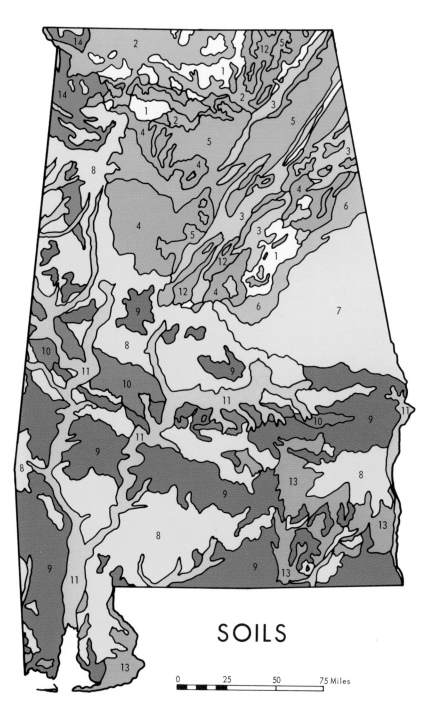

SOILS

0   25   50   75 Miles

1   RED SOILS OF INTERIOR LOW PLATEAU AND APPALACHIAN VALLEYS. *Red Podzolic:* Baxter, Cookeville, Dewey, Talbott; *Reddish-Brown Lateritic:* Decatur, Cumberland.

2   YELLOW PODZOLIC SOILS OF THE INTERIOR LOW PLATEAU: Dickson, Greendale. Includes Alluvial: Huntington, Ennis, Lindside.

3   YELLOW PODZOLIC SOILS OF THE APPALACHIAN VALLEYS: Includes Alluvial: Huntington, Lindside, and includes *Sols Bruns Acides:* Muskingum, Berks.

4   RED SOILS OF THE CUMBERLAND PLATEAU AND APPALACHIAN RIDGES. *Red Podzolic:* Enders, Townley; *Reddish-Brown Lateritic:* Hanceville, Greenville.

5   YELLOW PODZOLIC SOILS OF THE CUMBERLAND PLATEAU: Hartsells, Albertville.

6   SOILS OF THE BLUE RIDGE. *Lithosols:* Talladega, Chandler, Ramsey.

7   SOILS OF THE PIEDMONT PLATEAU. *Red Podzolic:* Cecil, Appling, Madison, Wickham; *Reddish-Brown Lateritic:* Davidson, Mecklenburg; *Sols Bruns Acides:* Louisa, Wilkes.

8   RED SOILS OF THE COASTAL PLAIN. *Red Podzolic:* Ruston, Orangeburg, Wickham, Cahaba, Carnegie, Dothan; *Reddish-Brown Lateritic:* Red Bay, Greenville.

9   YELLOW PODZOLIC SOILS OF THE COASTAL PLAIN: Norfolk, Susquehanna, Bowie, Cuthbert, Kalmia, Savannah, Tifton.

10   LIMESTONE AND CLAY SOILS OF THE BLACK BELT. *Reddish-Brown* acid clay soils: Oktibbeha, Vaiden, Eutaw; dark brown to black alkaline soils: Houston, Sumter, Binnsville, Bell, Catalpa.

11   SOILS OF THE COASTAL PLAIN, RIVER FLOODPLAINS, AND LOWER RIVER TERRACES. Floodplains: Iuka, Mantachie; Terraces: Flint, Wahee, Leaf, Augusta.

12   LITHOSOLS OF THE CUMBERLAND PLATEAU AND APPALACHIAN VALLEY AND RIDGE: Ramsey, Montevallo, Dandridge.

13   REGOSOLS ASSOCIATED WITH YELLOW PODZOLICS OF THE LOWER COASTAL PLAIN: Lakeland, St. Lucie, Alaga, Ocilla, Troup.

14   REGOSOLS OF THE INNER COASTAL PLAIN: Guin.

Source: Adapted from <u>Atlas of American Agriculture</u> <u>Part III</u>; U.S. Department of Agriculture.

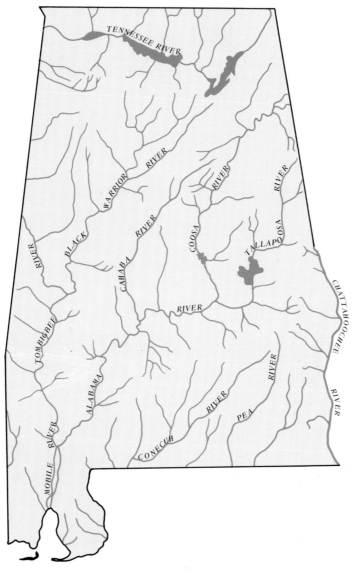

SURFACE WATER DRAINAGE SYSTEM

0   25   50   75 Miles

Source: Geological Survey of Alabama

WATER RESOURCES

Water is one of Alabama's most abundant—and most precious—natural resources. About one-twelfth of all the water that flows into the oceans from the 48 conterminous United States flows through Alabama during all or part of its journey to the sea. Rainfall, the source of both surface water and ground water, annually averages 50 inches in north Alabama and 65 inches in the southern part of the State along the Gulf Coast.

Surface Water.   Alabama is drained by two major river systems and numerous minor streams. The Tennessee River drains westward into the Ohio River across the northernmost ten counties of the State. The Tombigbee and its tributary, the Black Warrior River, drain western Alabama, while the Alabama River and its tributaries, the Cahaba, Coosa and Tallapoosa, drain the central and eastern parts of the State. The Tombigbee and the Alabama join to form the Mobile River, which flows southward into Mobile Bay. Southeastern Alabama is drained by the Conecuh, Yellow, Choctawhatchee, and Chattahoochee rivers.

Water to feed Alabama's plentiful streams results initially from rainfall, which enters streams in two ways—as surface runoff and as stored ground water. During periods between rains, streamflow is maintained by water already in the stream channel, by water seeping into the stream from the ground (ground water), and by flow from springs. During periods of prolonged drought, nearly all streamflow results from ground-water recharge. If no rain were to fall within the stream's drainage area and the water table declined to below the level of the stream bed, the stream would ultimately cease to flow.

Ground Water.   The amount of ground water available to streams and wells in a given area is dependent on the storage capacity of the rocks and soils underlying the area. Dense rocks, such as granite and slate, have very little pore space for the storage of water, and must contain cracks, joints, or solution channels if they are to serve as ground-water reservoirs. More porous rocks, such as sandstone and porous limestone, have greater storage capacity.

Alabama may be divided into three physical divisions, based on type and age of rocks: the Piedmont, the Plateau, and the Coastal Plain. The similarity of rock types within each division or province implies roughly a similarity of occurrence of ground water within each area, allowing for local variations in ground-water occurrence caused by differences in rock type.

The rocks in the Piedmont range in age from 200 to more than 500 million years old, and are the oldest in Alabama. These rocks are granite, schist, gneiss, quartzite, phyllite, slate, and marble. They are hard and non-porous, and weather to dense clay and tightly-packed sandy clay.

Well yields in the Piedmont are generally low. Yields from wells drilled into bedrock are dependent on the number and size of fractures or solution openings penetrated. Wells that produce water from the weathered (clay-rich) zone are generally dug wells and have yields limited by the slow rate at which water can flow through the fine, tightly-packed material. The average yield of a drilled well in the Piedmont is only about 30 gallons per minute, although some wells that penetrate solution channels in marble may yield up to 900 gallons per minute.

The Plateau region is underlain by sedimentary rocks ranging in age from 125 million to 500 million years. It is subdivided into three parts according to rock type: the limestone valleys, the coal measures, and the Valley and Ridge. In the limestone valleys, ground-water is developed from wells intersecting solution channels in the limestone. Wells and springs may yield up to 7,000 gallons per minute, depending on the number and nature of solution openings penetrated. In the coal measures water is found in cracks and crevices in the weathered mantle overlying the bedrock. Well yields vary from only a few gallons to 300 gallons per minute. Ground-water availability in the Valley and Ridge varies considerably according to rock type, with examples of occurrence being similar to those in both of the other subdivisions.

The Coastal Plain includes the youngest and least-consolidated rocks in Alabama; the oldest are about 125 million years old. Deposits of sand and gravel are plentiful and can store and yield large amounts of ground-water. Wells are easy to locate because waterbearing formations are numerous and widespread. The Coastal Plain is more abundantly supplied with water than any other area of the State.

Philip E. LaMoreaux

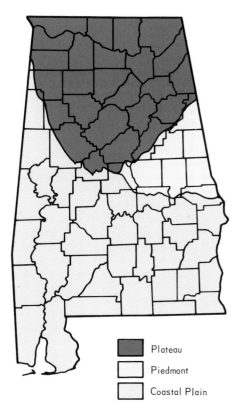

MAJOR PHYSIOGRAPHIC REGIONS

Plateau
Piedmont
Coastal Plain

Source: Geological Survey of Alabama

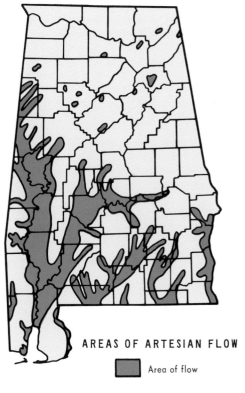

AREAS OF ARTESIAN FLOW

Area of flow

Source: Geological Survey of Alabama

WEATHER AND CLIMATE

The surface of Alabama rises gradually from the Gulf of Mexico in the south to the Appalachian uplands in the northern part of the State. The general elevation of the State ranges from sea level to 200 feet in the coastal plain, to 800 or 1000 feet in the northern Plateau section, and upward to 2,407 feet in the Talladega Mountains.

Alabama has a humid subtropical climate which reflects its eastern location in North America, its nearness to the Gulf of Mexico, and its latitude of approximately 30 to 35 degrees north. The weather and climate of Alabama are controlled by a combination of warm, moist Maritime air from the Gulf of Mexico and cool Continental air which originates in Canada and Alaska. During the summer season, the warm moist Gulf air dominates the weather pattern. Thundershowers occur frequently in the summer, and only very seldom does the cool continental air invade the State. During the winter and spring seasons, Alabama receives recurring waves of cold air which bring precipitation alternately with periods of clear dry weather and occasionally an extreme cold wave.

The geographic position, topography, and air mass activity of Alabama all contribute to a somewhat temperate climate. The summers are rather hot and humid, with average daytime high temperatures in the 90° F range and nighttime lows in the high 60's or low 70's. Extreme high temperatures in excess of 100° are unusual. In fact, some 27 states have recorded higher maximum temperatures than has Alabama. Thundershower activity during the summer season furnishes sufficient moisture for crops. Autumn is normally the driest period of the year.

Severe winter weather seldom occurs, and below

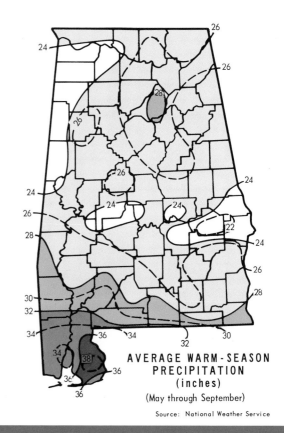

AVERAGE WARM-SEASON PRECIPITATION (inches)

(May through September)

Source: National Weather Service

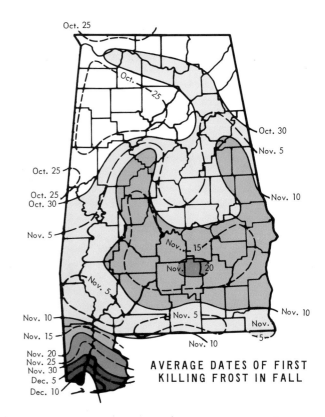

AVERAGE DATES OF FIRST KILLING FROST IN FALL

Source: U.S. Department of Agriculture

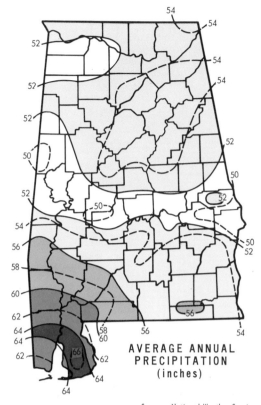

AVERAGE ANNUAL
PRECIPITATION
(inches)

Source: National Weather Service

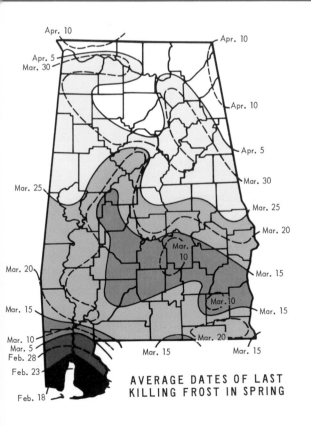

AVERAGE DATES OF LAST
KILLING FROST IN SPRING

Source: U.S. Department of Agriculture

freezing temperatures usually last less than 48 hours. Average January temperatures range from 42° in the north to 52° near the coast. Daytime highs and nighttime lows in January and February range from 55° to 30° in the north, and 60° to 40° in the south. The frost-free period averages 200 days in the extreme north to some 300 days near the coast.

Precipitation is rather evenly distributed throughout the year. Usually, however, the period from December through March receives slightly more precipitation, and when flooding occurs it is normally during this season. This is also the period of greatest cloudiness due to the conflict and mixing of cold northern air masses with warm, moist Gulf air.

Measurable snowfall occurs in the northern third of the State on the average of two to three days each winter, with the southern two-thirds receiving measurable snow only once every two or three years.

During the passage of cyclonic disturbances across and to the north of Alabama, there are occasionally destructive thunderstorms and tornados. Although tornados have been reported every month of the year in Alabama, their greatest frequency is in the spring from February through April.

An occasional hurricane will strike the coastal area of Alabama, but its destructive force seldom extends over 50 miles inland.

Alabama's climate is classified as humid subtropical, or "Cfa" under the Köppen system of climatic classification. This system best describes the climate of the state as being moderate. Winters are relatively mild and summers are warm to hot, with precipitation fairly well distributed throughout the year.

H. Don Hays

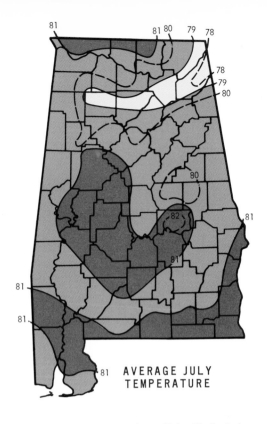

AVERAGE JULY
TEMPERATURE

Source: National Weather Service

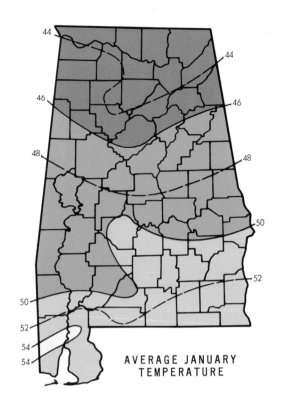

AVERAGE JANUARY
TEMPERATURE

Source: National Weather Service

SELECTED TEMPERATURE
RECORDS

Highest recorded
Average daily high
Monthly average
Average nightly low
Lowest recorded

Fahrenheit

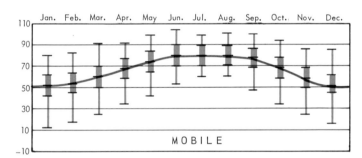

MOBILE

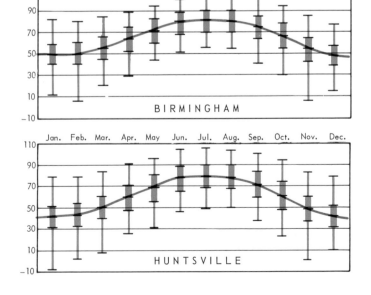

BIRMINGHAM

HUNTSVILLE

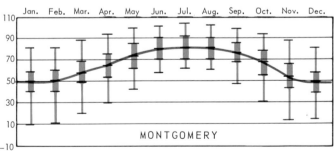

MONTGOMERY

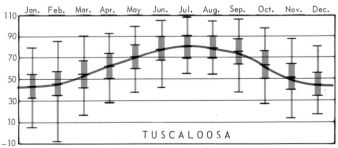

TUSCALOOSA

Source: National Weather Service

VEGETATION

The mild climate, abundant rainfall, and diversity of geological formations combine to provide suitable habitats in the State of Alabama to support vegetation which is remarkable for not only its beauty but also its variety in number of species and forest types. The present treatment is a very brief description of the major vegetation zones as delineated on the map of the *Potential Natural Vegetation of the United States* by A. W. Küchler.

Oak-Hickory Forest.   In the extreme north central and northwestern portion of the State, there is a well-developed oak-hickory forest which is the southern extension of a forest covering a large part of the central midwest of the United States, and extending as far north as central Michigan and west along river valleys to eastern Nebraska. The dominant species in this forest include white oak, red oak, southern red oak, black oak, shagbark hickory, mockernut, and pignut. Other species commonly found in this forest include basswood, winged elm, and black walnut. This forest is usually characteristic

of relatively dry sites and, in Alabama, is poorer in species than the areas surrounding it.

Oak-Hickory-Pine Forest.   Immediately south of the oak-hickory forest, the vegetation becomes more diverse and intergrades fairly rapidly with a mixed pine-hardwood forest which covers a large portion of the State. In its undisturbed state this forest is thought to have consisted primarily of hardwoods with single or small clusters of pines intermixed. The fact that pines quickly form essentially pure stands in areas following disturbances such as cultivation or fire has made it extremely difficult to describe the natural vegetation patterns in an area such as this in which fire is almost surely a sporadic but natural part of the ecology.

Thus, scattered stands of mostly pine are a common feature of this area, but in the absence of further disturbances these stands are eventually replaced by a mixed oak-hickory-pine forest. The dominant species of this forest include bitternut, mockernut, and pignut hickories, white oak, post oak, northern and southern red oak, loblolly and shortleaf pine. On drier ridges, especially in the northern portion, Virginia pine and scarlet oak become dominant, whereas on wetter sites yellow poplar, shumard oak, willow oak, live oak, and bay magnolia are of frequent occurrence.

This area is very rich in tree species, but many of these species are of limited distribution in the area and thus are not included in the above list of dominant or common species.

Cedar Glades. In extreme north-central Alabama and extending in scattered patches throughout the Tennessee Valley into northwest Alabama are areas of extremely shallow soil over limestone. In these areas red cedar is the dominant and often the only species of tree. These cedar glades support a beautiful spring flora of herbaceous species, many of which belong to the mustard family, and several flowering shrubs including St. John's Wort.

Mixed Mesophytic Forest. On rich, moist slopes and in cool ravines along the southern terminus of the Appalachian Highlands in northeastern Alabama is found a remnant of the mixed mesophytic forest. This is a very rich forest characterized by having a larger number of dominant species than any other forest type in the State. Plant geographers recognize this formation as the remnants of a vast forest that once extended over large portions of the northern hemisphere. Interestingly, there are similar remnants of this forest in southeastern Asia today. The dominant trees in this forest include several different species of oak, basswood, hickory, maple, beech, poplar, buckeye, chestnut, ash, magnolia, sweetgum, and hemlock. This southern extension of the Mixed Mesophytic Forest is best developed in moist ravines, particularly those with calcareous soil.

Black Belt. Extending in a narrow band approximately 20 miles wide across south-central Alabama from the vicinity of Montgomery through the northern half of Sumter County and northward into Mississippi is an area known as the Black Belt. This area is also referred to as the "cane-brake" or "prairie" region, and it coincides with the outcrop of soft limestone known as the Selma Chalk. This chalk weathers to a dark, heavy soil which supports a flora with many elements in common with the true prairies of the Midwest. In areas in which the soil is relatively deep, a rich forest develops similar to

that of the surrounding regions but including a number of species found primarily on limestone sites. These include: red cedar, overcup oak, shumard oak, chinquapin oak, durand oak, laurel oak, and nutmeg hickory. On areas of very thin soil and on other disturbed areas, the forest is replaced by glade-like areas that resemble prairies in many respects. Among the typical prairie species found in these open areas are the following: prairie sunflower, prairie cornflower, prairie rose, Cherokee sedge, tuberous milkweed, Torrey's rush, cut-leaf verbena, and big bluestem grass.

Southern Mixed Forest. In the extreme southern portion of the State, beginning approximately at the latitude of Clarke and Monroe Counties and extending south into Florida, is a forest zone often referred to as the Southern Mixed Forest. It is composed of tall trees with a mixture of broadleaf deciduous and evergreen species and four or more species of pines. The dominant trees in this forest include the following: southern magnolia, cucumber tree, sweetgum, beech, yellow poplar, white oak, laurel oak, swamp chestnut oak, turkey oak, red bay, shortleaf pine, loblolly pine, longleaf pine, southern white pine, white hickory, and ironwood. In sandy areas, particularly near the coast, the forest becomes more open, consisting largely of pines with a dense understory of shrubs including cabbage palms. This vegetation zone is sometimes referred to as a pine-oak savanna.

The Southern Mixed Forest covers an area with considerable ecological variation, from the red clay hill country in the northern part of the zone to the sandy pine flatwoods in the south near the coast. The different groups of species intergrade so extensively, however, that the entire area can be considered as a single complex forest type.

Southern Floodplain Forest. Along the middle and lower reaches of the Warrior, Tombigbee, Alabama and Mobile rivers there is a well developed Southern Floodplain Forest that remains distinct as this river system passes through three different forest types described above. This floodplain forest is typically dominated by tupelo gum, bald cypress, pecan, and several species of oak, particularly shumard oak, overcup oak, water oak, willow oak, laurel oak, and swamp chestnut oak. Other species that are common in this forest include swamp privet, red bay, water elm, American elm, cabbage palm, sugarberry, and rattan vine.

Joab Thomas

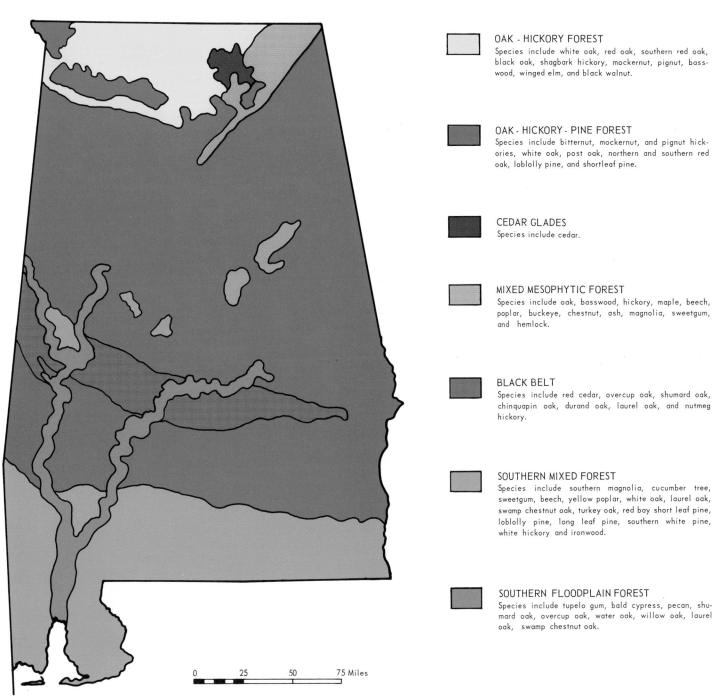

OAK - HICKORY FOREST
Species include white oak, red oak, southern red oak, black oak, shagbark hickory, mockernut, pignut, basswood, winged elm, and black walnut.

OAK - HICKORY - PINE FOREST
Species include bitternut, mockernut, and pignut hickories, white oak, post oak, northern and southern red oak, loblolly pine, and shortleaf pine.

CEDAR GLADES
Species include cedar.

MIXED MESOPHYTIC FOREST
Species include oak, basswood, hickory, maple, beech, poplar, buckeye, chestnut, ash, magnolia, sweetgum, and hemlock.

BLACK BELT
Species include red cedar, overcup oak, shumard oak, chinquapin oak, durand oak, laurel oak, and nutmeg hickory.

SOUTHERN MIXED FOREST
Species include southern magnolia, cucumber tree, sweetgum, beech, yellow poplar, white oak, laurel oak, swamp chestnut oak, turkey oak, red bay short leaf pine, loblolly pine, long leaf pine, southern white pine, white hickory and ironwood.

SOUTHERN FLOODPLAIN FOREST
Species include tupelo gum, bald cypress, pecan, shumard oak, overcup oak, water oak, willow oak, laurel oak, swamp chestnut oak.

0   25   50   75 Miles

Source: A. W. Kuchler, The National Atlas of the United States of America

NATURAL VEGETATION

ATLAS OF ALABAMA

CULTURAL AND SOCIAL PATTERNS

EARLY EUROPEAN EXPLORATION

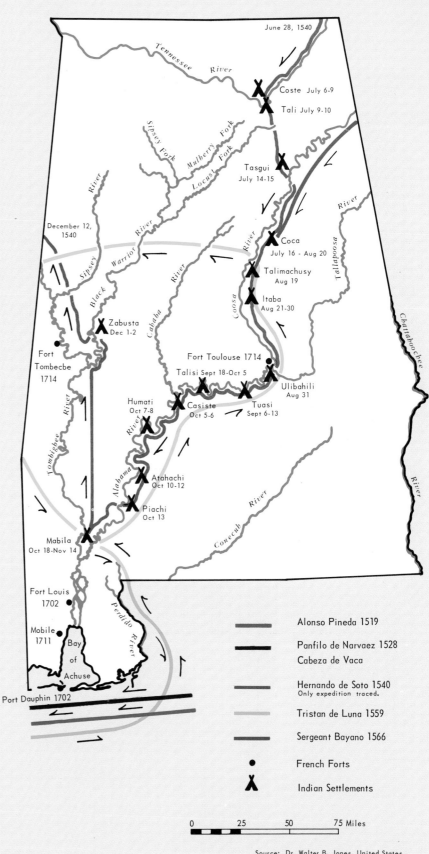

June 28, 1540

Coste July 6-9
Tali July 9-10
Tasgui July 14-15
Coca July 16 - Aug 20
Talimachusy Aug 19
Itaba Aug 21-30
December 12, 1540
Zabusta Dec 1-2
Fort Tombecbe 1714
Fort Toulouse 1714
Talisi Sept 18-Oct 5
Ulibahili Aug 31
Humati Oct 7-8
Casiste Oct 5-6
Tuasi Sept 6-13
Atahachi Oct 10-12
Piachi Oct 13
Mabila Oct 18-Nov 14
Fort Louis 1702
Mobile 1711
Bay of Achuse
Port Dauphin 1702

Alonso Pineda 1519
Panfilo de Narvaez 1528
Cabeza de Vaca
Hernando de Soto 1540
Only expedition traced.
Tristan de Luna 1559
Sergeant Bayano 1566

● French Forts
Indian Settlements

0   25   50   75 Miles

Source: Dr. Walter B. Jones, United States
DeSoto Expedition Commission

EARLY EXPLORATIONS

The record of European exploration of Alabama extends over two centuries. Martin Waldseemüller's map of 1507 shows an outline of Mobile Bay, yet the earliest identifiable voyage to Alabama was that of the Spanish explorer Alonso Álvarez de Piñeda in 1519. With four caravels Piñeda entered Mobile Bay, and a cartographer with the expedition made a map of the bay.

Nine years later, the exploration of Pánfilo de Narváez and Cabeza de Vaca reached Alabama. With 400 men and 80 horses, the Spanish expedition of Narváez moved overland through Florida. Thwarted in their search for gold, the Spaniards decided to leave by water. At present-day St. Marks, Florida, they built five flimsy boats. On September 22, 1528, the Spaniards departed and headed for New Spain. They hugged the coast to avoid being lost or swamped, and made repeated trips ashore for water and food. In Mobile Bay the Narváez party encountered Indians and made their usual request for water. Don Doroteo Teodoro, a Greek member of the Spanish expedition, and an unnamed black servant accompanied the Indians as hostages to get the water, and voluntarily or otherwise became the earliest-known non-Indian inhabitants of Alabama because of the Narváez-Vaca expedition sailed off without them.

The most extensive and also the most expensive of early explorations in the United States was that of Hernando de Soto; Soto (more often and less accurately written De Soto) entered Alabama on June 28, 1540, after having traveled from Cuba into Florida, and through other states into Tennessee. The Map of Hernando de Soto, 1539-1543, is the earliest known map showing any part of the interior of the United States.

When the Soto expedition crossed the Tennessee River into Alabama, the columns consisted of some 600 men, including blacksmiths, shoemakers, carpenters, seamen, priests, and the most numerous group, soldiers. There were also Indians serving as burden bearers, guides, and hostages. Horses were unknown to Alabama Indians when brought in by the Spaniards. Upon entering Alabama, Soto's men moved from the Tennessee River to the Coosa River, and down the valley to the village of Coosa, a center of Indian agriculture and the capital of the upper Creeks. From Coosa, the columns of Soto continued to the Alabama River and on to Mabila, probably located in Clarke County. There was fought one of the bloodiest of all engagements between Europeans and Indians. From Mabila the Soto columns moved north-ward up the valley of the Tombigbee River, and into what is now the State of Mississippi.

The explorations of Guido de las Bazares (1558), of Tristán de Luna y Arellano (1559-1560), and of Juan Pardo and Sergeant Boyano (1566-1567) were all related to a planned Spanish city on the northern coast of the Gulf of Mexico. Bazares entered Mobile Bay, about which he wrote a detailed report in 1558. While Bazares was exploring, Tristán de Luna y Arellano was preparing his large expedition which was expected to establish a colony. Luna departed Veracruz, June 11, 1559, with some 1,500 persons (including five who had accompanied Soto) in 13 vessels. Luna's expedition arrived at Achusi on September 19, 1559 and founded a settlement. Achusi has been identified as Pensacola, Florida, but another opinion places the settlement at Mobile. Luna sent exploring parties into present-day Alabama, up the Alabama River and the Coosa River to the village of Coosa, where Soto had found abundant food. Luna did not succeed in founding a permanent colony.

Another Spanish exploring expedition was sent out from Santa Elena (Beaufort, South Carolina) in 1566 and 1567, headed by Juan Pardo and Sergeant Boyano, for the purpose of discovering a land route to Texas which would by-pass the hazards to the treasure fleets offered by the Florida peninsula. The Pardo-Boyano expedition failed in its mission, but did explore into Alabama and did become the third group of Spanish explorers to reach the village of Coosa.

It remained for the French to found the first permanent settlement in Alabama, Mobile, founded at its present site in 1711. Earlier, in 1702, Fort Louis (named for Louis XIV) had been established at Twenty-seven Mile Bluff, but it was not a permanent settlement and was later moved to the site of Mobile. Port Dauphin was established in 1702 on Dauphin Island. In 1714 Fort Toulouse was founded at the junction of the Coosa and the Tallapoosa rivers at present-day Wetumpka. The French also established Fort Tombecbé on the Tombigbee River at White Rock Bluff near present-day Epes in Sumter County. The foundings of Natchez and New Orleans were accomplished from Mobile, which was then the capital of all of French Louisiana. The French period ended in 1763 with the Treaty of Paris, thus concluding the important early explorations in Alabama.

Charles Grayson Summersell

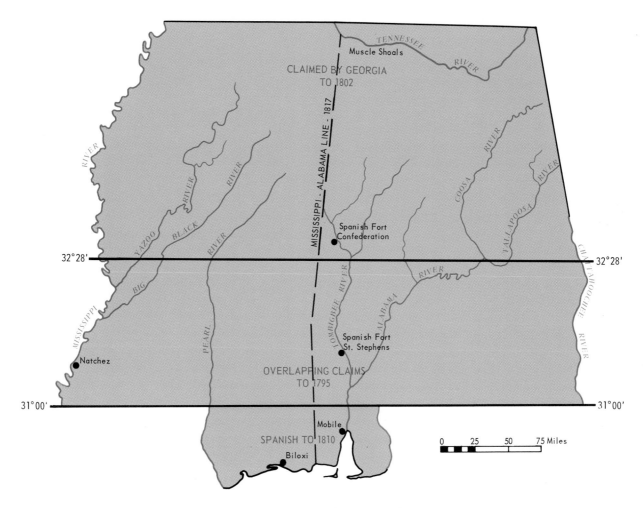

CLAIMED BY GEORGIA
TO 1802

MISSISSIPPI - ALABAMA LINE - 1817

Muscle Shoals

TENNESSEE RIVER

Spanish Fort
Confederation

32°28'

Spanish Fort
St. Stephens

OVERLAPPING CLAIMS
TO 1795

Natchez

31°00'

Mobile

SPANISH TO 1810

Biloxi

0   25   50   75 Miles

YAZOO RIVER

BLACK RIVER

BIG BLACK RIVER

MISSISSIPPI RIVER

PEARL RIVER

TOMBIGBEE RIVER

ALABAMA RIVER

COOSA RIVER

TALLAPOOSA RIVER

CHATTAHOOCHEE RIVER

THE MISSISSIPPI TERRITORY

EARLY BOUNDARIES AND SURVEYS

The Territory of Alabama was acquired by the United States in several stages. After the end of the American Revolution in 1783 the new nation, weak and poorly organized, claimed land as far south as Latitude 31°, which is the present boundary between Alabama and Florida. Spain claimed sovereignty over all the territory south of 32° 28'N, and from the Chattahoochee River to the Mississippi, in accordance with the boundaries of British West Florida, which Spain had conquered. The overlapping claims were settled in favor of the United States by the Treaty of San Lorenzo with Spain in 1795. Spain retained the coastal area for some years, but it was seized by the United States in 1810 and incorporated into the Mississippi Territory, except for the town of Mobile, which Spain held until 1813.

In 1798 Congress created the Mississippi Territory

in the area bounded by 32° 28'N on the north, 31° N on the south, the Chattahoochee River on the east and the Mississippi River on the west. However, the jurisdiction of the territorial government could be exercised only in the very limited areas to which Indian titles had been extinguished. In the Alabama portion of the territory, this jurisdiction existed only in a small area in the southwestern corner of the present State north of 31° N latitude. Title to the lands north of 32° 28'N was claimed by Georgia, as well as the Indians, until by the Compact of 1802 the Georgia claims were transferred to the United States. Two years later the Mississippi Territory's northern limit was extended to the Tennessee line, but most of the land involved was still subject to the aboriginal Indian titles.

The acquisition of the Louisiana Territory by the

United States in 1803 brought increased pressures on the Indians to permit the building of roads and the opening of water courses through their territory. This, coupled with the tensions associated with European wars and the influences of the white man's civilization among the Indians, led to the Creek Indian Civil War in 1813 and an invasion of the Creek country by the militia of Tennessee and Georgia. General Andrew Jackson of Tennessee forced the Creeks to cede a large part of their land to the United States by the Treaty of Fort Jackson, August 9, 1814. Within the next four years, treaties with the Choctaws, Chickasaws, and Cherokees pushed the Indian lines back still farther.

When the State of Mississippi entered the Union in 1817, the eastern portion of the Mississippi Territory was split off to become the Alabama Territory, with St. Stephens as its capital. Settlers poured in so fast that Alabama was able to enter the Union as a state in 1819.

Even before the Indian titles were extinguished, there had begun an influx of settlers from Tennessee, Georgia, and the Carolinas. Squatters established themselves on the public lands and sometimes on Indian lands. As the United States obtained title, the lands were surveyed according to the rectangular grid system into townships six miles square which were numbered east and west from the St. Stephens and Huntsville meridians and north and south from established base lines. Townships were subdivided into sections one mile square, containing 640 acres each, and the sections were subdivided into smaller lots.

The lands after being surveyed were offered for sale at public auction to the highest bidders. Lands not so taken were subsequently available at the minimum price of $2.00 per acre (changed to $1.25 in 1820). There were limited auction sales at Huntsville in 1809 and St. Stephens in 1811. The years 1817–1819 saw extensive sales accompanied by frenzied excitement and speculation, as good lands came into the market and settlers came in great numbers. By 1820 the land boom had collapsed, but the economic development of the new state had been firmly launched, and development rapidly continued.

James F. Doster

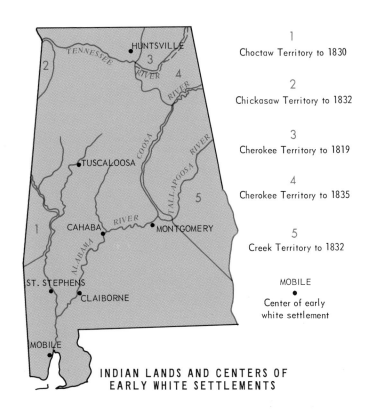

1
Choctaw Territory to 1830

2
Chickasaw Territory to 1832

3
Cherokee Territory to 1819

4
Cherokee Territory to 1835

5
Creek Territory to 1832

MOBILE
• Center of early white settlement

INDIAN LANDS AND CENTERS OF EARLY WHITE SETTLEMENTS

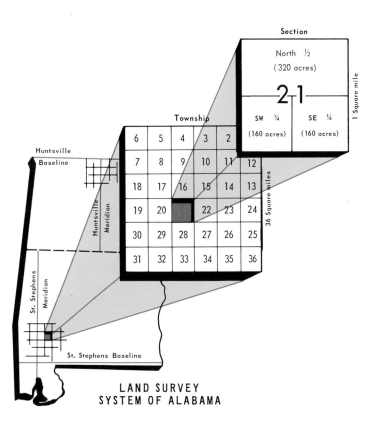

LAND SURVEY SYSTEM OF ALABAMA

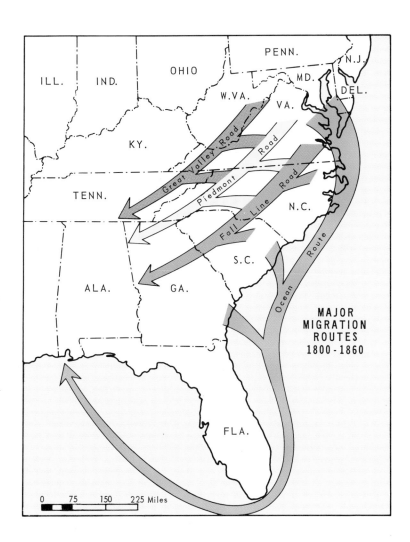

MAJOR
MIGRATION
ROUTES
1800-1860

0   75   150   225 Miles

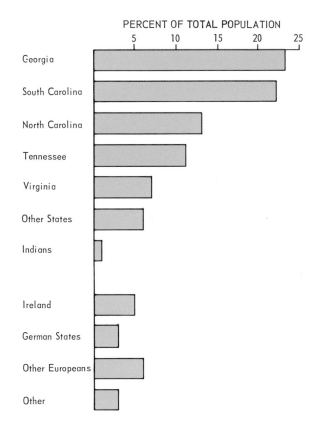

PERCENT OF TOTAL POPULATION

ORIGINS OF EARLY INHABITANTS

EARLY WHITE POPULATION IN-MIGRATION

The origins of the earliest Indian settlers of Alabama can possibly be traced to the Amur Valley area of northern China. After an extended migration, these people eventually established themselves along and inland from the Gulf Coast. Here the Indians found lands with a comparatively temperate climate where large numbers of buffalo, bear, and a multitude of edible native plants, including rice, fruits, and nuts, could be found. The original inhabitants of Alabama prospered and multiplied until the Gulf region possessed one of the largest concentrations of aborigines in North America. However, encroachment by the white man on Indian lands, continuous conflict, privation, disease (smallpox, measles) and, eventually, the relocation of the Indians to Oklahoma, erased much of the Indian cultural heritage from Alabama. Extensive contact with the white men was so effective in eliminating Indians from Alabama that in the 1860 census there were only 160 Indians counted in the entire State.

Dispersion of the Indians made available large areas of very productive land to white settlers. Furthermore, the Federal Government was giving, or selling for very low prices, 160-acre plots of agricultural land to anyone who would attempt to cultivate it. At the time the new lands became available in Alabama, factors were operating in the settled areas of Virginia, South Carolina, North Carolina, Georgia, and eastern Tennessee, which made them less attractive for farming. Some of the more important reasons for farm family migration from the older states included: (1) depletion of the rich tidewater soils that had been continuously planted to cotton and tobacco, and (2) possession of most of the productive areas by a relatively few established families.

There were basically three avenues of movement from the southern Atlantic States to Alabama. First, the river valleys were extensively used, primarily because of the ease of movement. As a result, the Tennessee, Tombigbee, Coosa, Tallapoosa, and upper Alabama River valleys were the first areas of extensive white settlement. The people who settled in the various river valleys were primarily backwoodsmen from the western part of the Carolinas, western Georgia, and eastern Tennessee.

Secondly, overland routes were developed as new passageways were marked through the Appalachians into the great interior valleys, and along the westward-bending Piedmont. Three interconnecting road complexes evolved. The two southernmost roads allowed easy penetration into eastern, central, and southwestern Alabama. Once again the backwoodsman from interior Virginia, the Carolinas, western Georgia, and eastern Tennessee moved into these areas. The third road was located in the lower Appalachian Valley, which terminates in north-central Alabama. This road helped focus settlement in the Huntsville, Decatur, and Tuscaloosa regions.

The third method of travel was by ocean-going vessels. Many of the wealthier residents of the Atlantic tidewater used this method of travel to relocate, with their slaves, on the productive lands of Alabama's Black Belt, on some of the unclaimed river lands of southern Alabama, and along the Tennessee River.

In 1850 Alabama's population (excluding slaves) rose to 428,779. Of this number forty-five percent were natives of the five states of Virginia, North and South Carolina, Georgia, and Tennessee. The influence of the immigrants on Alabama's economic, political, and social heritage can be noted by the fact that eighty-five to ninety percent of the pre-Civil War white population of the State originated, or had close ancestral ties, in one of these five states. Of the first sixteen governors of Alabama, fifteen were born in one of the five southeastern states. And of the 100 delegates at the Secession Convention in 1861 only seventeen were native-born Alabamians, while seventy-two were born in one of the five above states.

Alabama never had a large population of Europeans because they could not compete with the abundant and cheap black slave labor. In 1850 the foreign-born population amounted to only 1.6 percent of the State's total. The majority of the foreigners were refugees displaced as a result of the Irish potato famine and civil unrest and who had come to the South seeking farm land. The next largest foreign migration was from the German states. These states also had a period of intense civil unrest which resulted in a large scale emigration to America. Traces of the early French settlement of Mobile are still seen in area place-names, and local customs such as Mardi Gras.

Nicholas E. D'Andrea

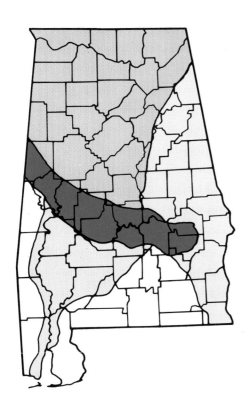

Area of large landholdings, settled by people from the tidewater regions of Virginia, North Carolina and Georgia. Most of the tidewater landholders from South Carolina had already moved into the Black Belt.

Area settled primarily by migrants from interior Virginia, North Carolina, South Carolina and east Tennessee. Many Germans and Irish moved down the Appalachian Valley into this area of Alabama.

Area settled by migrants from eastern Tennessee, South Carolina and western Georgia.

Area of large landholdings dominated by farmers from the tidewater areas of Virginia, North Carolina, South Carolina and Georgia.

SETTLEMENT PATTERNS
1860

23

THE WAR BETWEEN
THE STATES

In November, 1860, Abraham Lincoln was elected President on a platform demanding the exclusion of slaveholders with their property in slaves from the territories. Conservative and moderate leaders, North and South, unavailingly attempted to work out a compromise that would preserve the balance between the sections. This seems to have convinced Alabamians and Southerners generally that they could no longer preserve their constitutional rights in the Union. They withdrew and formed the Southern Confederacy. After unsuccessfully attempting to settle the difficulties between the two governments in a friendly manner and learning that an armed flotilla was approaching Fort Sumter, the Confederate Government bombarded it. This inaugurated hostilities.

With the exception of Mobile, there were no major battles in Alabama. Nevertheless, the State experienced many horrors of war including invasion, occupation, skirmishes, raids, and famine.

During the first year of the war, Alabama was free from invasion, but on April 11, 1862, the Federals under General Ormsby M. Mitchell entered Huntsville and captured nearly all the rolling stock of the railroads entering the city. Within the next few months Decatur, Athens, Tuscumbia, and the other towns of the Tennessee Valley were occupied. Despite the efforts of some Northern generals to enforce the laws of civilized warfare, Athens and Guntersville were sacked or bombarded and burned, along with villages from Town Creek to Tuscumbia.

The people of Alabama were never able to defend themselves adequately, for most of the State's troops were engaged along the main battle lines outside the State. General Phillip D. Roddy was finally able to raise a brigade, composed mostly of old men and boys, for the defense of North Alabama, and General Nathan B. Forrest and General Joe Wheeler were also able to provide some assistance.

In the Spring of 1863, Major General Abel B. Streight, with 2,000 mounted men, set out from Eastport on the northwestern boundary for Rome, Georgia, to cut the railroads from Chattanooga to Atlanta and Knoxville, which supplied Bragg's army, and to destroy large stores of Confederate supplies at Rome. Learning of Streight's movements, Forrest, with fewer than 600 Confederate troops, gave chase through the rugged terrain of North Alabama, compelling him to fight skirmishes and actions at Day's Gap, Crooked Creek, Hog Mountain, Blountsville, East Branch, Big Warrior River, Black Creek-Gadsden, Blount's Plantation, and Cedar Bluff, where he surrounded and bluffed Streigh into surrender.

Major General Lovell H. Rousseau carried the war into central Alabama. His purpose was to destroy iron works in Calhoun County, stores of Confederate supplies at Talladega, and to cut the Montgomery and West Point Railroad, which was supplying General Joseph E. Johnston, who was opposing Sherman in Georgia. Starting from Decatur on July 10, 1864, he fought skirmishes at Greenport and Ten Island Ford at the Coosa River, where he defeated General James H. Clanton, and then swept down the valley through Calhoun County and Talladega. Continuing south and west, he fought skirmishes at Cheaha and Auburn on July 18 and struck the railroad at Loachapoka. He destroyed miles of track and burned the depots there and at Notasulga, Auburn, and Opelika before being driven into Georgia.

A few weeks later Mobile was attacked. During the first week in August, General Granger with 15,000 Federal troops laid siege to Fort Gaines, and Admiral David H. Farragut, under a galling cross fire from forts Gaines and Morgan, blasted his way into Mobile Bay with the loss of one ship. Mobile's outer defenses had fallen, but the city held on until the Spring of 1865 when Spanish Fort on the eastern shore of Mobile Bay and Fort Blakely at its head fell under the combined attack of a pincer movement. Between March 20 and April 1, Major General Frederick Steel, with 15,000 Federals, had advanced from Pensacola by way of Pollard cutting railroads and destroying Confederate supplies, and on April 2 laid siege to Fort Blakely. General R. S. Canby advanced with 32,000 troops up the east side of the Bay and laid siege on March 27 to Spanish Fort, which surrendered twelve days later. The next day, after a siege of eight days, Fort Blakely surrendered. General Dabney

H. Maury, in charge of the defense of Mobile, realizing that he could no longer defend the city, withdrew with his troops and declared it an open city. The Federals occupied it on April 12, 1865.

Meanwhile Major General James H. Wilson had commenced his devastating raid into the heart of Alabama. Starting from Gravelly Springs in Lauderdale County in March, 1865, with a force of 13,500 cavalry, he arrived in the vicinity of Elyton on March 29, where he burned five iron works. Brigadier General John T. Croxton was dispatched toward Tuscaloosa, where he was engaged in action at Northport and at Tuscaloosa on April 3 by the home guard. He occupied the city the next day, destroying the iron foundry, shoe factory, nitre works, and cotton mills, as well as the University of Alabama. Moving on to Pleasant Ridge in Greene County, Croxton was checked in skirmishes at King's store and Lanier's mill, finally turning northeast into Georgia by way of Talladega and Jacksonville. Before reaching Georgia he destroyed nearly all of the remaining ironworks, cotton mills, and Confederate stores missed by Rousseau and Wilson.

On April 2, Wilson with 9,000 troops moved to Selma, an arsenal, by way of Montevallo, Randolph, Maplesville, Ebenezer Church, Plantersville, and Summerfield. Forrest had assembled a small force of 3,000, mostly old men and boys, to defend the city. Wilson swept through the thinly held lines and entered the city soon after dark. Private homes were entered and plundered; and, according to a newspaper correspondent with Wilson's army, Selma was the worst sacked city of the war. From Selma Wilson moved toward Montomery, skirmishing at Benton and Lowndesborough, and on April 12 he arrived in Montgomery. The mayor surrendered the city, but its industries, water and rail facilities, and a part of the business section were burned.

At Montgomery Wilson's force divided into two columns, one marching to West Point and the other to Girard. Each fought a skirmish at its destination on April 16, which ended the fighting on Alabama soil.

Austin L. Venable

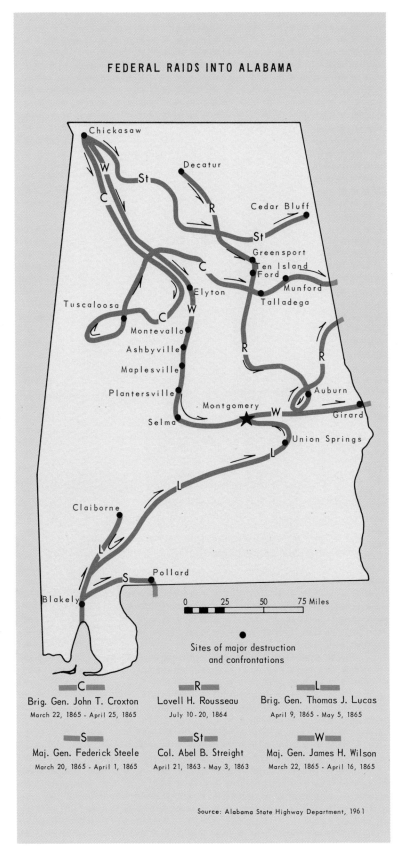

FEDERAL RAIDS INTO ALABAMA

0   25   50   75 Miles

● Sites of major destruction and confrontations

C Brig. Gen. John T. Croxton
March 22, 1865 - April 25, 1865

R Lovell H. Rousseau
July 10 - 20, 1864

L Brig. Gen. Thomas J. Lucas
April 9, 1865 - May 5, 1865

S Maj. Gen. Federick Steele
March 20, 1865 - April 1, 1865

St Col. Abel B. Streight
April 21, 1863 - May 3, 1863

W Maj. Gen. James H. Wilson
March 22, 1865 - April 16, 1865

Source: Alabama State Highway Department, 1961

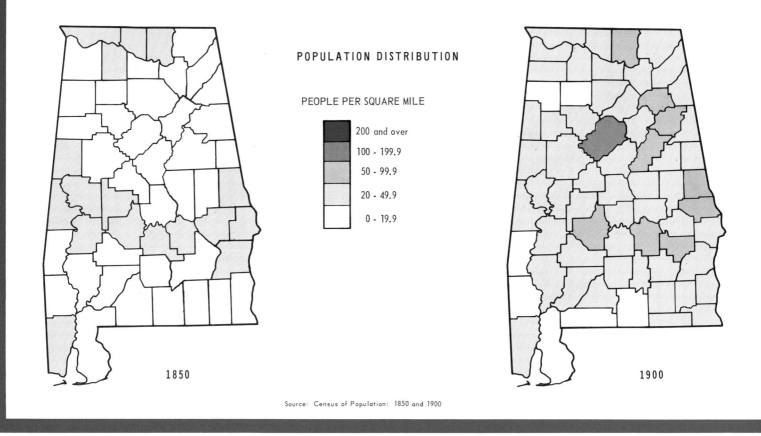

POPULATION DISTRIBUTION

PEOPLE PER SQUARE MILE

200 and over
100 - 199.9
50 - 99.9
20 - 49.9
0 - 19.9

1850

1900

Source: Census of Population: 1850 and 1900

POPULATION GROWTH, DENSITY, AND DISTRIBUTION

When Alabama became a state in 1819 it accounted for 1.3 percent of the nation's population. Rapid growth during the following twenty years raised the State's proportion to 3.5 percent in 1840. Since then Alabama has fallen behind national growth. In 1970 only 1.7 percent of the nation's population lived in Alabama.

Alabama became a territory in 1817 and a state two years later. The first census following statehood showed Alabama as the home of 127,901 persons in 1820. From 1820 to 1830 the number of inhabitants more than doubled, and during the following decade almost doubled again. During this period the state capital was Tuscaloosa, the head of navigation on the Warrior River. By 1850 there were 771,623 persons living in Alabama. The greatest number of incoming settlers, 58,887, came from Georgia, 48,663 came from North Carolina, 22,541 from Tennessee, and 10,387 from Virginia.

The map of population density in 1850 illustrates the importance of Black Belt soils and cotton agriculture in the Pre-Civil War economy of Alabama.

Density of population maps are usually good indicators of where people live. They illustrate the number of inhabitants in a given area unit. When the basic political unit is the county, as on the maps in this atlas, there is an inference that population is spread evenly throughout the county. Interpretation of population density maps must be made with an awareness that distribution is uneven, with somewhat greater densities near settlements and lesser densities in unproductive lands such as forests and swamps. County population density maps for the 19th century, when America's population was mainly rural, tend to be more accurate in reflecting true distribution than county maps illustrating the 20th century distribution. Increasing urbanization creates wide differences within county densities which are not reflected in county-wide maps.

Significant historical trends are indicated in the analysis of population maps for 1850, 1900, 1950, and 1970. In 1850 population densities were greatest in the belt of counties running from the Mississippi border to the Chattahoochee River between the Plateau Region and the lower Coastal Plain. Five of the seven most populous counties of the State—Greene, Dallas, Montgomery, Marengo, and Macon—form an almost continuous belt across the agricultural heart of Alabama. The other two

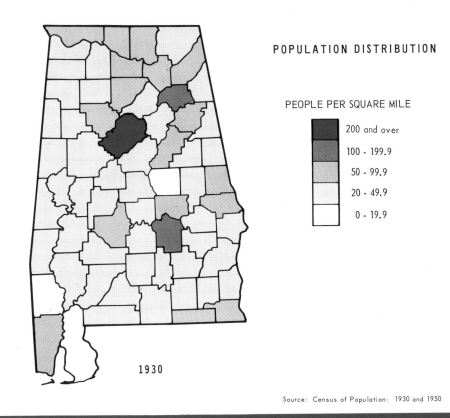

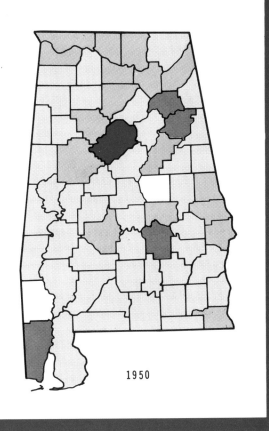

POPULATION DISTRIBUTION

PEOPLE PER SQUARE MILE

200 and over
100 - 199.9
50 - 99.9
20 - 49.9
0 - 19.9

1930

1950

Source: Census of Population: 1930 and 1950

leading counties, Mobile and Madison, reflected continued population accumulations at the primary points of immigration into the State. Political recognition of the concentration of population in the Black Belt occurred in 1846 when the state capital was transferred from Tuscaloosa to Montgomery.

There were two secondary agricultural regions with dense populations in 1850. One was in the northwest corner of the State in the Tennessee Valley. The other was in the Piedmont corridor entering Alabama from Georgia along the Coosa River. In 1850, Jefferson County, the present most populous county, had only 8,989 inhabitants and ranked 40th among the State's (then) 52 counties.

Between 1850 and 1900 Alabama's population rose by more than a million—from 771,623 to 1,828,697. The newcomers settled widely throughout the State on good farming lands. The continued dominance of agriculture is illustrated by the presence of five Black Belt and Wiregrass counties in the ranking of the ten most populous (Montgomery, Dallas, Marengo, Henry, and Lowndes). By 1900, however, the trend toward urbanization was already evident in the urban counties—Montgomery, Mobile, Tuscaloosa and, especially, Jefferson.

The development of the iron and steel industry in

Jefferson County following the Civil War gave this region an extraordinary increase in population. In 1860 Jefferson's 11,746 inhabitants placed it 38th among the State's counties; in 1870, with 12,345 people, it ranked 34th in the State. Between 1870 and 1880, while the State's population rose only 26.6 percent, Jefferson's population grew 85.5 percent to 23,272, moving the county to 19th place. In 1890, after a phenomenal rise of 280 percent to 88,501, Jefferson County was in first place, a ranking it has not relinquished since. Its 140,420 inhabitants in 1900 was almost twice the population of the second ranking county, Montgomery.

Between 1900 and 1930, the exodus from the rural counties that had begun in the 19th century continued. Although total population in Alabama rose 44.7 percent to 2,646,248, fourteen counties lost population. Six Black Belt counties—Lowndes, Wilcox, Perry, Greene, Hale, and Sumter—which had been among the State's population leaders in 1850 were the greatest losers: Lowndes lost 12,373 of its 1900 population of 35,651, and Wilcox decreased from 35,635 to 24,880. During the same period, the migration into the urban counties continued with Jefferson County recording a 207 percent increase to 431,493.

The period between 1930 and 1950 with its Great Depression and World War II witnessed an acceleration

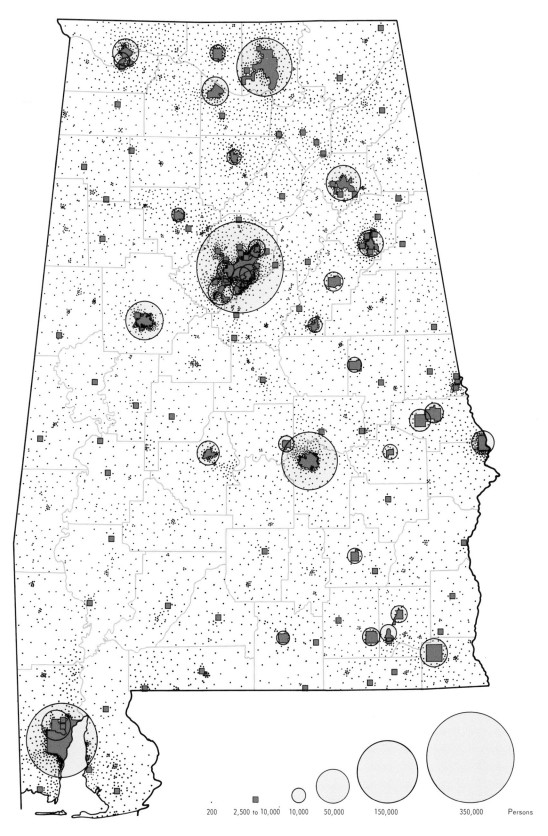

POPULATION DISTRIBUTION

200   2,500 to 10,000   10,000   50,000   150,000   350,000   Persons

Source: U.S Census of Population, 1970

of Alabama's demographic shifts. All the counties that lost population in the 1920's continued to lose during the 1930's. During the war years when defense plants provided increased attraction to farm workers, 44 of Alabama's 67 counties reported losses of population. In Alabama the loss by rural counties was more than compensated for by the growth of the industrial counties. Despite the rural exodus, State population rose 15 percent to 3,061,743 by 1950. Jefferson County rose to 559,928 (up 29.5 percent) and Mobile County almost doubled its population with a 95 percent rise to 231,105.

Between 1950 and 1970, Alabama's population grew slowly, gaining 12 percent compared to the national growth of 35 percent. Earlier demographic trends continued, with 39 counties losing population.

An analysis of population movements for the entire 1900–1970 period produces some definite patterns. The map showing population change during this period reveals that 25 counties had fewer people in them in 1970 than in 1900. Eight counties that lost almost half or more of their 1900 populations are in the agricultural sections of the State; seven in the Black Belt and one, Henry, in the Wiregrass. The percentages of loss recorded in each were: Greene, -56; Hale, -49; Sumter, -48; Perry, -52; Wilcox, -54; Lowndes, -64; Bullock, -63; and Henry, -64. On the other hand, population growth was most evident in the counties of the north-central region, the Tennessee Valley, and around Mobile Bay. While the State as a whole saw an 88 percent increase in population between 1900 and 1970, Mobile County's population rose 405 percent. Percentage increases for other leading counties were Baldwin, 350; Calhoun, 273; Etowah, 244; Madison, 327; and Tuscaloosa, 222. These increases led to a discernible concentration of population in a few urbanized counties. In 1900 it took 22 of the larger Alabama counties to account for half the State's population. By 1970 the nine counties of Jefferson, Mobile, Montgomery, Madison, Tuscaloosa, Calhoun, Etowah, Morgan, and Lauderdale contained over half Alabama's inhabitants. Furthermore, over 40 percent lived in the first five.

Analysis of the 1970 *Census of Population* suggests that the extraordinarily rapid migration into Alabama's larger metropolitan centers is slowing down and more people are moving into adjacent suburban counties. During the 1960's, while state population rose 5.4 percent, Jefferson County recorded an increase of only 1.6 percent and Mobile's population rose by a mere one percent. Furthermore, such urbanized counties as Montgomery

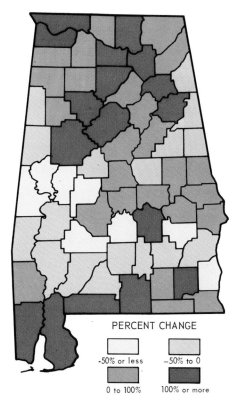

PERCENT CHANGE

-50% or less   -50% to 0

0 to 100%   100% or more

PERCENT CHANGE IN POPULATION
1900 to 1970

Source: U.S. Census of Population

and Etowah lost population, losing .8 and 2.9 percent respectively. Of the large urban counties only Madison, with a gain of 59 percent over 1960, indicated continued growth.

Between 1900 and 1970 the number of inhabitants in the United States increased 166 percent from 75,994,575 to 203,184,772. In the same period Alabama's population grew only 88 percent from 1,828,697 to 3,444,165. Alabama's population growth rate declined steadily from a 20.8 percent increase for the 1890–1900 decade to a 5.4 percent increase between 1960 and 1970. Correspondingly, national growth rates for the same periods declined from 21 percent to 13.3 percent. This disparity in growth rates caused Alabama to drop from 18th to 20th place in national population ranking. One consequence of Alabama's failure to keep pace with national population growth is the loss of representation in the U.S. Congress. In 1910 Alabama had ten members in the House of Representatives. The number of congressmen was reduced to nine following the 1930 census, to eight after 1960 and to seven by the 1970 census.

Walter F. Koch

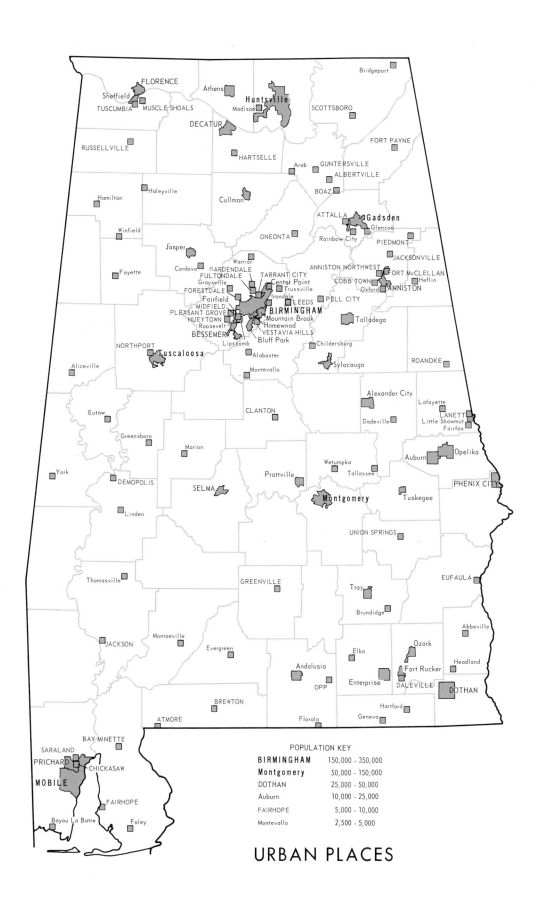

FLORENCE
Sheffield
TUSCUMBIA
MUSCLE SHOALS
Athens
Madison
Huntsville
SCOTTSBORO
Bridgeport

DECATUR
HARTSELLE
FORT PAYNE

RUSSELLVILLE
Arab
GUNTERSVILLE
ALBERTVILLE
BOAZ

Hamilton
Haleyville
Cullman
ATTALLA
Gadsden
Glencoe
PIEDMONT

Winfield
ONEONTA
Rainbow City
JACKSONVILLE

Fayette
Jasper
Cordova
Warrior
GARDENDALE
FULTONDALE
Graysville
FORESTDALE
Fairfield
MIDFIELD
PLEASANT GROVE
HUEYTOWN
Roosevelt
BESSEMER
Lipscomb
TARRANT CITY
Center Point
Trussville
Irondale
BIRMINGHAM
Mountain Brook
Homewood
VESTAVIA HILLS
Bluff Park
LEEDS
ANNISTON NORTHWEST
COBB TOWN
Oxford
FORT McCLELLAN
Heflin
ANNISTON
PELL CITY

NORTHPORT
Tuscaloosa
Alabaster
Montevallo
Childersburg
Talladega
ROANOKE

Aliceville
Sylacauga

Eutaw
CLANTON
Alexander City
Lafayette
LANETT
Little Shawmut
Fairfax

Greensboro
Marion
Dadeville

York
DEMOPOLIS
Wetumpka
Tallassee
Auburn
Opelika

Linden
SELMA
Prattville
Montgomery
Tuskegee
PHENIX CITY

Thomasville
GREENVILLE
UNION SPRINGS
EUFAULA

Jackson
Monroeville
Troy
Brundidge
Abbeville

Evergreen
Elba
Ozark
Headland

Andalusia
OPP
Enterprise
Fort Rucker
DALEVILLE
DOTHAN

BREWTON
Hartford
Geneva

ATMORE
Florala

BAY MINETTE
SARALAND
PRICHARD
CHICKASAW
MOBILE
FAIRHOPE
Bayou La Batre
Foley

POPULATION KEY
BIRMINGHAM 150,000 - 350,000
Montgomery 50,000 - 150,000
DOTHAN 25,000 - 50,000
Auburn 10,000 - 25,000
FAIRHOPE 5,000 - 10,000
Montevallo 2,500 - 5,000

URBAN PLACES

Birmingham Skyline

URBANIZATION

Over a period of one hundred and forty years, Alabama has changed in character from a rural to an urban state. When Alabama was admitted to the Union in 1819, the State was classified as 100 percent rural. Alabama's 1820 population was 127,901, ranking twentieth among the twenty-seven states and territories then comprising the Union.

During Alabama's greatest percentage growth (142 percent) between 1820 and 1830, she retained her rural character (about 95 percent). Following the War Between the States, the growth rate of Alabama declined in relation to national growth. By the beginning of the twentieth century, Alabama had a total of 1,828,697 residents, with only 12 percent classified as urban dwellers.

The most remarkable trends in urbanization have occurred in Alabama during the past seventy years. By 1960 the population had increased to 3,266,740 persons, of which 1,791,721 or 54.8 percent lived in urban areas. In 1960, for the first time in Alabama's history, more than half of the population was classified as urban, or as living in places with 2,500 or more population. At that time more than half of the population of Alabama was situated in only ten of the sixty-seven counties. Most urban dwellers resided chiefly in the seven Standard Metropolitan Statistical Areas of Birmingham, Huntsville,

Gadsden, Mobile, Montgomery, Tuscaloosa,and Columbus, Georgia—Phenix City, Alabama. The population per square mile in Alabama in 1960 was 63.3 persons as compared with 49.6 persons for the United States as a whole.

In 1970 there were 408 incorporated and unincorporated places of 1,000 or more people in Alabama. Of these, 61 were new additions, 246 experienced population growth, and 101 suffered a population decline during the previous decade. The places of 1,000 or more population experiencing the greatest percentage increases in population growth were generally small communities of less than 10,000 population. Among the communities with populations exceeding 25,000 in 1960, only Decatur, Florence, and Huntsville in the Tennessee Valley, Bessemer and Tuscaloosa in Central Alabama, and Dothan in South Alabama experienced population gains from 1960 to 1970. Huntsville with its space exploration installations recorded the greatest percentage gains in urban population by a wide margin. North and Central Alabama contained the greatest number of central places of 1,000 or more population, with Jefferson County leading all counties with 37 places. The fewest such places occurred in the rural counties of the Black Belt.

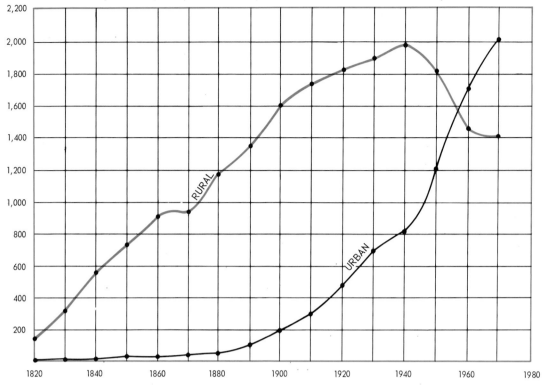

URBAN AND RURAL POPULATION GROWTH

By 1970 Alabama contained twelve urban areas with populations of over 20,000. Of these, nine are found in North and Central Alabama. It must be noted that the maximum numerical population growth between 1960 and 1970 occurred in the urban areas of over 20,000 population in the Tennessee Valley.

From 1960 to 1970 the Alabama metropolitan areas experienced a 6.5 percent increase in population as compared to a 16.6 percent increase for the metropolitan areas of the United States as a whole. The non-metropolitan areas of Alabama increased in population by 4.2 percent as compared to a 6.5 percent increase for the non-metropolitan areas of the United States as a whole. The 1970 population of Alabama totaled 3,444,165 with 2,011,941, or 58 percent, living in urban areas. It must be concluded that urbanization is occurring mostly in North and Central Alabama. Although urbanization is rapidly increasing in Alabama, it is not increasing so fast and has not reached the same level in Alabama as in the United States as a whole.

James M. Price
Neal G. Lineback

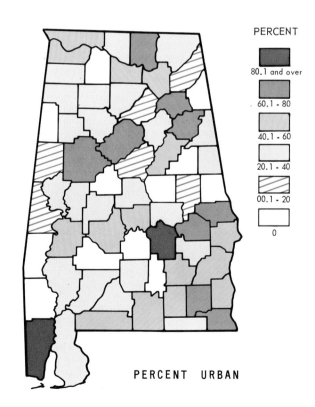

PERCENT

80.1 and over

60.1 - 80

40.1 - 60

20.1 - 40

00.1 - 20

0

PERCENT URBAN

BLACK POPULATION

The black population of Alabama can be studied from many points of view. Attention is here focused on numbers, distribution, residence and age. The black population of the State is now decreasing in numbers, moving to the cities, and showing a decrease in average age.

Blacks have been in Alabama probably as long as whites. The first census of Alabama in 1820 showed 42,450 blacks (571 free) and 84,451 whites. The early influx of blacks was involuntary—consisting mainly of slaves brought by their owners from Virginia, Maryland, and the Carolinas. Local planters purchased additional slaves from these areas. The availability of cheap fertile land in Alabama and declining productivity of lands on the Seaboard spurred this migration.[1]

The black population increased fivefold between 1820 and 1840, compared with a less than threefold increase for whites. By 1860 the Black Belt (named after its dark, rich soils) had developed its unique racial identity with a preponderance of blacks. Net immigration continued until the decade of the 1860's. In 1850

Alabama's black population was 345,122, of which 2,268 were "free men of color."

After the 1860's more blacks left the State than arrived. During the 1870's the major flow was to the adjoining West South Central States. This movement was from one rural area to another in search of agricultural opportunities.[2] The United States Census revealed a net loss of 36,100 blacks for this decade. The First World War sparked emigration for different reasons, but mainly for urban and industrial opportunities in the North and West. The East North Central States replaced the West South Central States as the leading destination of Alabama blacks. This northward and westward emigration of blacks has continued to the present, dampened by the Depression and then vitalized by the Second World War.

Over the past 20 years in Alabama, the trend in numbers of black people has been downward. In absolute terms, the total declined from 979,617 in 1950 to 903,467 in 1970; a decline of eight percent. The

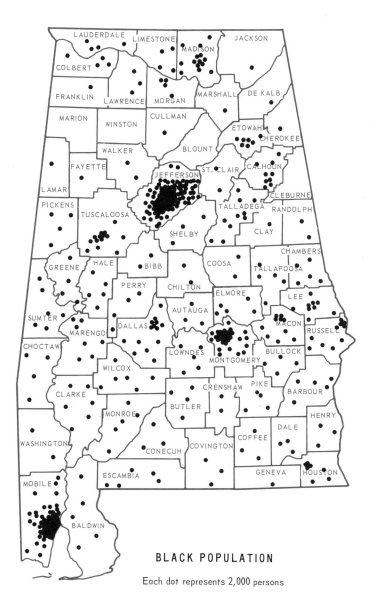

BLACK POPULATION

Each dot represents 2,000 persons

0   25   50   75 Miles

Source: U. S. Census of Population, 1970

trend between 1960 and 1970 was essentially the same as between 1950 and 1960.

There are two aspects of the black population: total numbers, and blacks as a percentage of the total population. The period from 1950 to 1970 is the first time during which there has been a persistent decline in total numbers. However, the percentage of blacks in the total state population has declined every census since 1900. In 1970 blacks comprised 26 percent of the total population, compared with 32 percent in 1950.

The main reason for the decrease in black population is emigration from the State. Not even relatively high fertility rates among black females have offset the negative effects of emigration. Between 1950 and 1960, the Bureau of Census reported a 224,000 net loss by migration of nonwhites and an even larger 231,000 net loss by migration between 1960 and 1970. Nearly all counties experienced net losses due to migration, but the effects of migration have been relatively more pronounced in the more rural counties.

Most of the State's black population is found in the more urbanized counties. Fifty-five percent of Alabama blacks reside in the Standard Metropolitan Statistical Areas containing Birmingham, Mobile, Montgomery, Huntsville, Tuscaloosa, Gadsden, and Columbus, Georgia—Phenix City, Alabama.

In 1970, 62 percent of the black population was classed as urban, compared with only 57 percent of the white population. This relatively more urban status of the black population was observed in every population census since 1930, and this margin increased during the 1950–1970 period. In 1950, 46 percent of the black population was urban, while 43 percent of the white population was so classified.

When the distribution of the rural black population is examined, the role of historical factors is evident.

Counties with the largest percentages of their total population classed as black are the Black Belt counties. No county north of Jefferson had as much as 25 percent of its population classed as black in 1970. In contrast there were 10 counties, all in the Black Belt, in which blacks represented 50 percent or more of the total population. Blacks form the majority of the population in all of the Black Belt counties except Montgomery. Despite the high black ratio in this area at the time of the 1970 census, there were indications that the Black Belt was becoming "less black." In 1950 there were fourteen counties where the blacks formed a majority, compared with only ten in 1970. The high emigration rate has been selective; blacks are leaving faster than whites.

Another feature of the black population of Alabama is its youthfulness, i.e. average age relative to that of the white population. A partial explanation for this is the selective migration of black persons in the 20–40 age group and relatively high black fertility rates. There is a higher percentage of blacks in all five-year categories under 20 years than of whites. For example, 12.2 percent of the black population was in the five- to nine-year old group, compared with 9.3 percent of the white population in 1970. In 1970 the state median age for blacks was 21.5 years, or seven years less than that for whites. In 1950 the black median age was only four years less than that for whites.

[1]The U.S. Census Bureau collected no data on black migration before 1870. The trends above were made by comparing the change in the Alabama population with rates of natural increase of all blacks in the United States.
[2]Thomas Jackson Woofter, Jr., Negro Migration: *Changes in Rural Organization and Population of the Cotton Belt* (New York: W.D. Gray, 1920) p.15.

Irene Nelson

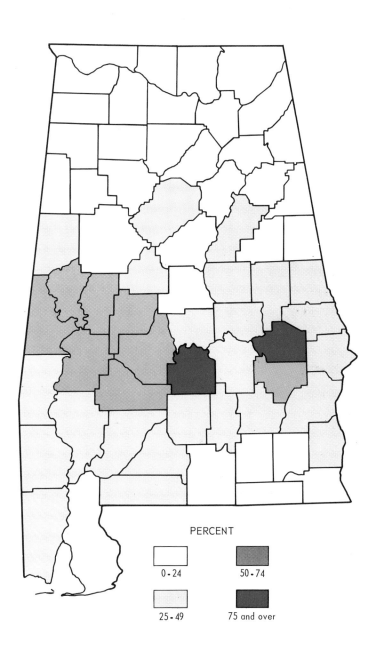

PERCENT

0 - 24   50 - 74

25 - 49   75 and over

POPULATION CLASSIFIED BLACK

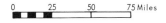

0   25   50   75 Miles

Source: U. S. Census of Population, 1970

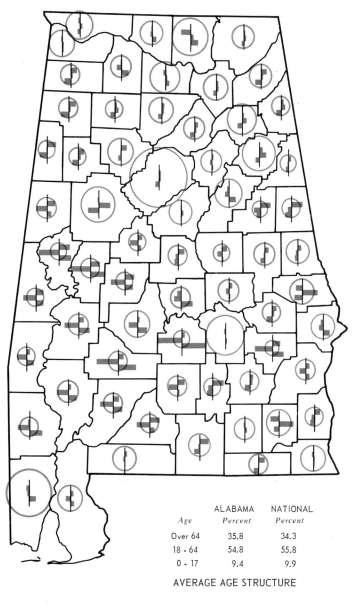

Age	ALABAMA Percent	NATIONAL Percent
Over 64	35.8	34.3
18 - 64	54.8	55.8
0 - 17	9.4	9.9

AVERAGE AGE STRUCTURE

COUNTY POPULATION

PERCENT DEVIATION FROM
STATE AVERAGE

AGE STRUCTURE

AGE STRUCTURE

In 1970 the median age of the population of Alabama was 27.0 years. This means that about half of the people living in the State were under 27 years of age and about half were over 27. The median age was slightly higher in most urban areas and lower in rural areas. Women averaged about three years older than men, and the average age of the white population was about seven years greater than that of the black population.

The median age of the population in the State has risen since 1900, when it was only 18.9 years, increasing by 8.1 years to the present figure of 27 years. Several factors account for this present older average age of the State's population. Among them are: (1) a general increase in life expectancy, (2) a decline in fertility rates, resulting in proportionately smaller numbers of children, and (3) the migration out of the State of substantial numbers of people of working age. The latter case is especially true among Alabama blacks, whose median age increased between 1900 and 1950, and thereafter decreased sharply. Marked changes have occurred in the age composition of Alabamians even within the past decade as a result of the large decline in proportionate numbers of children under 15 years of age, and the proportionate increase in numbers of persons 45 and over.

Geographic patterns are sometimes seen in the distribution of different age groups within the State. Of the total population of Alabama, 36 percent was less than 18 years of age in 1970. This age group was concentrated

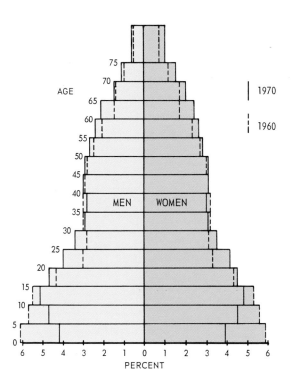

POPULATION PYRAMID 1960-1970

Source: U. S. Census of Population, 1970

in significantly greater-than-average proportions in the western rural Black Belt counties. The 18–64 group, which comprised 55 percent of the total, was proportionately underrepresented in those same counties, which also tended to have a larger-than-average population in the over-65 bracket. The latter age category accounted for 9 percent of the State's population in 1970.

Relatively large numbers of people over 65 are found not only in the western Black Belt but in all rural areas of the State. In contrast to this, four counties—Madison (NASA), Dale (Fort Rucker), Lee (Auburn University), and Autauga (probably a population spillover from Montgomery)—had conspicuously fewer people (each more than 20 percent below the State average) 65 years of age and older.

One fact is readily apparent from a cursory examination of age group distributions in Alabama. It is that the predominantly rural counties tend to have larger proportions of both children and elderly people than the State average. The population group between these two "dependent" age groups comprises the so-called "working population." Thus, in rural counties where the per capita income is relatively low, a contributing factor is the relatively small size of the "working population" group in the total county population. This means that rural counties have a somewhat lower percentage of economically productive people than do the more urban counties.

Selwyn Hollingsworth

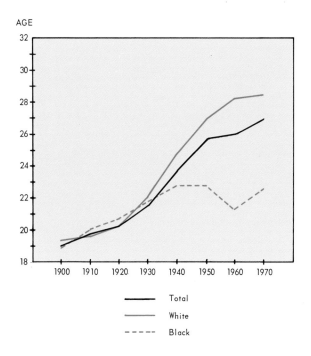

MEDIAN AGE BY RACE 1900-1970

Source: U. S. Census of Population, 1970

EDUCATION

The last three decades have seen significant changes in the nature and impact of education in Alabama. Since 1940, the percentage of persons 25 years or older who have received an eighth grade education has nearly doubled, the percentage completing a high school education has tripled, and the percentage completing 4 years of college has multiplied fivefold. While the percentages at each level are considerably below the national average, it is evident that there has been a significant increase in educational attainment at all levels in the State.

While this increase in educational attainment is evident for both blacks and whites, the relative advantage of whites over blacks has remained nearly constant. It should be kept in mind that these figures do not include persons under 25 years of age and that desegregation as well as the federally funded programs for the disadvantaged have only been implemented within the last decade. Those most affected by these programs would not have reached the age of 25 by 1970. It should also be noted that larger percentages of blacks who have completed their education beyond the eighth grade have migrated to other states than their white counterparts and that they frequently have done so before the age of 25. Only a relatively few migrate into Alabama from other states. There is, however, some evidence that migration patterns may be changing. The impact of federal funding, desegregation orders, and changing migration patterns cannot be adequately determined from the census data available at the present time.

The median educational attainment level in 1970 was higher for counties in Alabama with high population concentrations than for those with lower densities. The highest median grade levels completed for both blacks and whites were in the counties which included the large metropolitan areas of Birmingham, Huntsville, Tuscaloosa, Montgomery, and Dothan. The counties having populations with the lowest median years of school completed were concentrated in the rural Black Belt.

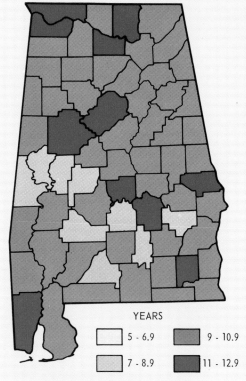

YEARS

| 5 - 6.9 | 9 - 10.9 |
| 7 - 8.9 | 11 - 12.9 |

MEDIAN SCHOOL YEARS COMPLETED BY ALL RACES

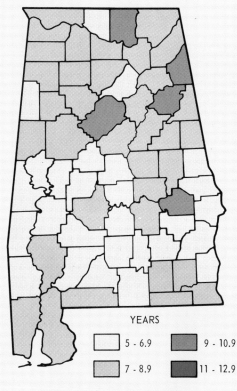

YEARS

| 5 - 6.9 | 9 - 10.9 |
| 7 - 8.9 | 11 - 12.9 |

MEDIAN SCHOOL YEARS COMPLETED BY BLACKS

Source: Census of Population, 1970

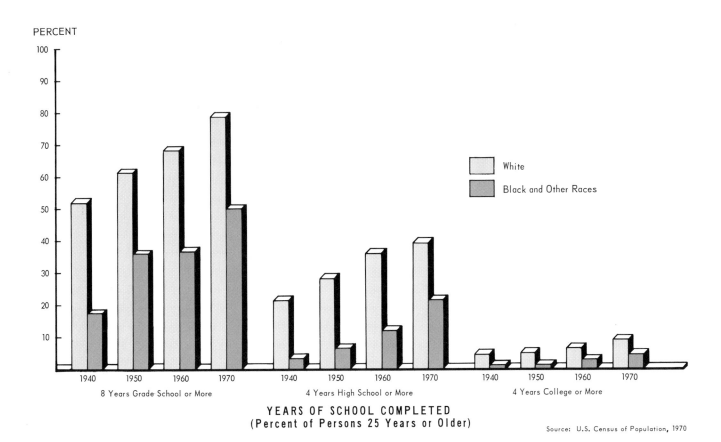

PERCENT

White
Black and Other Races

8 Years Grade School or More | 4 Years High School or More | 4 Years College or More

YEARS OF SCHOOL COMPLETED
(Percent of Persons 25 Years or Older)

Source: U.S. Census of Population, 1970

RODNEY HUEY

The median number of school years completed in 1970 for whites was 11.6 years, while that for the blacks was 8.1 years. There was also a consistent pattern on the basis of sex; females remained in school 1.1 years longer than males. For blacks, girls remained in school 1.9 years longer than boys. The school drop-out rate was lowest for white girls and highest for black males.

In summary, the educational attainment level, while lower than the national average, has increased significantly since 1940. The level of attainment is higher in urban areas than in rural areas. Whites attain a higher level of education than do blacks and females remain in school longer than males for both races. The data for the upcoming decade should provide an information base for correlating educational attainment with the federal funding, desegregation, and changing migration patterns of the 1960's.

Patrick M. Ferguson

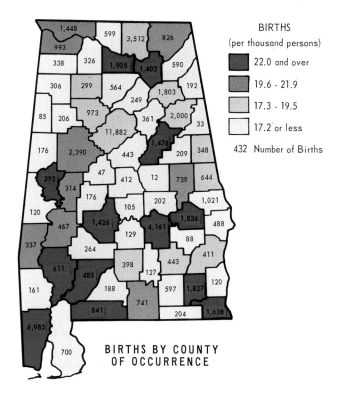

BIRTHS
(per thousand persons)

- 22.0 and over
- 19.6 - 21.9
- 17.3 - 19.5
- 17.2 or less

432 Number of Births

BIRTHS BY COUNTY
OF OCCURRENCE

Source: Bureau of Vital Statistics, 1970

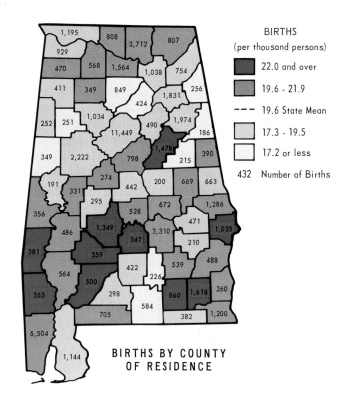

BIRTHS
(per thousand persons)

- 22.0 and over
- 19.6 - 21.9
- - - 19.6 State Mean
- 17.3 - 19.5
- 17.2 or less

432 Number of Births

BIRTHS BY COUNTY
OF RESIDENCE

Source: Bureau of Vital Statistics, 1970

BIRTHS AND DEATHS

The 1970 birth and death rates by county in Alabama provide some rather interesting contrasts, generally reflecting the age structure and socio-cultural backgrounds of the population.

Two methods were used to show births per thousand population—one was by the mother's county of residence and the other was by county of occurrence. Generally, the two geographic patterns did not conform, primarily, perhaps, because there seem to be several counties in the State which lack adequate medical facilities for obstetrics. As a result, it appears that women frequently chose to give birth at regional medical facilities in adjacent counties rather than in their county of residence. The pattern of births by place of occurrence is related, then, to the presence, proximity, or absence of complete medical facilities.

The birth rates by county of residence (residence of mother) provide a rather distinct geographic pattern.

The northern tiers of counties generally had birth rates above the state mean of 19.6 births per thousand, while a northeast-southwest diagonal band with birth rates below the mean stretched from north Georgia to the Mississippi border, generally corresponding to an industrial belt across the State. The southern one-half of Alabama being more rural and agricultural possessed birth rates generally higher than the rest of the State, reflecting, perhaps, rural mores for larger families and high concentrations of black population.

Higher death rates by place of residence were found in the southern two-thirds of the State, particularly in the predominantly rural agricultural counties. Where the rates were highest, there were frequently large proportions of aged persons in the counties, resulting from heavy out-migrations of young adults.

The national trend of the birth rate has been downward in recent years, and Alabama is no exception. Since

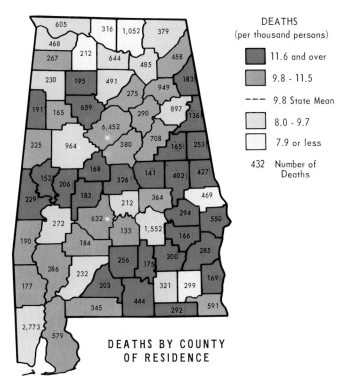

DEATHS
(per thousand persons)

11.6 and over

9.8 - 11.5

– – – 9.8 State Mean

8.0 - 9.7

7.9 or less

432 Number of
Deaths

**DEATHS BY COUNTY
OF RESIDENCE**

Source: Bureau of Vital Statistics, 1970

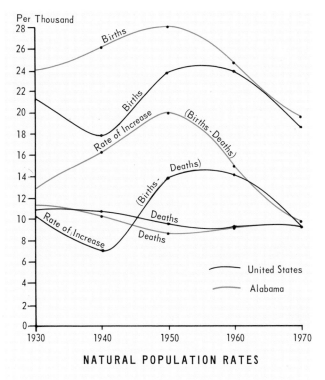

NATURAL POPULATION RATES

Source: Bureau of Vital Statistics, 1970

the 1950's it has become apparent that family planning is postponing some pregnancies, the rate of illegitimacy is decreasing, the number of children born per family is declining, and more persons are living further beyond the child-producing age than ever before.

The national trend in the death rate has been slowly downward for many years, but in Alabama the trend began to creep upward during the 1950's. This perhaps was in response to the aging population; for as more people lived longer and longer and as outmigration of young adults occurred, the death rate began to reverse and has continued slightly upward into the 1970's.

The total result of Alabama's births and deaths has been a decline in the rate of natural population increase. In other words, the population of the State is increasing through births at a slower rate than ever before.

Ross Palmer

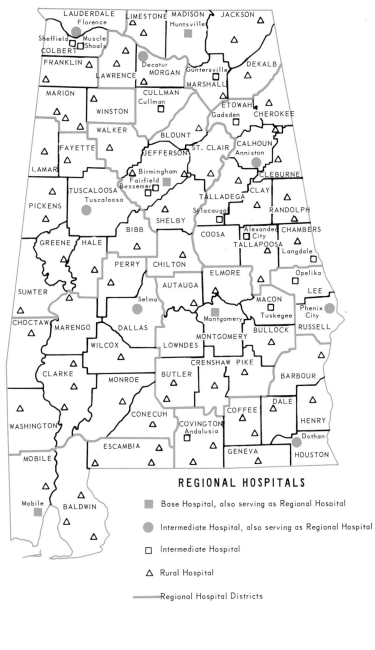

REGIONAL HOSPITALS

■ Base Hospital, also serving as Regional Hospital

● Intermediate Hospital, also serving as Regional Hospital

□ Intermediate Hospital

△ Rural Hospital

── Regional Hospital Districts

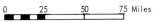

0   25   50   75 Miles

Source: Alabama Department of Public Health

PHYSICAL HEALTH FACILITIES

Increasingly health care in America today is provided by medical institutions such as hospitals and public health centers. This is also true in Alabama where regional hospitals, intermediate hospitals, and rural hospitals serve the population of the State. The regional hospitals are in the larger cities, and are equipped with the latest electronic monitoring devices for use by cardiac and other patients. Other remarkably sophisticated laboratory equipment is also available, and eighteen different tests may be run automatically on a single sample of blood serum; the results of these tests are printed on a chart as part of the patient's record. X-ray and other equipment has also become more effective in operation. Through a cooperative effort, referrals are made from the rural hospitals to the larger regional hospitals where more sophisticated equipment and medical expertise are available to meet the needs of the patient.

In 1971 Alabama had 138 hospitals of all types, with a total of 28,962 beds. There were 121 short-term general hospitals in Alabama with 16,286 beds, into which a total of 530,588 patients were admitted in 1970. All hospitals, both short-term and long-term, had an average daily census of 24,447 patients, and employed 38,786 persons, with total operating expenses amounting to $338,000,000 in that year.

The growth of hospital care in Alabama has involved not only the enlargement of centralized medical complexes, but also an increase in the number of rural hospitals. The major-medical complexes include the renowned University of Alabama Medical Center in Birmingham, as well as major-medical complexes in Mobile, Montgomery, Tuscaloosa, Huntsville, and the Florence-Sheffield area. Hospitals in Alabama have undergone internal growth in order to meet the State's increasing health needs. Emphasis has been placed both on the development of new services and on increased utilization of these service departments. The larger hospitals have intensive-care units with coronary care monitor-

- ● District Tuberculosis Hospitals
- ▲ Other Facilities
- — Districts

TUBERCULOSIS CENTERS

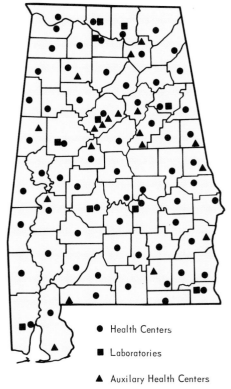

- ● Health Centers
- ■ Laboratories
- ▲ Auxilary Health Centers

PUBLIC HEALTH CENTERS

Source: Alabama Department of Public Health

ing equipment. Several hospitals in Alabama today have full-time emergency room staffing by physicans, which is important, because out-patient departments and emergency rooms have shown a tremendous increase in utilization in the last several years, and this means better health care for the individual.

The hospital licensure program in Alabama has helped to maintain high standards, both in construction and operation, with a remarkable degree of efficiency. Each hospital is required to have a fire safety and disaster plan. One hospital in Alabama recently won a first-place award in the entire nation for its fire safety program.

With the growth of physical plants, the stimulus of the medical center and school in Birmingham, and the new programs in medical education in Mobile, Tuscaloosa, and Huntsville, the people of Alabama can look forward in the coming years to a continued improvement in its overall program of medical and hospital care.

D.O. McClusky

HIGHER EDUCATION

Alabama's concern for the education of its youth beyond the high school level dates from admission to statehood. One of the first acts of the Alabama legislature was to authorize the establishment of a state university at Tuscaloosa. Construction on The University of Alabama campus began in 1827, and the first students were admitted in 1831. In the meantime various religious bodies established institutions of higher learning to augment the state system. The Jesuit order of the Roman Catholic Church founded Spring Hill College at Mobile in 1831. Methodists established colleges at LaGrange and Athens, and the Baptists opened Judson College for Women and Howard College at Marion. In 1970 twelve of the State's senior colleges were sponsored and controlled by religious bodies.

Over the past 150 years Alabama's system of colleges and universities has grown steadily both in the public and private sectors. In 1971 there were sixteen state-operated senior colleges, universities and university centers, with a total enrollment of 65,416. Fifteen private senior colleges served an additional 14,368 students. Despite the presence of thirty-one institutions, however, enrollment was still dominated in 1971 by the two largest state universities, The University of Alabama and Auburn

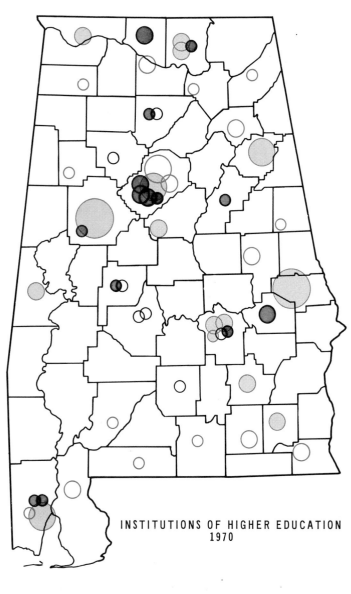

INSTITUTIONS OF HIGHER EDUCATION
1970

UNIVERSITIES AND COLLEGES

State

Private

JUNIOR COLLEGES

State

Private

Less than 1,000   1,000 - 3,999   4,000 - 9,999   10,000 and over
ENROLLMENT

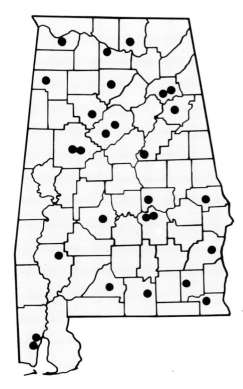

TRADE SCHOOLS AND TECHNICAL INSTITUTES

SCHOOL	LOCATION	1970 ENROLLMENT

SENIOR COLLEGES AND UNIVERSITIES

School	Location	1970 Enrollment
Alabama A & M University	Normal	2,755
Alabama State University	Montgomery	2,524
Athens College	Athens	1,080
Auburn University	Auburn	14,229
Montgomery Branch	Montgomery	992
Birmingham-Southern College	Birmingham	1,040
Florence State University	Florence	3,235
Huntingdon College	Montgomery	784
Jacksonville State University	Jacksonville	5,900
Judson College	Marion	458
Livingston University	Livingston	2,000
Miles College	Birmingham	1,139
Mobile College	Mobile	506
Oakwood College	Huntsville	572
St. Bernard College	St. Bernard	652
Samford University	Birmingham	2,663
Southeastern Bible College	Birmingham	180
Spring Hill College	Mobile	970
Stillman College	Tuscaloosa	660
Talladega College	Talladega	531
Troy State University	Troy	3,458
Fort Rucker Center	Ozark	1,175
Maxwell-Gunter Center	Montgomery	1,099
Tuskegee Institute	Tuskegee	2,918
University of Alabama at		
Birmingham	Birmingham	6,629
Huntsville	Huntsville	2,630
Tuscaloosa	University	13,017
University of Montevallo	Montevallo	2,454
University of South Alabama	Mobile	4,526

JUNIOR AND COMMUNITY COLLEGES

Public

School	Location	1970 Enrollment
Alexander City Junior College	Alexander City	1,151
Albert P. Brewer Junior College	Fayette	444
John C. Calhoun State Technical Junior College	Decatur	2,087
Jefferson Davis Junior College	Brewton	613
Enterprise Junior College	Enterprise	1,387
James H. Faulkner Junior College	Bay Minette	1,086
Gadsden Junior College	Gadsden	2,727
Patrick Henry Junior College	Monroeville	528
Jefferson Junior College	Birmingham	4,753
Theodore A. Lawson Junior College	Birmingham	1,205
Mobile Junior College	Mobile	915
Northeast Alabama Junior College	Rainsville	695
Northwest Alabama Junior College	Phil Campbell	579
Snead Junior College	Arab	882
Southern Union Junior College	Wadley	612
George C. Wallace State Technical Junior College	Dothan	1,027
Lurleen B. Wallace Junior College	Andalusia	595

Private

School	Location	1970 Enrollment
Alabama Christian College	Montgomery	282
Alabama Lutheran		
Academy and Junior College	Selma	
Cullman College	Cullman	136
Lomax-Hannon Junior College	Greenville	6
Marion Institute	Marion	303
Selma University	Selma	380
Walker County Junior College	Jasper	

Source: Alabama Department of Education, 1971

University. These two university systems accounted for 37,977 students, 47.5 percent of Alabama's senior college enrollment and 36.9 percent of the State's entire college population. The two main campuses at Tuscaloosa and Auburn served directly 34.1 percent of all senior college students and 26.5 percent of all college students in Alabama.

The unprecedented expansion of the college network in Alabama during the 1960's has afforded almost all the inhabitants the opportunity to continue their education beyond the high school level. A comparison of the school network with the population distribution for 1970 reveals that about 97.9 percent of Alabama's population lives within sixty miles of a senior college, and 99.4 percent lives either within twenty miles of a junior college or within sixty miles of a senior college.

An analysis of enrollment and trends in higher education reveals a total 1970–71 enrollment of 102,909 in Alabama's sixty-five junior and senior colleges and universities. This represented an increase of 150 percent over 1960–61. During the decade, enrollment in state-supported institutions rose 195.4 percent, from 29,344 to 86,702, with almost a quarter of the 1970 enrollment being accounted for by the new junior colleges. Enrollment in private colleges grew by 37.3 percent during the 1960's, increasing from 11,798 to 16,207 students.

The most striking development in higher education in Alabama during the 1960's has been the phenomenal growth of enrollment in the junior colleges, especially in those of the state system established in 1964. In 1960 there were no state-supported junior colleges. Eight private junior colleges had 1,680 students, 3.9 percent of all college enrollment in the State. In 1970 private school enrollment had increased to 1,839, even though two of the larger private junior colleges had become state institutions. Enrollment in the seventeen state junior colleges was 21,286. The combined enrollment in all junior colleges represented a 1,320 percent increase over 1960, and junior college enrollment accounted for 22.4 percent of all college students in the State. This rapid growth reflected a trend in college attendance patterns that demands a reappraisal of relationships between the four-year and two-year institutions.

In addition to the universities and colleges, Alabama has an extensive system of twenty-seven trade schools and technical institutes. These schools offer Alabamians opportunities to train for a wide variety of technical and semiprofessional occupations such as barbering, practical nursing, data processing, and aircraft mechanics. The expansion of the trade school system began in 1964, and the enrollment growth rate has paralleled that of the new state junior colleges.

Walter F. Koch

Air University

MILITARY

There are numerous military reservations and facilities, both active and reserve, throughout Alabama. Many of them engage in rather specialized activities, and have roles which are not duplicated elsewhere in the United States.

ARMY

The major active Army installations in Alabama are: the Army Aviation Center and School, Fort Rucker; Army Missile and Munitions Center and School, Redstone Arsenal; and the Army School/Training Center at Fort McClellan.

Fort Rucker. The Army Aviation Center and School is at Fort Rucker, located between Enterprise and Ozark. The Aviation School provides training not only for Army student aviators, but also for those of the Navy, Marine Corps, and Air Force. Military personnel of allied nations also receive training here. Approximately 10,500 military people and 7,800 civilians are employed at Fort Rucker, which covers over 59,000 acres.

Redstone Arsenal. Redstone Arsenal is a combination of two U.S. Army arsenals, the Redstone Ordnance Plant and the Huntsville Arsenal. Redstone Arsenal serves as the nerve center for the Army's missile and rocket programs. The Army Missile Command and the Army Missile and Munitions Center and School are located on the Arsenal. Also on the Arsenal are the George C. Marshall Space Flight Center of the National Aeronautics (nonmilitary) and Space Administration and a government-owned, contractor-operated facility engaged in rocket propellant research and manufacture. Located off post are the Army Safeguard Logistics Command and the Army Engineer Division, Huntsville. The Army employed approximately 5,000 military personnel and over 10,000 civilians at Redstone and in Huntsville; while the civilian personnel, both of N.A.S.A. and government contractors working on the base, numbered over 25,000 people in early 1972. The Arsenal covers 38,881 acres.

Fort McClellan. Fort McClellan is distinguished by being the home of two Army Corps—the Army Chemical

GSA

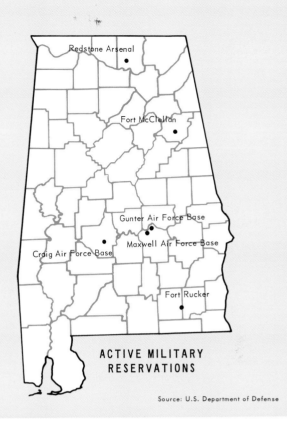

ACTIVE MILITARY
RESERVATIONS

Source: U.S. Department of Defense

Corps and the Women's Army Corps. Here are located the Army Chemical Center and School and the Women's Army Corps Center and School. Other activities at Fort McClellan are the Army Combat Command Chemical-Biological-Radiological Agency, and the U.S. Third Army Noncommissioned Officer Academy. Fort McClellan covers 46,374 acres, has an average military population of 6,000, and employs about 1,300 civilian personnel.

AIR FORCE

Maxwell Air Force Base. Maxwell A.F.B. is the home of the Air University. This school conducts professional and technical education programs in its role as the professional educational center of the Air Force.

The base, located on the northwest edge of Montgomery, Alabama, is 2,400 acres in area, and has an average military population of 5,000.

Gunter Air Force Base. Gunter A.F.B. has two major activities as its present mission. The Extension Course Institute (ECI) is the correspondence school of the Air Force. It provides course materials to over 400,000 officers and airmen each year.

The U.S.A.F. Data Systems Design Center develops automated data systems and computer programs for worldwide use by the Air Force. The population of Gunter is approximately 1,500. The base is on the northeastern edge of Montgomery, Alabama, and is 347 acres in area.

Craig Air Force Base. Craig's mission is to train jet pilots for the Air Force. The military population of the base is approximately 2,700 and it is located five miles southeast of Selma, Alabama.

NAVY

There are no major naval installations in Alabama. However, Naval Reserve Training Centers are located in Birmingham, Gadsden, Huntsville, Mobile, Montgomery, Sheffield, Troy, and Tuscaloosa. Navy Recruiting Stations are also located in Anniston, Cullman, and Dothan, as well as in the above cities. The Naval Training Unit of the Army Chemical Center and School is at Fort McClellan. Naval officers at Hayes International Corporation in Dothan and at NASA in Huntsville engage in liaison activities.

Bill R. Blalock
Robert A. Jackson

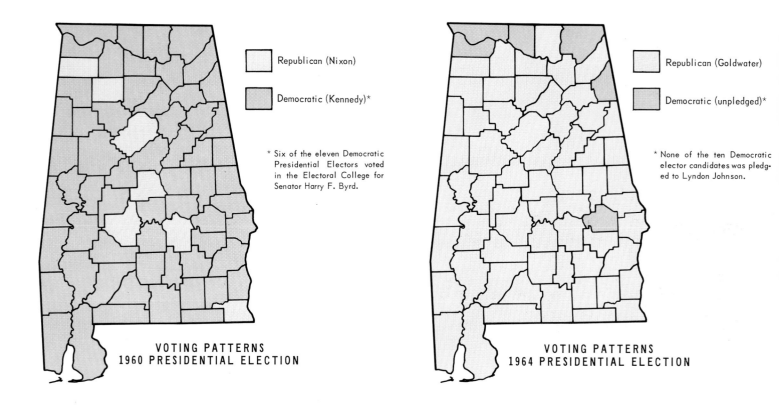

VOTING PATTERNS
1960 PRESIDENTIAL ELECTION

VOTING PATTERNS
1964 PRESIDENTIAL ELECTION

POLITICS

For many years following the end of the Reconstruction Era, Alabama was a firm member of the bloc of Democratic-voting Southern states termed the "Solid South." Not until 1948 did Alabama give its electoral vote to any candidate other than the Democratic nominee for President. In 1948 Alabamians voted for Strom Thurmond, the States' Rights Democrat. In 1952 and 1956 national Democratic loyalties revived in support of Adlai Stevenson.

John F. Kennedy was the choice of Alabamians in 1960. However, six of the 11 Democratic electors supported Senator Harry F. Byrd of Virginia instead of their party's national nominee. Complicated by problems related to race relations, Democratic loyalties declined again in 1964 when Republican Senator Barry Goldwater won 61 Alabama counties and 69.5 percent of the popular vote, while there were no electors pledged to

President Johnson on the ballot.

In 1968 Alabamian George C. Wallace (whose wife, the late Governor Lurleen Burns Wallace, was state chief executive at the time) was a national presidential candidate. His fellow-Alabamians supported him with 65.9 percent of the popular vote and a victory in all but three of the State's 67 counties. Electors pledged to him were those of the regular Democratic Party of Alabama; two other slates of electors were pledged, one to Hubert H. Humphrey and one to Richard M. Nixon. The Humphrey and Nixon popular vote percentages were 18.7 and 14.0, respectively.

Inter-party competition has been keener for federal offices than for state and local offices. Republicans have contested vigorously, although unsuccessfully, for United States Senate seats, and in 1964 won five of the eight U.S. House seats then allocated to Alabama. Two

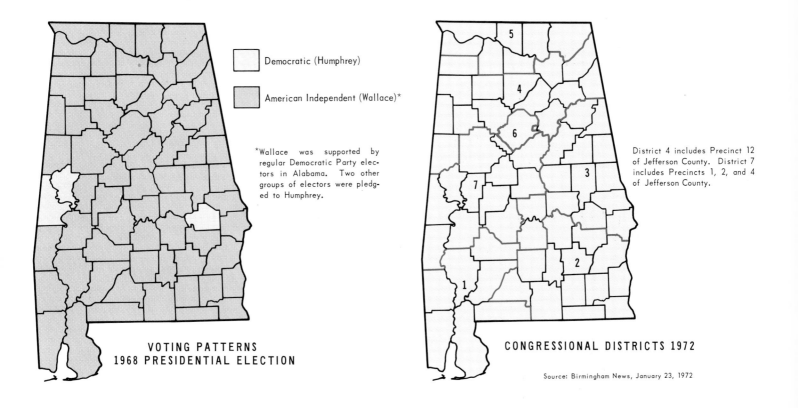

Democratic (Humphrey)

American Independent (Wallace)*

*Wallace was supported by regular Democratic Party electors in Alabama. Two other groups of electors were pledged to Humphrey.

VOTING PATTERNS
1968 PRESIDENTIAL ELECTION

District 4 includes Precinct 12 of Jefferson County. District 7 includes Precincts 1, 2, and 4 of Jefferson County.

CONGRESSIONAL DISTRICTS 1972

Source: Birmingham News, January 23, 1972

of these seats were lost in 1966. Since 1967 Alabama has been represented in Congress by five Democrats and three Republicans. Effective January, 1973, Alabama will have seven House seats.

Elections in 1970 saw 104 Democrats and two Republicans elected to the State House of Representatives and 35 Democrats and no Republicans chosen for the State Senate. The executive branch of Alabama State Government is also dominated by Democrats. The Governor, Lieutenant-Governor, Attorney General, Secretary of State, State Auditor, State Treasurer, and Commissioner of Agriculture and Industries were all elected on the Democratic ticket. The highest state courts, the Supreme Court and the Courts of Criminal and Civil Appeals, are composed solely of justices and judges who are members of the Democratic party.

The powers exercised by the legislative, executive, and judicial branches are based on the State Constitution, the sixth such constitution, which was adopted in 1901. The Alabama Constitution is one of the longest in the nation; it has been amended 310 times. Most of the amendments relate to the functions exercised by local governments. The executive branch of the State government is composed of approximately 160 agencies, the most common designations of which are board (47), commission (38), and department (22). The Governor of Alabama is able to give leadership to state government through his appointive and budget powers. These, coupled with veto powers and tenure provisions, give him more formal powers than any other Deep South governor. The Legislature meets in regular session only every two years, with the Governor being empowered to call special sessions and indicate the agenda for such sessions.

William H. Stewart

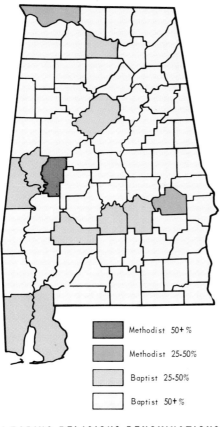

**LEADING RELIGIOUS DENOMINATIONS
1950**

Methodist 50+%

Methodist 25-50%

Baptist 25-50%

Baptist 50+%

Source: The National Atlas of the United States of America

"Blessing of the Fleet"   ABPI

RELIGIONS

The population of the State of Alabama is almost exclusively Protestant in religious preference. Since the frontier days, the Baptist and Methodist denominations have maintained a continuing strength and popularity. Concentrations of Roman Catholics are found primarily in Birmingham and Mobile. Early European settlement in Mobile accounts for its large Catholic element, while the increase in numbers of Catholics in Birmingham has been due to the influx of people of varied persuasions because of the city's industrial growth. The sizeable German-Catholic community in Cullman County dates back to an agricultural "colony" established during the 19th century. In Alabama Catholics constitute approximately five percent of the total population, and the percentage of Jews is considerably smaller. The Jewish population is located almost entirely in metropolitan areas and small towns. Jews are most numerous in Birmingham, where the first congregation was organized almost a century ago.

The Protestant domination is numerically overwhelming. Although exact percentages are not available, it is likely that Protestants, both church members and non-members of Protestant preference, constitute from 80 to 90 percent of the population of Alabama. Among the Protestant denominations, the various Baptist groups have the largest membership among both the white and black populations. That there are approximately 850,000 members of the Southern Baptist Church alone reveals the extent of Baptist dominance. This figure includes only those baptized, and it excludes both children and

MAJOR CHURCH GROUPS
1970

BAPTIST

METHODIST

CATHOLIC   EPISCOPALIAN   PRESBYTERIAN

NON-AFFILIATED,
NON-PREFERENCE
AND OTHER RELIGIONS

40%   15%   5%   3%   2%   35%

PERCENT OF TOTAL POPULATION
(Estimates by author)

older adherents who are not baptized. Total Baptist memberships are equal to approximately 35 to 40 percent of the population. A county by county breakdown shows a uniform strength in the Baptist churches in both urban and rural areas. As the State has increased in population, the Baptist churches have enjoyed a large and proportionate growth in membership.

The various Methodist churches share with the Baptists, although on a smaller scale, a vigorous frontier history followed by a significant membership increase along with the population growth. The various Methodist churches have a membership of approximately 350,000 (the total does not include baptized children, or adherents). Unlike the Baptists, the Methodist churches, while maintaining a steady urban membership, have experienced slight losses in rural areas.

The combined membership in the primarily urban-centered Presbyterian and Episcopalian churches is about 5 percent of the population, about a third of the Methodist membership. The Churches of Christ in the last several decades have grown rapidly, although no figures are available due to the congregational structure of the denomination. Pentecostal and other sectarian groups form a small percentage of the Protestant category.

John E. Shelton

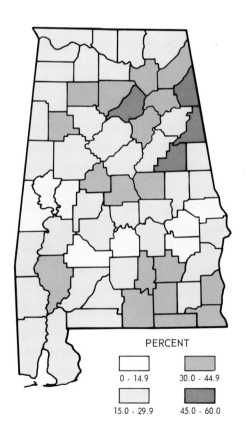

PERCENT

0 - 14.9   30.0 - 44.9

15.0 - 29.9   45.0 - 60.0

SOUTHERN BAPTIST MEMBERSHIP
1971

ATLAS OF ALABAMA

ECONOMIC
CHARACTERISTICS

INCOMES

The amount of income received by the people of Alabama is an indication of how well Alabamians live. To be sure, income does not determine happiness or well being, however, it does portray a standard or level of living. For example, it gives an indication of the amount of food, clothing, shoes, and books that Alabamians are able to purchase and of how comfortably they live. Each of the several different income statistics now available measures a particular facet of the total income picture.

The mean (average) income of families in the United States in 1969 was $10,577. The comparable figure for Alabama, $8,412, was considerably lower. It is meaningful to understand the way income is distributed among residents of the State. The associated map displays the variance in mean income found throughout Alabama counties. Eight Alabama counties had a mean family income of between $4,000 and $6,000, 28 had a mean family income between $6,000 and $7,000, 15 fell in the $7,000 to $8,000 bracket, and 11 counties were in the $8,000 to $9,000 range. The five counties with the highest income belong in the over $9,000 category—Jefferson, Morgan, Montgomery, Mobile, and Madison. The highest income areas represent the three largest metropolitan areas as well as the prime industrial centers of the State—Birmingham, Mobile, and Huntsville. Nonetheless, only Madison County with a $11,455 figure had a family income that surpassed, or for that matter equaled, the national average.

Statistics on the income of all families, and of unrelated individuals who are members of households although not related to anyone else in the household, present National and State figures that are lower than family income means. In 1969 this income figure was $7,185 for Alabama. In regard to county incomes, only Madison had a mean income for households of over $9,000, three counties fell between the $8,000 and $9,000 range, nine belonged to the $7,000 to $8,000 classification, and 23 registered in the $6,000 to $7,000 group. Thirty-one, or about 46 percent of the counties, had a mean income for families and unrelated individuals of between $4,000 and $5,000. From the map depicting these data, it is clear that most of the low income areas in the State are located within a band covering the south-central portion of the State from Mississippi to Georgia, generally corresponding to the Black Belt.

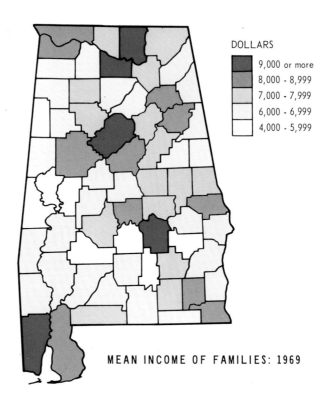

DOLLARS

- 9,000 or more
- 8,000 - 8,999
- 7,000 - 7,999
- 6,000 - 6,999
- 4,000 - 5,999

MEAN INCOME OF FAMILIES: 1969

Source: U. S. Census of Population, 1970

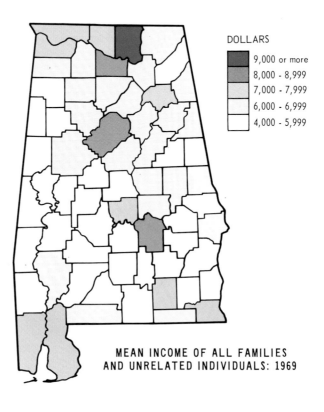

DOLLARS

- 9,000 or more
- 8,000 - 8,999
- 7,000 - 7,999
- 6,000 - 6,999
- 4,000 - 5,999

MEAN INCOME OF ALL FAMILIES
AND UNRELATED INDIVIDUALS: 1969

Source: U. S. Census of Population, 1970

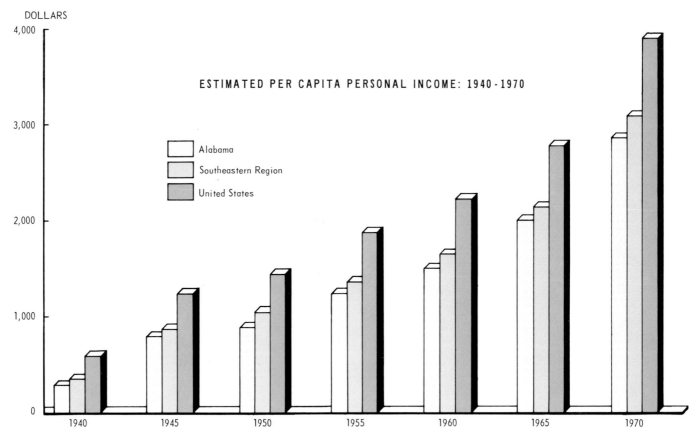

ESTIMATED PER CAPITA PERSONAL INCOME: 1940-1970

Source: Abstract of Alabama

INCOMES

Personal income is defined as income of residents from all sources. The term includes income and other direct personal taxes, but does not include deductions for individual contributions to social security, government retirement, and other social insurance programs. Per capita personal income is computed by dividing total personal income by total population. Since 1939 this figure has steadily increased in the United States, in the Southeast region, and in Alabama. At the outset of World War II, per capita personal income was $282 in Alabama; by 1950 it had risen to $880, by 1960 to $1,489, and by 1970 to $2,853. Making no allowances for changes in the price level, which of course lowers the increase substantially, per capita personal income in Alabama increased during this period by $2,571. Looking at com-

parable figures for the Southeast region—which includes the states of Florida, Georgia, Tennessee, and Mississippi as well as Alabama—per capita personal income increased from $343 to $3,195; that is to say, by $2,852. The United States figure for the same time period depicts a gain from $595 to $3,921 or an increase of $3,326. Since 1940 the amount of growth experienced by Alabama has been less than that of the United States and slightly less than that of the Southeast region. Thus, Alabama has not only a lower per capita personal income, but also less growth of income than the Southeast region and the United States.

The United States Department of Commerce classifies families as living above or below the poverty level on the basis of a poverty index which is revised each year as the Consumer Price Index changes. The poverty index considers in addition to income several factors such as size of family and farm-nonfarm residence. The establishment of the poverty level is based on an "economy" food plan developed by the Department of Agriculture for "emergency or temporary use when funds are low." A family is classified as living in poverty when its total money income is less than approximately three times the cost of the "economy" food plan. While 10 percent of the families in the United States were poor in 1969, 20 percent of Alabama families were living below the poverty level at the same time. Within the State, 46 percent of the black families lived in poverty, yet only 13 percent of whites were similarly classified. Two counties had 50 percent or over of their families living below the poverty level, Greene County with 54 percent and Lowndes County with 50 percent. Forty-seven counties had less than 30 percent of families below the poverty level and 18 counties had less than 20 percent. There is less poverty in the northern and the southern parts of the State, although select counties in the southern part have relatively more poor. Those counties with a high percent of black residents generally had a higher poverty index.

By looking specifically at the families with incomes over $10,000, a clearer picture of the size and distribution of the upper-middle and upper income groups is provided. Most recent census statistics indicate 31 percent of Alabama families had incomes over $10,000, 36 percent of the white and 21 percent of the Negro families. However, large differences exist among counties. Madison County again had the highest record with 52 percent of families with incomes over $10,000. No Alabama county fell into the 40 to 50 percentile. Thirteen counties had 30 to 40 percent of the families with incomes above $10,000, 30 counties were in the 20 to 30 percent range, and 23 fell within the 10 to 20 percent bracket. The middle and upper income families appear to reside in scattered pockets throughout the State instead of clustering in one or two areas. Although some of the counties that lacked a substantial number of families in the middle or upper income ranges had a high percent of poor families, others had a substantial percent of families with incomes above the poverty level yet below $10,000.

Mary Fish

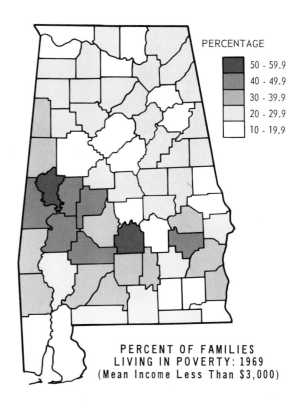

PERCENT OF FAMILIES
LIVING IN POVERTY: 1969
(Mean Income Less Than $3,000)

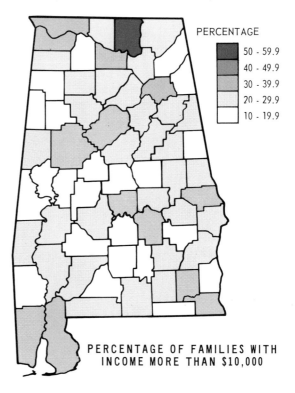

PERCENTAGE OF FAMILIES WITH
INCOME MORE THAN $10,000

Source: U. S. Census of Population, 1970

55

TAX BASE: 1969-1970
(millions of dollars)

☐ 0 - 49.9 ☐ 50.0 - 99.9

▨ 100.0 - 499.9 ▨ 500.0 - 999.9 ■ over 1000.0

Source: 1967 Census of Government

TAX BASE

As the economic role of government as a purchaser and dispenser of goods and services and as a source of employment increases, the ability of state and local governments to obtain needed tax revenue to finance their activities becomes ever more crucial. State governments derive their revenues from several sources, but especially from income and sales taxes. Local governments generally derive the bulk of their tax revenues from property taxes, supplemented by charges and fees for services. For that reason, identification of the tax base for any state or portion of a state is at best a sophisticated guess. Yet, a reasonably good estimate of the basic tax base of the state is provided by data on the main sources of tax revenue—retail sales, personal income, and gross assessed value of property. The total dollar value of these three can be termed the "basic tax base."

Alabama's basic tax base in 1969–70 was approximately $19.4 billion, which was heavily concentrated within four of the 67 counties of the State—Jefferson, Madison, Mobile, and Montgomery. Together these four counties accounted for about one-half of the total of the base. Many of the other counties, particularly those in predominantly rural areas, ranked extremely low, relative to the top four. This fact makes the provision of quality public services in education, health, welfare, and highway transportation quite difficult for many Alabama communities.

With respect to taxable dollars represented by the components of the basic tax base, personal income was first, followed by retail sales and gross assessed value of property. Revenue accruing to the State from the retail sales tax is considerably greater than that from the personal income tax because, simply, the tax rates for the two are different. Tax rates on value of property vary from county to county, and the gross assessed value for tax purposes is only a fraction of its true market value. In several rural counties the assessed value of property exceeded the value of retail sales, whereas in more urbanized areas total retail sales are relatively more important.

For the State as a whole, Alabama's tax base is rather limited in relation to the tax bases of other states. One

State Capitol   ABPI

meaningful method of comparing state tax bases is through the use of an index which expresses the base of each state in terms of comparable data, and eliminates population differences by using per capita figures. On such an index, Alabama's tax base was about nine-tenths as large as the average for all southern states in 1970; among eleven southern states, Alabama ranked 9th. In comparison with the rest of the nation, Alabama's tax base was one of the lowest among all 50 states.

The limited tax base creates special economic problems for Alabama. State and local government expenditures for education, health services, and others normally encourage economic growth. In order to provide funds for those expenditures, the tax base must be either enlarged or utilized more effectively. In terms of the latter, Alabama has not demonstrated an inclination to make a particularly strong tax effort, that is, more completely utilize the tax base, which, in effect, would increase the tax rate. On a scale with 100.0 indicating the national average, Alabama's tax effort rated 84.7; the State's tax effort ranked 7th among nine neighboring states.

The alternative to increasing the tax rate is to enlarge the tax base, preferably through a higher economic growth rate. Some of the requirements for this growth must be met by government expenditures. One possibility for an increase in revenue lies in redefining the tax base. Property is evaluated at only a fraction of its market value for tax base purposes. In Alabama, the property tax base—the gross assessed value of property—is quite low relative to other states.

Another issue of major importance is the equity or equality of the distribution of the tax burden. Tax burden is the percentage of income used to pay taxes. In Alabama the state-local tax structure takes a larger percentage of the income of the lower income groups than of the higher income groups.

Greater equality in the distribution of the tax burden may be achieved if, when additional tax revenue is needed, heavier taxation of income and productive property receives priority over any increase in sales taxes.

Charles G. Leathers

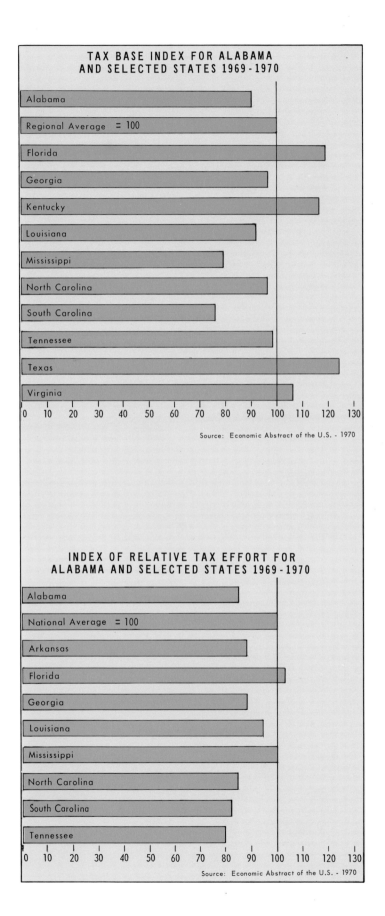

TAX BASE INDEX FOR ALABAMA AND SELECTED STATES 1969-1970

Source: Economic Abstract of the U.S. - 1970

INDEX OF RELATIVE TAX EFFORT FOR ALABAMA AND SELECTED STATES 1969-1970

Source: Economic Abstract of the U.S. - 1970

On the Tennessee River

AGRICULTURAL REGIONS

Physical, biological, social, and economic forces have influenced the development of agricultural regions in Alabama. Within the agricultural regions, broad overall differences are found in size of farms, proportion of land in farms, and land use, as well as major crop, livestock, and poultry enterprises.

Alabama is divided into nine agricultural regions based on the factors which have shaped and continue to influence Alabama's agricultural and economic development.

Tennessee Valley and Limestone Valleys. Level to gently rolling land predominates. Farms are mechanized and individual landholdings are larger than the state average of about 190 acres. Renting of additional land is common in order to obtain large enough acreages to economically operate mechanical equipment. Cotton is the chief cash crop, and this region produces close to half of Alabama's cotton. Corn, soybeans, and hay are other major crops. With proper management, excellent pastures and forage crops are possible and significant numbers of beef cattle are raised.

Sand Mountain. This region, including most of the Appalachian Plateau area of Alabama, varies from rugged

hill country to gently rolling plateau surfaces. Plateau soils generally are sandy loams that have a fairly high water-holding capacity. They respond well to fertilization, and high yields are feasible for most crops. Farms are small in size; and, with the development of industry, many members of farm families work off the farm all or part of the year. Leading crops are cotton, corn, hay, and some vegetables. Broiler and egg production are the chief sources of agricultural income in several counties, and this region alone produces most of Alabama's income from poultry enterprises. The southern part of this region is largely in forest; here farming plays a role subordinate to coal mining and forestry.

Talladega Mountains. Rugged topography is common and the area is largely devoted to the utilization of forest resources. Some poultry production and general farming occur in this region.

Piedmont Plateau. The land is gently rolling to hilly. In the late 1930's cotton was an important crop. At present row-crop production is very limited, and much cropland has reverted to forest and pasture. Soil exhaustion, erosion, and the difficulty of adapting to commercial mechanized farming have all played a role in the decline of row crops. Farms are small; and, in addition to cotton, corn, and hay crops, there is some broiler production and beef cattle raising.

Upper Coastal Plain. This region is mostly in forest, and it exhibits a variety of soils and types of landscape. It is a rolling to hilly area with cropland and pasture located on the more level areas of valley floors, river terraces, and hilltops. Cotton, corn, and hay are major crops. Beef cattle are the chief livestock enterprise.

Black Belt. Dark gray to black soils originally gave this region its name. The land is level to rolling and is mostly cleared and in agricultural uses. Average farm size is the largest in the State, and extensive development of pasture land and hay production on the limey soils has helped make this the leading dairy and beef cattle region of the State. Since 1964 a sizeable amount of pasture land has been plowed and planted in soybeans, and the area is a leader in soybean production.

Southwestern Piney Woods. This area is mostly in forest, and the land varies from wooded flat plains (flatwoods) to very low hills. Value of farm production is well below that of pulpwood and lumber. Corn, cotton, and hay lead in crop acreage. Deer, turkey, and other wildlife abound in the region.

Lower Coastal Plain. In the eastern part of this region, commonly known as the Wiregrass Area, peanuts are the major cash crop. Soils are generally sandy loams or loamy sands that are adapted to peanut production. Cotton and corn are also important. Almost all farms are mechanized, with operators having substantial investments in machinery and equipment. Some truck crops such as tomatoes, melons, beans, squash, and potatoes are produced in the region. Beef cattle and hogs are significant livestock enterprises.

Gulf Coast. Of all the regions, the Gulf Coast has the longest growing season, ranging up to 300 days per year. This favors the production of several vegetables and truck crops. Soybean production is of major importance in this region, and pecans are also of economic significance. Value of land and buildings is relatively high, and few farms are tenant-operated.

J.H. Yeager

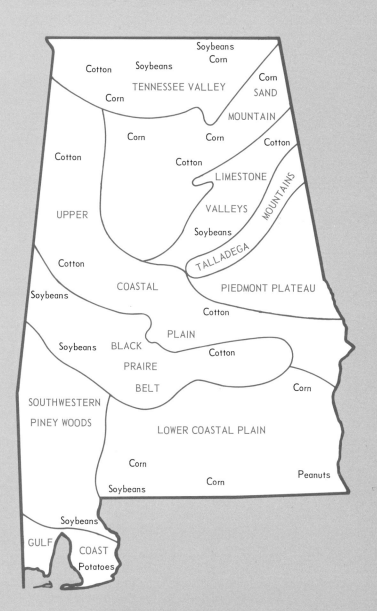

AGRICULTURAL REGIONS

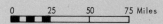

0   25   50   75 Miles

Source: U.S. Department of Agriculture

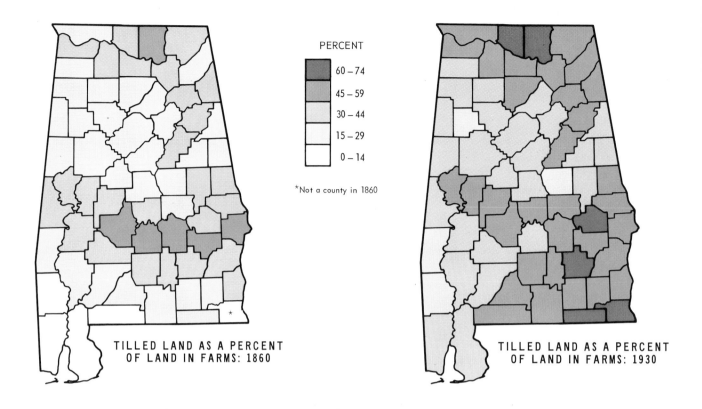

PERCENT

60 – 74
45 – 59
30 – 44
15 – 29
0 – 14

*Not a county in 1860

TILLED LAND AS A PERCENT
OF LAND IN FARMS: 1860

TILLED LAND AS A PERCENT
OF LAND IN FARMS: 1930

HISTORICAL CHANGES IN AGRICULTURAL LAND USE

Between 1860 and 1900, land in farms in Alabama increased almost 11 percent and most counties shared in the increase. Increases were greatest in the Sand Mountain and Wiregrass areas, while counties with decreases were in the Black Belt.

Land in farms in the State decreased 15 percent between 1900 and 1930, and by 1930 there were 7 percent fewer acres in farms than in 1860. Reductions were greatest in the Black Belt and Piedmont counties. Several counties in the Sand Mountain and Wiregrass areas experienced no decline but, in fact, continued to show an increase in land in farms.

Ninety-four percent of the land in farms in 1860 was either in woodland and forest or tilled land. Fifty-five percent was woodland and forest, and 39 percent was tilled. Only four counties had more than half the land in farms in tilled acres, while six counties had more than 80 percent of farm acreages in woodland and forest.

In 1930, only 84 percent of the land in farms was in woodland and forest and tilled land. The proportion in woodland and forest had decreased to 37 percent while the proportion of tilled land increased to 47 per-

cent. Twenty-three counties had more than half the farm land in tilled acres. Counties with the highest proportion of tilled acres were in the Tennessee Valley and Wiregrass areas.

Cotton and corn combined occupied approximately three out of five acres of tilled land in Alabama in 1860. Cotton and corn were grown on 31 and 28 percent of the tilled land, respectively. Half or more of the tilled acres in five counties was planted to cotton. Among areas of the State, counties in the Black Belt had the greatest proportion of land in cotton. Each of the counties in this area had more than 40 percent of tilled acres in this crop. No cotton was reported planted in Mobile County, only 300 acres were reported in Escambia County, and low acreages were reported in Baldwin and Cullman counties.

Corn was a more universally grown crop than was cotton. Although five counties had more than half the tilled acres planted in corn, these counties were not in one general area. The proportion of tilled acres planted in corn varied between 18 percent in Macon and Mobile counties, and 55 percent in Covington.

Acres devoted to the production of corn and cotton increased between 1860 and 1900. Corn acreage increased by a third while cotton acreage increased 37 percent.

By 1930, the proportion of land in farms that was tilled land reached 47 percent for the State. Together, cotton and corn utilized three-fourths of the tilled land. Cotton was planted on 43 percent of the tilled land. The total acreage of cotton in 1930 was 11 percent greater than in 1900, and was 53 percent greater than in 1860. Cotton acreage increased most in those counties where tilled acreage increased. The areas in which cotton acreage increased most between 1860 and 1930 were the Sand Mountain and Wiregrass areas. In 14 counties, acreage planted in cotton declined. Most of the counties in which there was a reduction in cotton acreage were in the Black Belt, where all but three counties had fewer acres of cotton in 1930 than were planted in 1860.

Corn was planted on 32 percent of the tilled acres in 1930, and although the total acres of corn was 4 percent less than the total in 1900, it was 28 percent greater than in 1860. Counties that had the greatest acreages of corn were in the Tennessee Valley and Wiregrass areas, but some counties in other areas had the higher proportion of tilled land in corn.

Morris White

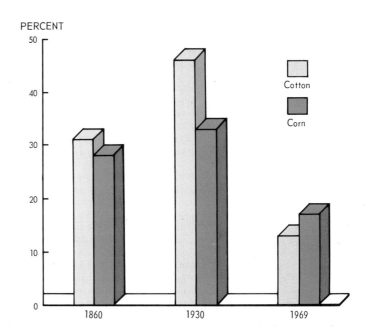

PERCENT OF TILLED LAND
IN COTTON AND CORN
1860-1969

Source: U. S. Census of Agriculture, 1969

61

Black Belt Cattle   GSA

FARM SIZE AND LAND IN FARMS

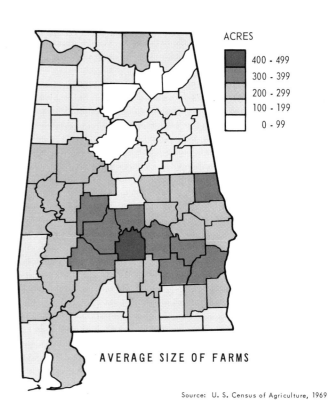

ACRES

- 400 - 499
- 300 - 399
- 200 - 299
- 100 - 199
- 0 - 99

AVERAGE SIZE OF FARMS

Source: U. S. Census of Agriculture, 1969

From 1964 to 1969 the average farm size in Alabama increased from 164.5 acres to 188.3 acres, an increase of 23.8 acres or 14.5 percent. Even so, average farm size in Alabama is still much smaller than that for the nation, which approached 400 acres in 1969. Thus, Alabama's farm size is approximately one-half that of the national average.

There were only slight changes in the average size of farms for the United States from 1900 until about 1930. After the depression the average farm size for the United States started to increase fairly rapidly. In contrast, the average size of farms in Alabama actually declined from 1900 until the depression, and then started a slower rate of increase than for the United States as a whole.

In 1964 Montgomery County had the largest farms, with an average of 330.0 acres. But average farm size in Lowndes County increased by 180.9 acres between 1964 and 1969 to an average of 449.8 acres. By 1969 Lowndes was the only county with an average size of farms over 400 acres. In 1969 there were nine counties where average farm size ranged between 300 and 400 acres. These were: Montgomery, 370 acres; Barbour, 351 acres; Wilcox, 349 acres; Bullock, 327 acres; Perry, 325 acres; Pike, 323 acres; Chambers, 318 acres; Dallas,

313 acres; and Autauga, 308 acres.

In general, the Black Belt area had the largest farms in the State in 1969. Between 1964 and 1969 the largest increases in farm size in terms of both total acres and percentage increase were found here. The increases in this area ranged from a low of 44 acres for Bullock County, to a high of 181 acres for Lowndes County. A larger concentration of beef cattle farms and large scale mechanization of agriculture in this area probably contributed to the great increase in size of farms. This area is considered the major beef cattle producing region of the State, and probably has more beef cattle farms (farms producing only beef cattle) than any other area in the State. Another factor that contributed to larger increases in farm size in the Black Belt was the exodus of population and thus the combining of small farm acreages.

The Sand Mountain area had the smallest farms in the State. Cullman County had the smallest average farm size of any county with an average of only 75 acres, followed by Marshall with 76 acres, and DeKalb with 86 acres. Jefferson (99 acres) was the only other county that had an average farm size of less than 100 acres. Sand Mountain counties had a very small percentage

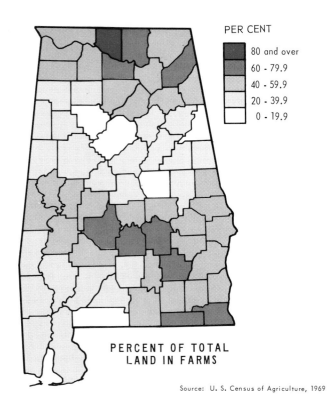

PER CENT

80 and over

60 - 79.9

40 - 59.9

20 - 39.9

0 - 19.9

PERCENT OF TOTAL
LAND IN FARMS

Source: U. S. Census of Agriculture, 1969

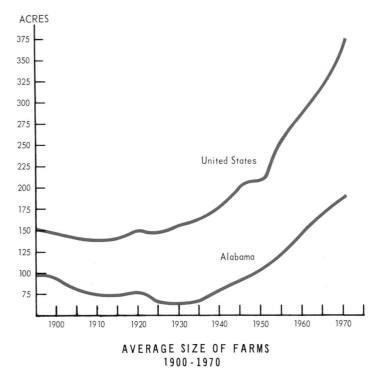

AVERAGE SIZE OF FARMS
1900 - 1970

Source: U. S. Census of Agriculture, 1969

increase in farm size from 1964 to 1969, ranging from a 2 percent increase in DeKalb, up to a 28 percent increase for Marshall. This indicated a stable farm population, and a very small number of farms sold for the purpose of combining farms.

Five counties, most of them in the Piedmont, experienced a decrease in farm size during the period of 1964 to 1969. They were Winston, Cherokee, Russell, Cleburne, and Coffee, all with decreases of 4 percent or less.

The Wiregrass region in Southeast Alabama, and the Tennessee Valley area in the northern part of Alabama experienced a moderate increase in farm size from 1964 to 1969. The Wiregrass ranged from a decrease of .1 percent for Coffee County up to an increase of 24 percent for Henry County. The Tennessee Valley counties ranged from a 9 percent increase for Colbert County to an 18 percent increase for Madison County.

Farm sizes in the Wiregrass and Tennessee Valley were close to the State average, approximately 200 acres per farm. The farms in these two areas are devoted principally to row-crops, including peanuts, corn, and small grains in the Wiregrass area, and cotton, corn, and soybeans in the Tennessee Valley area. In both areas farmers

supplement their crop income with hogs and cattle.

Limestone County, with 86 percent, had the highest percentage of total land in farms in 1969. There were only four other counties with more than 70 percent of total land in farms. These were Montgomery with 78 percent, Lowndes with 76 percent, Pike with 74 percent, and Houston with 73 percent.

Jefferson County had the smallest percentage of total land in farms in 1969 with only 9 percent. Cleburne with 18 percent, and Coosa and Escambia counties each with 20 percent, were the only other counties with less than 20 percent of total land area in farms.

The percentage of land area in farms for the State decreased from 46.6 percent in 1964 to 43.5 percent in 1969. There were 12 counties that had only a slight increase in percentage of land in farms from 1964 to 1969.

All in all, farms in Alabama are increasing in size as the migration of small landholders effects a consolidation of farms and, thus, large scale mechanization. The total land in farms, however, is diminishing as many small acreages are increasingly being placed in forest production or allowed to lie idle.

Sidney C. Bell

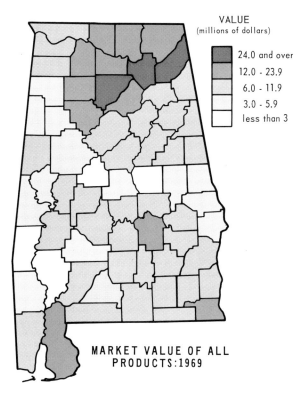

VALUE
(millions of dollars)

24.0 and over
12.0 - 23.9
6.0 - 11.9
3.0 - 5.9
less than 3

MARKET VALUE OF ALL
PRODUCTS:1959

Source: U. S. Census of Agriculture, 1969

VALUE
(millions of dollars)

24.0 and over
12.0 - 23.9
6.0 - 11.9
3.0 - 5.9
less than 3

MARKET VALUE OF ALL
PRODUCTS:1969

Source: U. S. Census of Agriculture, 1969

AGRICULTURAL VALUE
AND EMPLOYMENT

Farm population in Alabama in 1970 was 270,000; only eight percent of the total population in the State. Furthermore, farm population constituted only about a fifth of Alabama's rural residents.

Until the 1960 *Census of Population,* the majority of residents lived in rural areas. In the 1860 Census, rural population was 915,000, or about 95 percent of the total population of Alabama. Practically all of these people farmed for a living. Rural population increased to a peak of 1,977,000 in 1940. Between 1940 and 1970, rural population declined to 1,416,000, or 42 percent of the state total.

Most people living in rural areas do not farm. These residents, who are dependent on non-agricultural employment, are classified as rural nonfarm. The rural nonfarm segment of Alabama's population has grown dramatically in the past two decades. Many of these people have left farming for industrial employment while maintaining a rural residence.

The total agricultural employment in Alabama was 56,100 in March, 1970, as reported by the Department of Industrial Relations. This was 4.6 percent of the total number of people employed within the State. Counties where agricultural employment was largest were located in the Sand Mountain, Tennessee Valley, Gulf Coast, and Wiregrass areas. These are major farming regions of the State. In some metropolitan areas, agricultural employment is only reported for a combination of counties. The level of agricultural employment by area is dependent on a number of factors, including available industrial employment, size of farm, and type of farm enterprise. For example, farm employment is most concentrated in those counties where labor-intensive farm enterprises are located. Horticultural crops in the Sand Mountain area and nursery enterprises along the Gulf Coast are examples of labor-intensive enterprises. Cotton and soybean farmers, and livestock producers as well, are substituting mechanical equipment and other labor saving devices for increasingly expensive farm labor. In counties where these crop and livestock enterprises predominate, the farm work force has declined sharply.

Since the late 1940's a large number of farmers and farm workers have left agriculture. The migration was especially pronounced in the Black Belt counties and around metropolitan areas. Small production units which failed to provide an adequate family income caused many farmers to seek other employment. Suburban growth provided farmers owning land close to town an opportunity to sell their farms at values far above

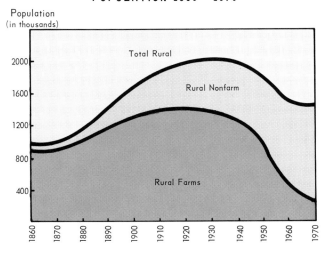

FARM, NONFARM, AND TOTAL RURAL
POPULATION 1860 - 1970

Population
(in thousands)

Source: U.S. Census of Population, 1970

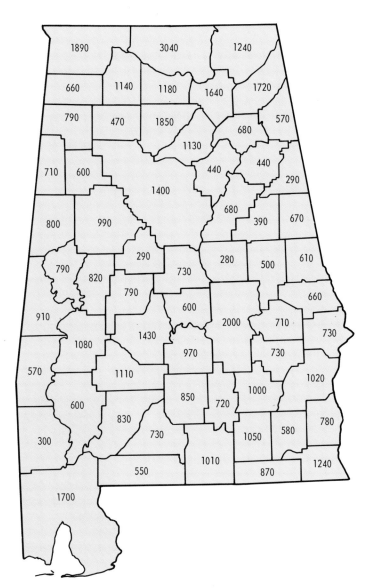

AGRICULTURAL EMPLOYMENT
1970

Total Agricultural Employment, 56,100

Some Metropolitan Areas are
reported as combined counties

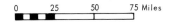

0   25   50   75 Miles

Source: Alabama Department of Industrial Relations

their worth for agriculture. Farm laborers were also attracted to industrial employment by substantially higher wages.

According to the *Census of Agriculture,* market value of all agricultural products sold by Alabama farmers in 1969 amounted to $670.3 million. This was about 1.2 percent of the value of all farm products sold by farmers in the United States. Value of farm products in the State rose from $414.3 million in 1959, a 62 percent increase. The increase in value during the 1960's resulted both from larger quantities of products marketed and from rising farm prices.

Cullman County with farm sales of $80.6 million, 12 percent of total sales, was by far the leading agricultural county. Other leading agricultural counties were DeKalb, Lawrence, Marshall, and Morgan in the Tennessee Valley, and Blount and Baldwin counties. Between 1959 and 1969, value of farm products sold increased in 62 counties, but declined slightly in five counties. The largest increase, 278 percent, occurred in Cullman County.

Average value of agricultural products sold per farm was $9,247 in 1969. Average farm sales in excess of $10,000 were reported for 19 counties; average sales were between $5,000 and $10,000 in 39 counties and under $5,000 in only nine counties. In 1959 average sales per farm were under $5,000 in 61 counties.

Lowell E. Wilson

MAJOR CROPS

In 1970 the leading field crops in Alabama by value of production were cotton, peanuts, soybeans, hay, and corn, in that order. Vegetables and nuts and fruit also contributed significantly to the value of crop production.

Crop agriculture accounts for about 30 percent of the cash receipts of Alabama farmers; 70 percent of the sales involve livestock and livestock products. The chief cash crops are cotton, peanuts, and soybeans. Most of the corn and hay is used as livestock feed on the farm where it is grown.

The most significant changes between 1950 and 1970 have to do with cotton, corn, and soybeans. Cotton acreage is less than half, and corn acreage less than a third, of what it was two decades ago. Soybean acreage, however, has increased tenfold in response to the demand for vegetable oil and livestock feed. In short, Alabama's crop agriculture has undergone a period of adjustment, and the State is concentrating on those crops where cost of production is competitive with the rest of the United States.

The major crop-growing areas of the State are the Tennessee Valley (cotton-soybeans), Sand Mountain (cotton-corn-vegetables), Black Belt (soybeans-hay), Wiregrass (peanuts-corn), and the Mobile Bay area (soybeans–vegetables–pecans). Each of these areas has developed a commercial agriculture that requires large investments in production facilities. Level land, large farms, and productive soils are factors which make areas suitable for a mechanized crop agriculture.

Cotton has been the chief cash crop of the State since records have been kept. In 1850, Alabama was the leading cotton-producing state, but today it ranks 6th. Because of acreage controls, production remains fixed on about 600,000 acres. The Tennessee Valley is the leading area, acccounting for about 45 percent of the State's production.

Peanuts are grown in southeastern Alabama where, in the 1920's, farmers planted them as an alternative cash crop to cotton, which was plagued by the boll weevil. This peanut area extends into southwestern Geor-

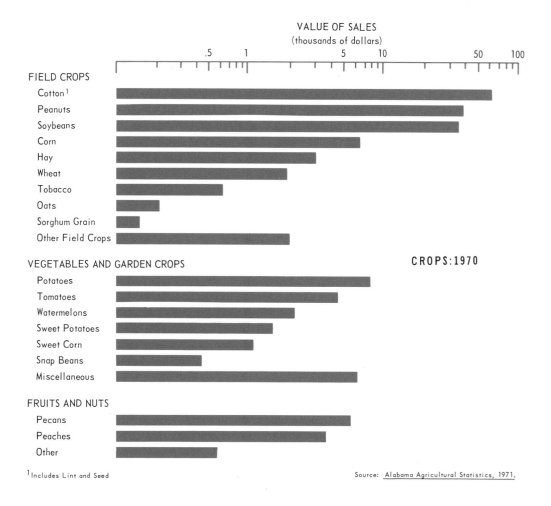

VALUE OF SALES
(thousands of dollars)

FIELD CROPS
Cotton[1]
Peanuts
Soybeans
Corn
Hay
Wheat
Tobacco
Oats
Sorghum Grain
Other Field Crops

VEGETABLES AND GARDEN CROPS
Potatoes
Tomatoes
Watermelons
Sweet Potatoes
Sweet Corn
Snap Beans
Miscellaneous

FRUITS AND NUTS
Pecans
Peaches
Other

CROPS:1970

[1] Includes Lint and Seed

Source: Alabama Agricultural Statistics, 1971.

66

gia, and constitutes one of the major peanut-producing regions of the United States. Alabama ranked 4th in peanut production in 1970.

Soybeans are the present "glamor crop" of Alabama. In the past decade, soybean acreage has increased by almost five times to over 650,000 acres harvested. Soybeans are the leading cash crop in acreage. They have had a considerable effect on the farm economy, involving farm machinery sales, the establishment of storage and marketing facilities, and farm real estate activity. Soybeans are a popular crop in Alabama because of the high price and both good yields and low land prices relative to Midwest soybean land. Much Black Belt pasture land has been plowed and planted to soybeans, where the large farm ownership units make it feasible to invest in soybean production. The chief soybean areas are the southwest (Mobile Bay area), the Black Belt, and the Tennessee Valley.

The trends in the production of corn reflect the disappearance of the small, submarginal farm and the fact

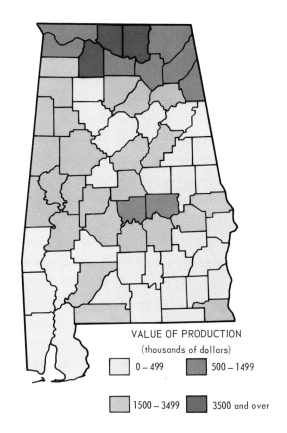

VALUE OF PRODUCTION
(thousands of dollars)

☐ 0 – 499 ▨ 500 – 1499

▨ 1500 – 3499 ▨ 3500 and over

COTTON AND COTTONSEED: 1970

Source: Alabama Department of Agriculture and Industry

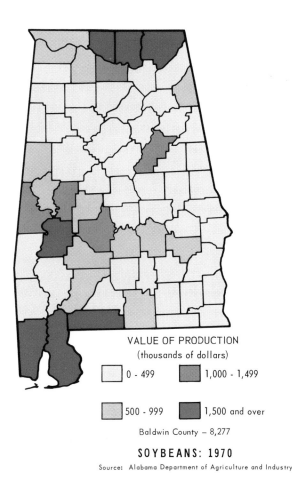

VALUE OF PRODUCTION
(thousands of dollars)

☐ 0 - 499 ▨ 1,000 - 1,499

▨ 500 - 999 ▨ 1,500 and over

Baldwin County – 8,277

SOYBEANS: 1970

Source: Alabama Department of Agriculture and Industry

GSA

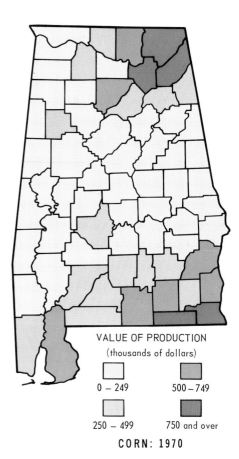

VALUE OF PRODUCTION

(thousands of dollars)

0 – 249

250 – 499

500 – 749

750 and over

CORN: 1970

VALUE OF PRODUCTION

(millions of dollars)

No Production

less than 1

1 – 2.9

3 – 6.9

7 and over

PEANUTS: 1970

Source: Alabama Department of Agriculture and Industry

that Alabama corn yields are not very competitive with imported Midwest corn as a livestock feed. Locally, corn is receiving increasing competition from sorghum for use as silage. Corn is mainly grown in Alabama in association with livestock feeding programs, such as in the production of poultry in the Sand Mountain region and hogs in the Wiregrass region.

Hay is a major crop in Alabama. The chief area of hay production is the Black Belt, where two factors have promoted this development. The limey soils are excellently suited to grass, and the early problems associated with cotton production in the 1920's (soil depletion, boll weevil) facilitated the transition to a cattle economy based primarily on grass for pasture and hay. In relation to the State's total cropland, more land is now devoted to hay than was the case 20 years ago. Total hay acreage has been steady, while much land has gone out of cotton and corn, much of it reverting to pasture and woodland, and some converting to hay production.

Alabama also has a significant production of vegetables, Irish potatoes, sweet potatoes, and fruits and nuts. These are all produced on many farms for home consumption, but this discussion deals only with those crops produced for market.

In 1970 Alabama ranked in the top ten states nationally in the production of the following crops: pecans, 3rd; tomatoes, 6th; watermelons, 6th; sweet potatoes, 8th; and peaches, 9th. In 1970 the value of production of each crop (in order of importance) was: Irish potatoes, pecans, tomatoes, peaches, sweet potatoes, watermelons, and sweet corn. For many of these crops, a very small number of counties—in some cases, a single county—accounts for most of the value of production.

The Gulf Coast area produces early Irish potatoes, with Baldwin County being the State's leading producer. Baldwin County also accounts for more than half of Alabama's commercially produced sweet corn and pecans.

Tomatoes, Irish potatoes, sweet potatoes, and peaches are important crops in the Sand Mountain

region. The Sand Mountain region accounts for most of the State's tomatoes, about half of the Irish potato crop (a later variety than the Baldwin County potato), and most of the sweet potato crop. Most of the State's commercially grown sweet potatoes are produced in one county—Cullman.

There is a third area of important vegetable production, and that is the Wiregrass area, especially Houston and Geneva counties. Houston is the leading watermelon-growing county and also has significant production of tomatoes, peas, lima beans, and melons.

The Gulf Coast, Sand Mountain, and Wiregrass regions have light sandy soils that respond well to fertilization, a history of commercial agriculture, and access to urban markets. These are all factors favoring production of commercial vegetables and other food crops.

Frank D. Huttlinger

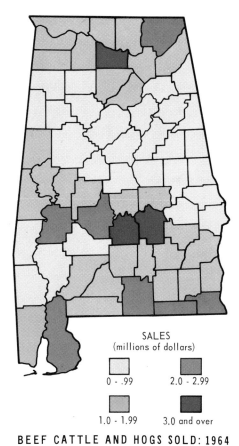

SALES
(millions of dollars)

☐ 0 - .99   ▨ 2.0 - 2.99

▨ 1.0 - 1.99   ■ 3.0 and over

BEEF CATTLE AND HOGS SOLD: 1964

Source: U.S. Department of Agriculture

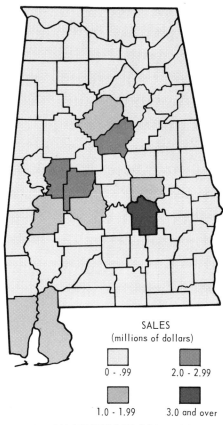

SALES
(millions of dollars)

☐ 0 - .99   ▨ 2.0 - 2.99

▨ 1.0 - 1.99   ■ 3.0 and over

DAIRY PRODUCTS SOLD: 1964

Source: U.S. Department of Agriculture

LIVESTOCK

An on-the-farm revolution has occurred in Alabama agriculture over the past three decades. The number of farms and farmers has decreased, while average size of farm operations has increased, and mechanization has replaced much of the animal power and hand labor. Perhaps the most dramatic change has been the development of a more diversified agriculture, with the emergence of animal or livestock agriculture as the dominant segment of farming in Alabama. During the period 1940–44, the cash farm sales of cotton contributed nearly 47 percent of the total cash farm income. Over 70 percent of all cash sales were from cotton and other crops, while the sale of livestock and livestock products contributed less than $54,000,000 or only about 29 percent of the total sales. By contrast, in 1970 the sales of livestock and livestock products amounted to

$534,750,000 and contributed over 71 percent of the total cash sales, while all crops accounted for just under 29 percent.

Poultry was an infant industry in 1940, accounting for less than $13,000,000 annually in cash sales during the 1940–44 period. By 1970 poultry had become the dominant agricultural enterprise, accounting for nearly 35 percent of total cash sales. In that year cash sales from broilers alone amounted to nearly $159,000,000, and the sale of eggs contributed an additional $63,000,000.

Beef cattle were of little importance to Alabama agriculture in 1940, and annual cash sales during the period 1940–44 averaged only slightly above $13,000,000. By 1970 beef cattle had become the second most important source of agricultural income, with cash sales amounting to $156,667,000, or nearly 21 percent of the total from all products.

Dairy and hog operations in 1940–44 were about equal to beef as sources of cash sales, each contributing about $13,000,000 annually. By contrast, in 1970, the cash sales of hogs exceeded $63,000,000, and sales of dairy products were almost $52,000,000.

It is predicted that animal agriculture will continue to expand and increase in importance in Alabama. A great potential exists, especially through the efficient utilization of forages by ruminant animals. Continued improvement in forage quantity and quality, accompanied by a continued improvement in animal performance, can be obtained. The full utilization of resources, including those of agriculture, is essential to balanced economic development.

W. M. Warren

LIVESTOCK AND LIVESTOCK PRODUCTS:1970

	CASH RECEIPTS
	(thousands of dollars)
Broilers	158,992
Cattle and Calves	156,667
Eggs	96,775
Hogs	63,034
Dairy Products	51,750
Chickens, Other Than Broilers	5,761
Honey and Beeswax	550
Turkeys	87
Other	931

Source: Alabama Agricultural Statistics, 1971.

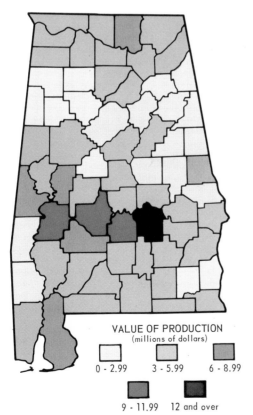

VALUE OF PRODUCTION
(millions of dollars)

0 - 2.99   3 - 5.99   6 - 8.99

9 - 11.99   12 and over

VALUE OF CATTLE AND CALVES: 1970

Source: U.S. Department of Agriculture

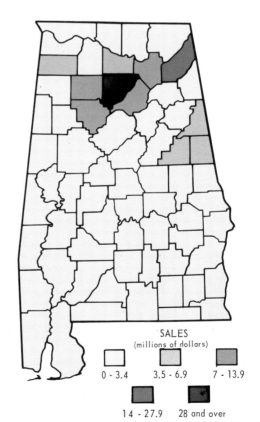

SALES
(millions of dollars)

0 - 3.4   3.5 - 6.9   7 - 13.9

14 - 27.9   28 and over

POULTRY AND POULTRY PRODUCTS SOLD: 1964

Source: U.S. Department of Agriculture

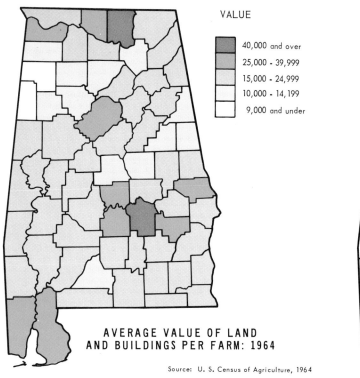

VALUE

40,000 and over
25,000 - 39,999
15,000 - 24,999
10,000 - 14,199
9,000 and under

AVERAGE VALUE OF LAND
AND BUILDINGS PER FARM: 1964

Source: U. S. Census of Agriculture, 1964

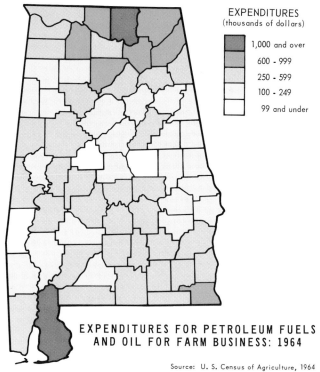

EXPENDITURES
(thousands of dollars)

1,000 and over
600 - 999
250 - 599
100 - 249
99 and under

EXPENDITURES FOR PETROLEUM FUELS
AND OIL FOR FARM BUSINESS: 1964

Source: U. S. Census of Agriculture, 1964

AGRICULTURAL LAND VALUES
AND EXPENDITURES

Agriculture has always played a significant role in the economy of Alabama. From the days of "King Cotton" until the present time, farming has been the main source of income for large, but decreasing, numbers of people. Today, agriculture is still "big business" in Alabama, but it is more diversified, with production of cotton, soybeans, peanuts, corn, and livestock all contributing significantly to the value of farm production. The saying, "Cotton is going west, cattle are coming east, blacks are going north, and Yankees are coming south," is descriptive of some of the economic and cultural changes that have taken place over the past forty years, both in the Southeast and in Alabama.

Large scale mechanization of agriculture has changed not only the landscape of Alabama, but the farm economy as well. Certain areas where large acreages can be utilized, the land is fairly level, and the soils can be made productive have seen a literal invasion of gang plows and grain crops, especially soy-

beans. The destruction of hedge and fence rows, and the clearing and plowing of pasture land are all evidence of the increasing degree of farm mechanization.

Principally, these changes have occurred in the Black Belt, the Tennessee Valley, and the Piney Woods regions of the State. But nowhere has the impact been greater than in parts of the Black Belt, that zone of limey clay soils which remains, in spite of this diversification, the leading beef cattle and dairying area of the State. High expenditures for petroleum products are indicative of the intensive use of farm machinery in these areas.

Expenditures for fertilizers have increased more than ten-fold in the past twenty years. Fertilizers are especially used in areas of the State where row crops such as peanuts, soybeans, cotton, and corn prevail. Alabama stands as one of the leading Southeastern states in the application of fertilizer materials.

Expenditures for livestock feed are strongly affected by the poultry industry in the northern part of the State.

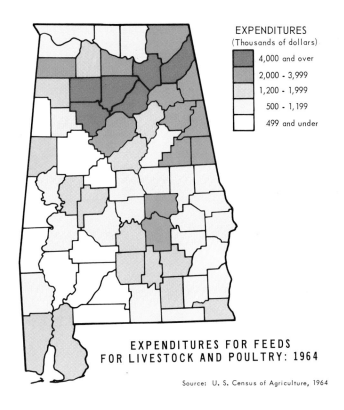

EXPENDITURES
(Thousands of dollars)

4,000 and over

2,000 - 3,999

1,200 - 1,999

500 - 1,199

499 and under

EXPENDITURES FOR FEEDS
FOR LIVESTOCK AND POULTRY: 1964

Source: U. S. Census of Agriculture, 1964

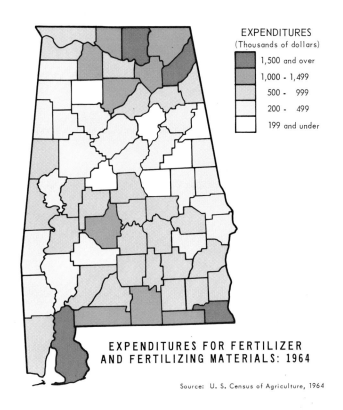

EXPENDITURES
(Thousands of dollars)

1,500 and over

1,000 - 1,499

500 - 999

200 - 499

199 and under

EXPENDITURES FOR FERTILIZER
AND FERTILIZING MATERIALS: 1964

Source: U. S. Census of Agriculture, 1964

The large-scale broiler production carried on in Cullman and Walker counties demands tremendous volumes of commercially processed and pelletized feeds.

The value of productive farm land has increased significantly during the past decade. A contributing factor to this increase has been the demand for available, low-cost land suitable for soybean production. This trend has been most pronounced in the Black Belt. Yet the counties with the highest overall average value of farm land and buildings have been urban counties where suburban developers have inflated the demand and thus the price of the best agricultural lands. Galloping urban development has squeezed the remaining farmers in urban counties to the point where greater financial gains are realized by selling to the developer than continuing to farm the land. As this trend continues, agricultural land close to the cities spirals upward in value, and the number of productive farms declines.

Neal G. Lineback

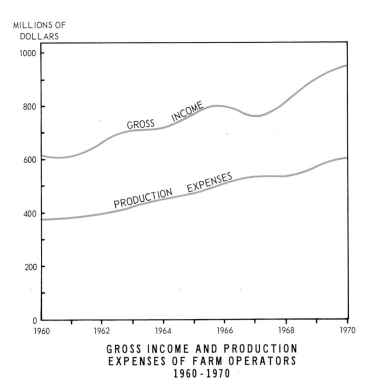

GROSS INCOME AND PRODUCTION
EXPENSES OF FARM OPERATORS
1960 - 1970

Source: Alabama Department of Agriculture and Industry

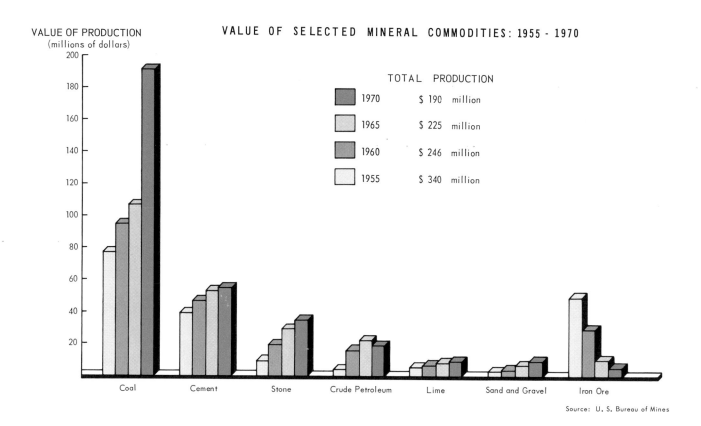

VALUE OF PRODUCTION
(millions of dollars)

VALUE OF SELECTED MINERAL COMMODITIES: 1955 - 1970

TOTAL PRODUCTION

1970	$ 190 million
1965	$ 225 million
1960	$ 246 million
1955	$ 340 million

Coal   Cement   Stone   Crude Petroleum   Lime   Sand and Gravel   Iron Ore

Source: U. S. Bureau of Mines

MINERAL PRODUCTION

The population explosion and the affluent nature of our societies are placing unprecedented demands on the limited mineral and fuel resources of our world. Within eight short years, by 1980, the United States will require twice as much energy (petroleum, natural gas, coal, hydroelectric power and nuclear fuels) as today. By the year 2000 the world's population will have doubled and, with increased standards of living, we will need many times the amount of mineral resources produced today. The urbanization of our country makes the immediate availability of building materials a necessity; in eight years only 10 percent of our people will live outside urban areas, and by the year 2000 the United States will need twice as many cities as we have today. We must take stock of our resources in order to plan for the future and achieve the greatest return from the earth with a minimum of environmental degradation. Truly every state must consider its mineral and fuel resources as a major investment for the future.

Fortunately, Alabama has been blessed with varied and substantial mineral and fuel deposits, and the value of these mined products has grown steadily through the years. In 1970 the total value of Alabama's mineral production reached $340 million, a new record, and a 19 percent increase over the previous year. This represents an increase of 196 percent since World War II. The value of the mining industries is, however, far greater than the production figures indicate. In 1970 over $63 million were paid as wages to 8,300 Alabama citizens employed by the minerals industries.

The record value of $340 million represents a wide range of mineral products produced from every county in the State. Coal, cement (raw materials), stone and petroleum lead the list with $303 million in value, or 91 percent of the total. Most mineral production comes not from the mineral-bearing crystalline igneous and metamorphic rocks of the Piedmont, but rather from the sedimentary rocks of the Coastal Plain, the Valley and Ridge, and the Plateau provinces. The Piedmont represents an area of great potential deposits which should be revealed as improved exploration techniques evolve.

The greatest production value in Alabama stems from the mineral fuels which constituted 63 percent of the 1970 value of production. Coal leads the list, ($190 million) followed by petroleum ($20 million). Alabama's recoverable reserves of coal are estimated at 13.7 billion tons, enough for several hundred years at the present rate of consumption. Coal occurs in the northern portion of the State in sedimentary rocks which were formed in lush and luxuriant swamps about 300 million years ago. Today it is mined from 138 mines in 12 counties, with Jefferson, Walker and Tuscaloosa counties yielding the greatest production from the Warrior Coal Field.

Alabama may develop as a major oil and gas producing state in the coming years. The first gas production was in the early 1900's from the Silurian rocks underlying Huntsville. In 1944, after 350 dry wells, the first producing oil well was drilled in Choctaw County. Today there are almost 600 producing oil wells in Alabama, concentrated predominantly in southwestern counties. In this portion of the State, production is from the Jurassic sediments (Smackover) at depths as great as 16,000 feet below sea level and from the shallower Cretaceous strata. Lamar County, in the Black Warrior Basin in northern Alabama, has oil production from the older Mississippian rocks. Hundreds of acres in the Basin are presently under lease in Lamar, Pickens, Tuscaloosa, Fayette, Marion, Walker, Winston, Cullman, and Blount Counties; these counties hold tremendous fuel potential, which will eventually be developed. Presently the greatest oil production, valued at more than $18 million annually, is from the Citronelle field of Mobile County, where Cretaceous sediments overlying salt domes furnish oil from over 400 producing wells. Gas production from the Flomaton field in Escambia County awaits only the completion of extracting plants which will remove dangerous hydrogen sulfide in order that the gas may be safely consumed. Off-shore oil and gas fields are attracting much attention and should develop rapidly, pending environmental safeguards. Other mineral fuels produced in Alabama include asphalt and coke; but, compared to coal and petroleum, these are of relatively minor importance.

The increased urban growth and development of highways is directly reflected by the production of many of the non-metallic mineral commodities (often called industrial minerals), which represent 36 percent of Alabama's 1970 mineral production. Alabama produces over $55 million worth of cement (17 percent of the total annual mineral production), and ranks second nationally in tonnage of masonry cement. Seventy-eight percent of the State's masonry cement is shipped to other southeastern states. Jefferson, Mobile, and Shelby

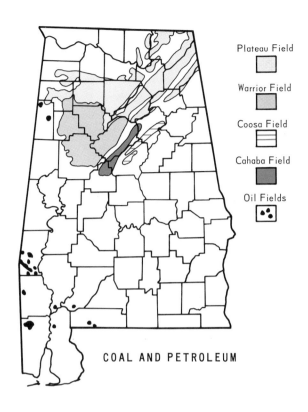

Plateau Field

Warrior Field

Coosa Field

Cahaba Field

Oil Fields

COAL AND PETROLEUM

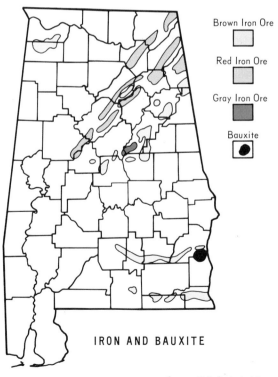

Brown Iron Ore

Red Iron Ore

Gray Iron Ore

Bauxite

IRON AND BAUXITE

Source: U. S. Geological Survey

Strip Mining

Counties are the leading producers.

Nineteen counties, led by Shelby, Jefferson and Morgan, produce marble, dolomite, limestone, and sandstone, with a value of over $37 million. Principal uses for this stone include such things as concrete aggregate, in lime and cement manufacturing, and as a flux in the manufacture of iron.

Sand and gravel are building materials necessary to urban development. Both are widely distributed in the sediments throughout the State, and 31 counties produce sand and gravel valued at almost $9 million. Montgomery, Macon, and Clarke Counties top the list, producing sand and gravel for paving and fill.

Clay and lime round out the non-metallic mineral products that are produced in large amounts in the State. Both are of prime importance to the construction industry. Clay is used primarily for brick, building block, sewer pipes, cement, and lightweight aggregate (a filler to produce lightweight concrete), and is mined principally from the Paleozoic and Cretaceous rocks of Jefferson, Shelby, Russell, Walker, and Calhoun Counties. The value of clay production, over $7 million, is somewhat less than that of lime, which is almost $10 million. Shelby County

is the sole producer of lime, which is used by a diverse group of industries. The lime is produced by heating limestone at high temperatures. The paper industry consumes over 30 percent of the State's lime production, and the construction industry uses about 15 percent in the manufacture of mortar and plaster. Lime is also widely used in metallurgical processes and sewage treatment.

Many other non-metallic deposits exist, widely dispersed throughout the State. Some are mined in small quantities, while, for others, mining is not now economically feasible. Collectively these include phosphate rock, salt, mica, talc, barite, asbestos, beryl, fluorite, and graphite.

Alabama is also a producer of metallic ores. Many years ago it was the ready availability of the State's iron ore in close proximity to coal and limestone (used as a flux) which provided the iron and steel for the Confederacy. Today the iron and steel industry has brought immeasurable benefit and growth to Alabama. However, the value of iron ore production is today declining (in 1970 it was $5.7 million, 11 percent lower than in 1969) due to increased competition from South American imports. Iron ore production is currently from the Silurian sedimentary rocks of Franklin, Blount, Jefferson, and Pike Counties, but iron ore deposits are widely distributed throughout the State.

Alabama's other principal metallic ore mineral is bauxite, an ore of aluminum. All of Alabama's bauxite production is used, however, in the manufacture of refractories (fire brick) and aluminous chemicals (aluminum sulfate-alum) for the paper industry. Deposits in the Tertiary rocks (formed about 40 million years ago) in Barbour and Henry Counties make Alabama the second largest bauxite producer in the country.

Other metallic mineral deposits may exist in the Piedmont. These include gold, chalcopyrite (an ore of copper), sphalerite (zinc), galena (lead), and arsenopyrite (arsenic). Major exploration companies are presently engaged in seeking out economic deposits of many of these minerals.

Considering these resource production figures on a county basis, Jefferson and Shelby, followed by Talladega, Tuscaloosa, and Walker, counties stand out as principal mineral producers. These counties form a broad area in the central portion of the State corresponding to the location of coal, iron, and cement resources. Most counties have some mineral production; the counties with the smallest production lie in east-central and west-central Alabama.

The State's interest in its resources is intimately tied to the maintenance of the environment as shown by the recently enacted "Alabama Surface Mining Act." The Act prohibits unlicensed strip mining (one of the most economical means of recovering Alabama's shallow mineral resources) and requires reclamation of surface mined areas in order to protect land value and our physical environment.

In summary, the sedimentary rocks of the State furnish the foundations for a firm and economical mineral and fuel industry that will continue to grow and offer Alabama increasing returns from our earth resources. The Piedmont, the ancient crystalline mountains of east-central Alabama, sparkles with the glint of hidden mineral wealth and tantalizingly beckons the geologist to uncover her deposits of gold, copper, mercury, zinc, and other valuable resources. Truly the mineral industries of Alabama are a life-giving segment of the State's existence.

Stephen H. Stow

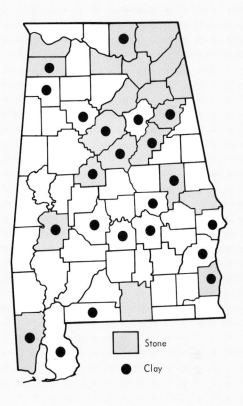

PRODUCTION OF NON-METALLIC
MINERAL RESOURCES

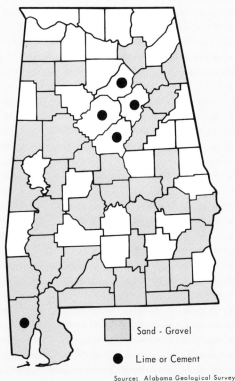

Source: Alabama Geological Survey

Shrimp Fleet

DAVID BLAKEMAN

COMMERCIAL FISHING

The commercial fisheries of Alabama are based on Gulf Coast ports in Mobile and Baldwin counties. Freshwater species comprise but a very insignificant portion of the landings. In April 1970 fishing in the Alabama and Tombigbee rivers was totally suspended because of mercury pollution.

In 1970 there were 29.6 million pounds of salt-water species landed in Mobile and Baldwin counties. These had a dockside value to fishermen of $9,925,000. The oyster catch, with a dockside value of $1,008,000 in 1967, was worth but $158,000 in 1970 as the chief oyster beds had to be closed for 141 days because of domestic pollution.

The importance of the different types of gear and methods of fishing relative to value of catch is shown in the accompanying graphics. There are five fisheries of major importance. The otter trawl fishery is the most important and depends chiefly on shrimp, but is now (1970) taking large quantities of croakers which are shipped on ice to East Coast markets. Hand lines are used for red snappers and groupers, and this fishery operates mainly out of Mobile. Tongs are the only oyster gear permitted except on private beds, or for taking seed

oysters. The majority of the crabs are taken in pots. Trammel and gill nets are used chiefly for mullet and spotted sea trout.

In 1970 because of the depressed economic conditions in the southern part of Mobile County, an analysis was made of the role of commercial fishing in the area. The survey showed that the industry in 1970 furnished about 312,000 man-days of employment to fishermen, and that the processing of oysters and crabs resulted in wages of $846,000 to local labor. One promising aspect is the upswing in landings of croakers by the otter trawl vessels. This helps the economy, especially during the winter and spring months when shrimp are scarce.

During 1970, 350 otter trawl vessels made 6,207 landings in south Mobile County. These vessels fish both in the protected waters of Mobile Bay and Mississippi Sound, and on the high seas. Trawl vessels land shrimp from as far away as the Tortugas ground off Key West, areas offshore of Louisiana and Texas, and the Campeche banks off the west coast of the Yucatan Peninsula in Mexico.

George A. Rounsefell

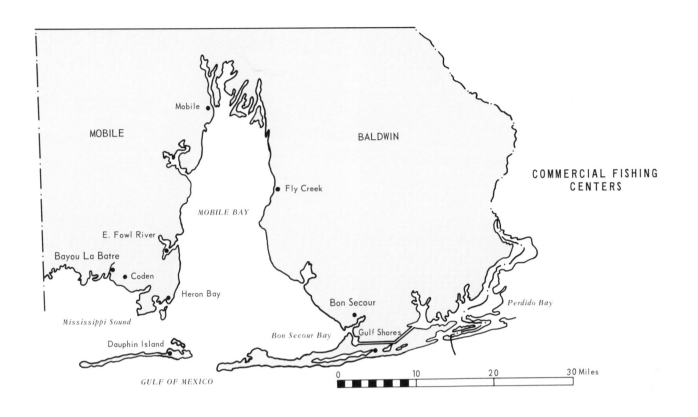

COMMERCIAL FISHING
CENTERS

MOBILE

BALDWIN

Mobile

Fly Creek

MOBILE BAY

E. Fowl River

Bayou La Batre

Coden

Heron Bay

Bon Secour

Perdido Bay

Gulf Shores

Mississippi Sound

Bon Secour Bay

Dauphin Island

GULF OF MEXICO

0   10   20   30 Miles

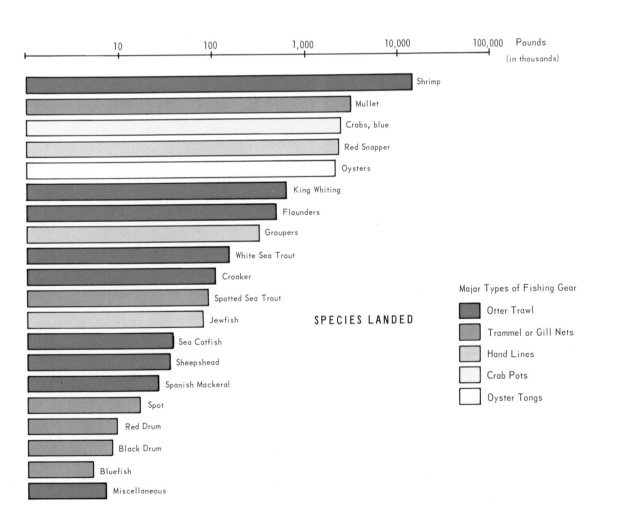

10   100   1,000   10,000   100,000   Pounds

(in thousands)

Shrimp

Mullet

Crabs, blue

Red Snapper

Oysters

King Whiting

Flounders

Groupers

White Sea Trout

Croaker

Spotted Sea Trout

Jewfish

SPECIES LANDED

Sea Catfish

Sheepshead

Spanish Mackeral

Spot

Red Drum

Black Drum

Bluefish

Miscellaneous

Major Types of Fishing Gear

Otter Trawl

Trammel or Gill Nets

Hand Lines

Crab Pots

Oyster Tongs

GSA

AFC

FORESTRY

Alabama is fortunate to have the land resources for increased forest production. Sixty-seven percent, or 21.7 million of the State's 32.7 million acres, is in forest. Although not all acres are fully productive, the land base for greater production does exist. The average per-acre, per-year growth of Alabama's forests is about ½ cord, or 64 cubic feet. Research has shown that land planted to pines may be expected to produce in excess of one cord per acre per year. The challenge, therefore, to forest landowners and managers is to double production on land now in forest, because the technology required has been developed. To reach production goals forecast for the next 30 years, incentives must be created that will make investment in forest operations more profitable.

An estimated $1.37 billion was added to Alabama's economy in 1970 by the growing, harvesting, transporting, and manufacturing of forest products. The stumpage value of commercially harvested forests, or the value of all commercial wood harvested, was estimated to be $90.3 million in 1970.[1]

With the exception of Limestone County in the Tennessee Valley, each of Alabama's 67 counties has more than one hundred thousand acres of commercial forest land. Counties in west central and southwest Alabama are considered to have the greatest potential and highest yield records of harvested wood products. Forecasters predict that hardwood lumber production will decline and pine lumber will level off in the years immediately ahead. Round pulpwood production of both pine and hardwood will continue to increase.

Forest land managers are in general agreement that well-stocked pine stands can be harvested by any system of cutting. There is the selection (or selective) system, in which individual trees or groups of trees are harvested, and the clear-cut method. Because the latter system completely destroys the forest cover within the clear-cut area,

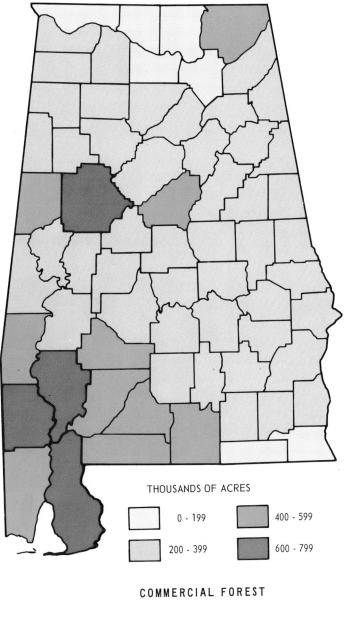

THOUSANDS OF ACRES

0 - 199	400 - 599
200 - 399	600 - 799

COMMERCIAL FOREST

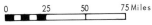

0   25   50   75 Miles

Source: Alabama Forestry Commission

it is opposed by conservationists. However, clear cutting of understocked stands may be the only practical and economical way of getting land into full production, when it is followed by direct seeding or planting. Replanting, as in row crop agriculture, is an accepted practice when the initial stand is judged inadequate.

The southwestern corner of the State, sometimes referred to as the Piney Woods, has the largest concentration of commercial forest acreage, lumber production, and roundwood sold for pulp. Unlike most of the land of other counties, the Piney Woods area has not been cleared for agriculture and has continued to be a heavily forested portion of the State since its settlement. Considerable acreages of the land are held by major paper companies, which utilize all types of current reseeding practices.

Pulpwood and chips for pulp in large commercial amounts are produced almost totally in the southern two-thirds of the State, and more specifically in the coastal plain. The immature sandy soils are far more suited to pines than hardwoods (oak, maple, hickory, etc.). Thus, the pattern of pulpwood cut corresponds to the pattern of commercial pine forests.

Lumber production, or wood sold commercially other than for pulp and firewood, can be broken into two divisions, pine and hardwood. Most of the pine board-feet are utilized directly in the construction industry, while hardwood has a multiplicity of uses, including veneer, pallets, flooring, furniture, mold-board (made from chips), and railroad ties. Hardwood lumber production, unlike pine, is scattered over the State, with large amounts being produced in the Plateau counties where pines give way to a predominance of hardwoods.

National forests, including Talladega, William B. Bankhead, Tuskegee, and Conecuh, are sources of some wood production, cut under controlled conditions specified by the Forest Service. Both pulp and lumber are harvested, using both selective and clear cutting methods.

Since forests cover 67 percent of the land area of the State, it may be said that 67 percent of the State's environment is affected by what is done within the forest ecosystem. This concept places a real responsibility on the forestland owner and manager to treat forest lands

AFC

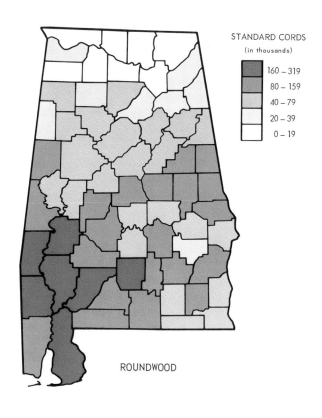

STANDARD CORDS

(in thousands)

160 – 319
80 – 159
40 – 79
20 – 39
0 – 19

ROUNDWOOD

PULPWOOD CUT: 1970

in the public interest. Forests represent but one kind of vegetative cover found on wild lands. Because both people and wildlife need and use lands in forest, treatment and harvesting methods must be concerned with these and other multiple uses.

Alabama's forests should be made more productive. The base for expansion of existing forest-related industries and for establishing new industry is an ample supply of the raw material, wood. Without an increase in forestland, the present acreage must be managed to produce higher yields. One way to accomplish this goal is to convert understocked stands into stands that are fully stocked. On lands where this is done, production is more than doubled. Yields may be further increased by planting seedlings, produced through genetic research, that have superior growth rates. These superior seedlings may increase growth as much as 25 percent over that obtained by nursery-run seedlings. Growth can

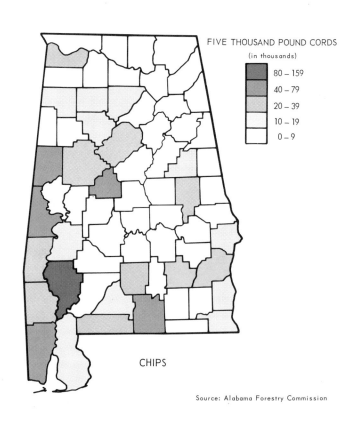

FIVE THOUSAND POUND CORDS

(in thousands)

80 – 159
40 – 79
20 – 39
10 – 19
0 – 9

CHIPS

Source: Alabama Forestry Commission

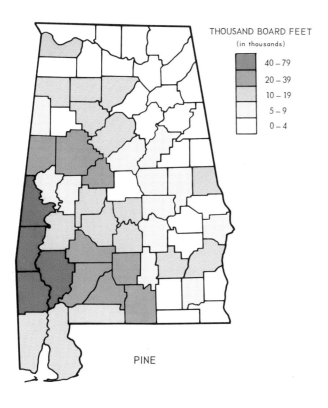

THOUSAND BOARD FEET
(in thousands)

40 – 79
20 – 39
10 – 19
5 – 9
0 – 4

PINE

LUMBER PRODUCTION: 1970

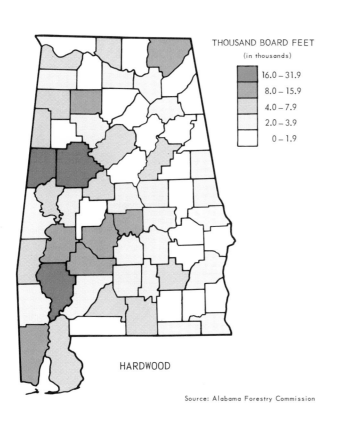

THOUSAND BOARD FEET
(in thousands)

16.0 – 31.9
8.0 – 15.9
4.0 – 7.9
2.0 – 3.9
0 – 1.9

HARDWOOD

Source: Alabama Forestry Commission

be further increased by fertilization. Although research results vary, an increase of 15 percent in the growth rate may result from fertilization.

The potentials for increased yields vary with the quality of the soil and the species being planted. Most pine species can be planted on pine sites with the confidence that they will grow. Although less is known about hardwoods, they yield well on good hardwood sites; but such sites are frequently used for agricultural crops other than trees.

It will be necessary to double timber growth in Alabama and other southern states before the end of the current century if southern forests are to meet population needs anticipated by the year 2000.

[1]Alabama Forest Products Association, Joe W. Graham, Executive Vice President.

W. B. DeVall

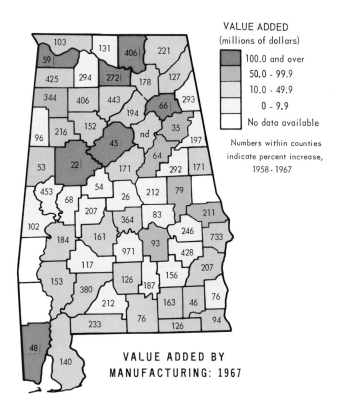

NUMBER OF EMPLOYEES

- 50,000 and over
- 10,000 - 49,999
- 4,000 - 9,999
- 1,000 - 3,999
- 0 - 999

Numbers within counties indicate percent increase, 1960 - 1970

EMPLOYMENT IN MANUFACTURING: 1970

Source: Department of Industrial Relations State of Alabama, July, 1971

VALUE ADDED
(millions of dollars)

- 100.0 and over
- 50.0 - 99.9
- 10.0 - 49.9
- 0 - 9.9
- No data available

Numbers within counties indicate percent increase, 1958 - 1967

VALUE ADDED BY MANUFACTURING: 1967

Source: 1967 Census of Manufactures

MANUFACTURING

The manufacturing economy of Alabama has exhibited an impressive vitality in recent years. Throughout the 1960's the pace of economic expansion in Alabama's manufacturing sector has exceeded that for the United States as a whole. Manufacturing employment in Alabama rose from 233,400 in 1960 to 321,800 in 1970, an increase of 37.9 percent, compared to an increase of only 15.5 percent for the country. Value added by manufacture in Alabama rose from $1.77 billion in 1958 to $3.53 billion in 1967, for a gain of almost 100 percent in the space of eight years. During the same time, value added by manufacture increased by only 85.2 percent for the entire nation.[1] Alabama ranked nineteenth among the 50 states in percentage increase in "value added" during the period 1958–1967.

The basic character of Alabama's manufacturing economy can be seen by reference to the accompanying graphics. These provide a good indication of the pattern and trends in manufacturing activity within the State. The map, Employment in Manufacturing, reveals a dominant concentration of manufacturing employment in the northern half of the State. In fact, more than two-thirds of the 321,800 persons employed in manufacturing work in firms located in the northern half of Alabama. Particularly heavy concentrations of manufacturing employment are found in Jefferson County (65,803), Mobile County (21,345), Madison County (12,155), Calhoun County (12,079), Etowah County (11,263), Morgan County (11,066), Talladega County (10,109), and Tuscaloosa County (10,069). In 1970 these eight counties contained 47.8 percent of the State's manufacturing employment, and seven of the eight (Mobile County being the exception) are in the northern portion of the State.

One of the most dramatic trends in Alabama's manufacturing sector is the strong expansion of employment in the less urbanized counties, as shown by the percentage changes in manufacturing employment for the 1960–1970 period. Nineteen counties in Alabama realized more than a 100 percent gain in manufacturing employment between 1960 and 1970; seventeen of these were counties in which there was no community with a 1970 population of as much as 15,000 persons. Still another eleven counties with no sizeable urban community had percentage increases in manufacturing employment which exceeded the state-wide average of 37.9 percent. At the same time, except for Madison County, the percentage gains in manufacturing employment in the most urbanized and heavily populated counties were far below the state-wide average. A total of 52,300 of the 88,400 new jobs in manufacturing, or 59.2 percent, were in counties other than those containing Alabama's seven largest cities.

Statistics for value added by manufacture by county for 1967 indicate large concentrations of manufacturing activity in the following counties: Jefferson ($852.8 million), Mobile ($279.9 million), Etowah ($223.6 million), Madison ($210.9 million), Morgan ($206.0 million), Colbert ($146.0 million), and Tuscaloosa ($108.4 million). The dominance of these seven counties is amply indicated by the fact that they accounted for 57.4 percent of the total value added by manufacture in Alabama in 1967. Again, however, the largest percentage gains in value added occurred in the less populous rural counties, reflecting the increasing degree to which industrialization and economic growth are penetrating and enveloping the rural sections of the State.

The accompanying table shows value added by manufacture by major industry groups for the years 1958, 1963, and 1967, with related percentage changes. The industry breakdown reveals that manufacturing in Alabama is concentrated in food and kindred products, textiles, apparel, paper and allied products, chemicals, rubber and plastics, primary metals, fabricated metals, and nonelectrical machinery. The expansion of these particular industries in Alabama is a direct reflection of the abundant supply of unskilled and semiskilled labor and, in the case of the paper and chemical industries, the ready availability of forest and water resources.

[1]Value added by manufacture is a measure of the market value of the economic activity which takes place at particular manufacturing establishments. It is derived by subtracting the total cost of materials from the value of shipments and adjusting the resulting amount by the net change in inventories. Value added by manufacture is considered to be the best available indicator for comparing the relative economic importance of manufacturing among industries and geographic areas.

Arthur A. Thompson

VALUE ADDED BY MANUFACTURE BY INDUSTRY
WITH RELATED PERCENTAGE CHANGES: 1958, 1963, 1967

		VALUE ADDED BY MANUFACTURE				
		Amount (millions of dollars)			Percent Change	
INDUSTRY CODE	INDUSTRY	1958	1963	1967	1958 to 1963	1963 to 1967
19	Ordnance and Accessories	---	---	---	---	---
20	Food and Kindred Products	151.8	203.4	261.6	33.9	28.6
21	Tobacco Manufactures	4.2	---	---	---	---
22	Textile Mill Products	178.2	219.3	322.1	23.0	46.9
23	Apparel	89.8	157.8	254.8	75.7	61.5
24	Lumber and Wood Products	77.9	100.9	142.8	29.5	41.5
25	Furniture and Fixture	15.3	24.3	36.8	58.8	50.6
26	Paper and Allied Products	112.3	165.6	323.2	47.5	95.2
27	Printing and Publishing	44.6	54.2	82.8	21.5	52.8
28	Chemical and Allied Products	139.7	216.5	418.2	54.9	93.2
29	Petroleum and Coal Products	9.5	14.1	18.4	48.4	30.5
30	Rubber and Plastics Products	96.8	133.6	190.5	38.0	42.6
31	Leather and Leather Products	---	---	---	---	---
32	Stone, Clay and Glass Products	84.4	94.2	113.7	11.6	20.7
33	Primary Metals	469.5	500.2	638.6	6.5	27.7
34	Fabricated Metal Products	107.7	132.4	216.5	22.9	63.5
35	Machinery, Except Electrical	28.9	51.7	100.4	78.9	94.2
36	Electrical Equipment and Supplies	33.8	37.5	70.3	10.9	87.5
37	Transportation Equipment	104.1	142.4	163.4	36.8	14.7
38	Instruments and Related Products	---	---	3.4	---	---
39	Miscellaneous Manufacturing	---	10.0	22.2	---	122.0
	All Industries, TOTAL	1,770.5	2,325.2	3,525.5	31.3	51.6

MANUFACTURING TYPES

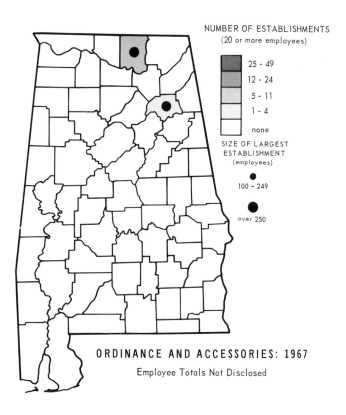

NUMBER OF ESTABLISHMENTS
(20 or more employees)

25 - 49
12 - 24
5 - 11
1 - 4
none

SIZE OF LARGEST
ESTABLISHMENT
(employees)

100 - 249

over 250

ORDINANCE AND ACCESSORIES: 1967

Employee Totals Not Disclosed

Source: Census of Manufactures

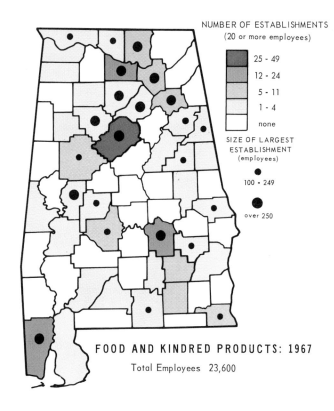

NUMBER OF ESTABLISHMENTS
(20 or more employees)

25 - 49
12 - 24
5 - 11
1 - 4
none

SIZE OF LARGEST
ESTABLISHMENT
(employees)

100 - 249

over 250

FOOD AND KINDRED PRODUCTS: 1967

Total Employees 23,600

Source: Census of Manufactures

ORDNANCE AND ACCESSORIES establishments with 20 or more employees in 1967 were located in only two counties in Alabama.[1] Madison (Huntsville) and Etowah (Gadsden) counties possessed five and three firms, respectively.

Most firms engaged in manufacturing ordnance are attracted to government-impacted areas, such as military bases, space flight centers, and missile bases. Locations near the center of demand for the more sophisticated types of ordnance are necessitated by the need for detailed and continuous communication between the users and suppliers of weapons and weapon parts.

		Percent of State Total
TOTAL ESTABLISHMENTS	9	.1
WITH 20 OR MORE EMPLOYEES	8	.5
VALUE ADDED BY		
MANUFACTURE (millions)	. . .	
EMPLOYEES	2500 or more	
PAYROLL (millions)	. . .	
PRODUCTION WORKERS (thousands)	. . .	
WAGES (millions)	. . .	
AVERAGE HOURLY WAGE	. . .	
AVERAGE HOURLY WAGE OF ALL		
STATE INDUSTRIES	$2.49	

FOOD AND KINDRED PRODUCTS companies with 20 or more employees were found in 39 of Alabama's 67 counties in 1967. The largest number of firms were engaged in producing bottled and canned soft drinks, dairy products, meat products, and bakery goods. In general, the highly urbanized counties had the most food processing companies, which supplied processed food products to both the urban centers and the rural areas.

		Percent of State Total
TOTAL ESTABLISHMENTS	475	9
WITH 20 OR MORE EMPLOYEES	209	14
VALUE ADDED BY		
MANUFACTURE (millions)	$203.4	6
EMPLOYEES (thousands)	23.6	8
PAYROLL (millions)	$114.5	7
PRODUCTION WORKERS (thousands)	14.2	6
WAGES (millions)	$ 56.9	5
AVERAGE HOURLY WAGE	$ 1.91	

[1]The significance of establishments with 20 or more employees lies in the fact that errors in enumeration by the Bureau of the Census were perhaps more prevalent with smaller firms.

TEXTILE MILL PRODUCTS, mainly yarn and thread, were produced by 119 plants with 20 or more employees in 1967. Textile mills, which generally pay lower wages than most other types of manufacturing, are attracted to areas where abundant unemployed or underemployed labor is available. Highly urban areas are thus usually avoided, except where other factors result in economies sufficient to offset the more costly labor.

		Percent of State Total
TOTAL ESTABLISHMENTS	141	3
WITH 20 OR MORE EMPLOYEES	119	8
VALUE ADDED BY		
MANUFACTURE (millions)	$322.1	9
EMPLOYEES (thousands)	40.0	14
PAYROLL (millions)	$178.0	11
PRODUCTION WORKERS (thousands)	37.2	16
WAGES (millions)	$154.2	13
AVERAGE HOURLY WAGE	$ 2.02	

TOBACCO MANUFACTURES INDUSTRIES included only three establishments in Alabama in 1967, and were of relatively minor importance.

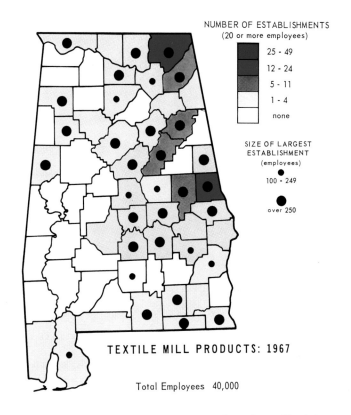

TEXTILE MILL PRODUCTS: 1967

Total Employees 40,000

Source: Census of Manufactures

APPAREL AND OTHER TEXTILE PRODUCTS were manufactured by plants with 20 or more employees in 56 of 67 counties in 1967. Most of the 220 apparel companies produced shirts for men and boys, nightwear, trousers, and work clothes. Production facilities were found in both rural and urban counties, and were not concentrated in any one part of the State.

The apparel industry brings economic benefits to rural counties where there are only limited resources to develop other industries. Wives and daughters of working men, called "by-product labor," are extensively utilized by the apparel industry, and the wages are relatively low.

		Percent of State Total
TOTAL ESTABLISHMENTS	220	4
WITH 20 OR MORE EMPLOYEES	168	12
VALUE ADDED BY		
MANUFACTURE (millions)	$254.8	7
EMPLOYEES (thousands)	42.7	15
PAYROLL (millions)	$140.1	9
PRODUCTION WORKERS (thousands)	39.4	17
WAGES (millions)	$122.6	11
AVERAGE HOURLY WAGE	$ 1.71	

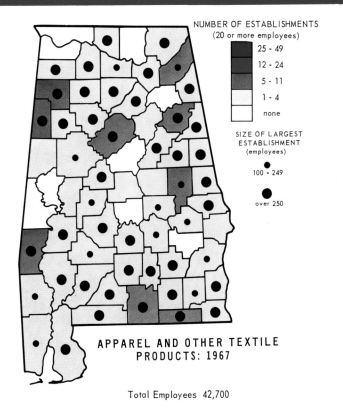

APPAREL AND OTHER TEXTILE PRODUCTS: 1967

Total Employees 42,700

Source: Census of Manufactures

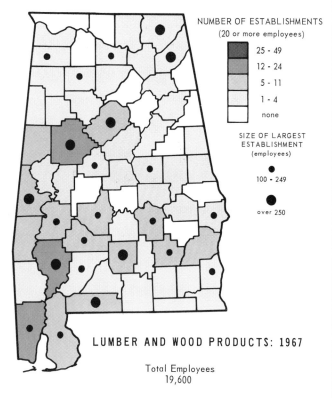

NUMBER OF ESTABLISHMENTS
(20 or more employees)

25 - 49
12 - 24
5 - 11
1 - 4
none

SIZE OF LARGEST
ESTABLISHMENT
(employees)

● 100 - 249

● over 250

LUMBER AND WOOD PRODUCTS: 1967

Total Employees
19,600

Source: Census of Manufactures

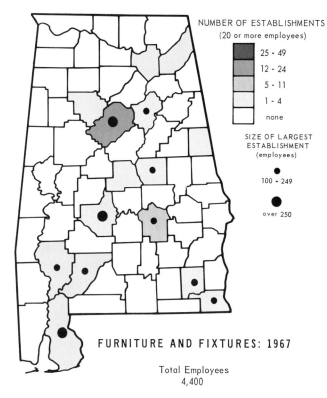

NUMBER OF ESTABLISHMENTS
(20 or more employees)

25 - 49
12 - 24
5 - 11
1 - 4
none

SIZE OF LARGEST
ESTABLISHMENT
(employees)

● 100 - 249

● over 250

FURNITURE AND FIXTURES: 1967

Total Employees
4,400

Source: Census of Manufactures

LUMBER AND WOOD PRODUCTS establishments were noticeably restricted to the west central and southwestern sections of Alabama, areas with a heavy forestation of pines and hardwoods. In 1967 there were 213 establishments with 20 or more employees, and many hundreds of smaller firms were scattered across the State. These included the so-called "pecker wood sawmills," which are highly mobile and in almost continuous movement from one stand of timber to another.

		Percent of State Total
TOTAL ESTABLISHMENTS	2,200	44
WITH 20 OR MORE EMPLOYEES	213	15
VALUE ADDED BY		
MANUFACTURE (millions)	$142.8	4
EMPLOYEES (thousands)	19.6	7
PAYROLL (millions)	$ 73.8	5
PRODUCTION WORKERS (thousands)	18.1	8
WAGES (millions)	$ 61.7	5
AVERAGE HOURLY WAGE	$ 1.70	
AVERAGE HOURLY WAGE OF ALL STATE INDUSTRIES	$ 2.49	

FURNITURE AND FIXTURES companies with 20 or more employees were found in 15 counties in Alabama in 1967. Most of these enterprises manufactured household furniture.

Good transportation facilities with access to urban markets, and available raw materials are the principal location factors for the furniture industry. Alabama, having an abundant supply of hardwoods and softwoods, has the raw materials to support a greater furniture production.

		Percent of State Total
TOTAL ESTABLISHMENTS	122	2
WITH 20 OR MORE EMPLOYEES	39	3
VALUE ADDED BY		
MANUFACTURE (millions)	$36.6	1
EMPLOYEES (thousands)	4.4	2
PAYROLL (millions)	$19.0	1
PRODUCTION WORKERS (thousands)	3.9	2
WAGES (millions)	$14.8	1
AVERAGE HOURLY WAGE	$1.83	
AVERAGE HOURLY WAGE OF ALL STATE INDUSTRIES	$2.49	

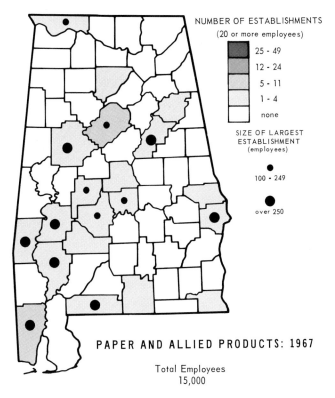

PAPER AND ALLIED PRODUCTS: 1967

Total Employees
15,000

Source: Census of Manufactures

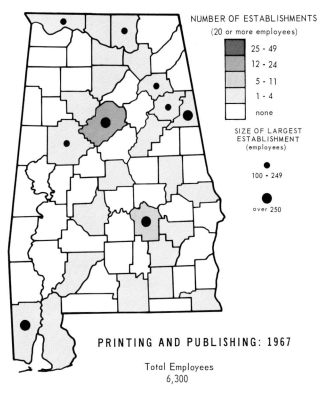

PRINTING AND PUBLISHING: 1967

Total Employees
6,300

Source: Census of Manufactures

PAPER AND ALLIED PRODUCTS plants, each employing 20 or more persons, were located in 20 counties in Alabama in 1967. Most of the companies manufactured paperboard containers, boxes and miscellaneous converted paper products.

The industry in Alabama is highly dependent on access to pulpwood, rail transportation and large amounts of water. Thus most of the plants are located along the major rivers of the State.

		Percent of State Total
TOTAL ESTABLISHMENTS	51	1
WITH 20 OR MORE EMPLOYEES	43	3
VALUE ADDED BY		
MANUFACTURE (millions)	$323.2	9
EMPLOYEES (thousands)	15.0	5
PAYROLL (millions)	$113.6	7
PRODUCTION WORKERS (thousands)	12.4	5
WAGES (millions)	$ 89.9	8
AVERAGE HOURLY WAGE	$ 3.42	
AVERAGE HOURLY WAGE OF ALL		
STATE INDUSTRIES	$ 2.49	

PRINTING AND PUBLISHING establishments numbered 334 in Alabama in 1967, of which 273 were commercial printers and newspapers employing fewer than 20 persons.

Printing and publishing are almost totally urban activities. Although newspaper publishing can be found in hundreds of small towns and large cities across the State, most commercial printers are found in the large cities, reflecting the highly urban demand for this type of service.

		Percent of State Total
TOTAL ESTABLISHMENTS	334	7
WITH 20 OR MORE EMPLOYEES	61	4
VALUE ADDED BY		
MANUFACTURE (millions)	$82.8	2
EMPLOYEES (thousands)	6.3	2
PAYROLL (millions)	$37.0	2
PRODUCTION WORKERS (thousands)	4.2	2
WAGES (millions)	$23.0	2
AVERAGE HOURLY WAGE	$2.84	
AVERAGE HOURLY WAGE OF ALL		
STATE INDUSTRIES	$2.49	

CHEMICAL AND ALLIED PRODUCTS establishments in 1967 numbered 133, approximately half of which employed 20 persons or more. The largest number of companies were engaged in the manufacture of agricultural and industrial chemicals, such as fertilizer, plastics, and paints.

Chemical plants primarily are located where there is good access to raw materials. This involves location near a natural source, near a plant that produces a by-product used in the chemical industry, or next to good transport facilities. The locations of plants in Alabama reflect these factors. Plant sites along rivers give access to water to those industries requiring large amounts of it, and have facilitated the removal of liquid waste materials in some cases.

		Percent of State Total
TOTAL ESTABLISHMENTS	133	3
WITH 20 OR MORE EMPLOYEES	64	4
VALUE ADDED BY		
MANUFACTURE (millions)	$418.2	12
EMPLOYEES (thousands)	11.7	4
PAYROLL (millions)	$ 80.1	5
PRODUCTION WORKERS (thousands)	8.0	3
WAGES (millions)	$ 48.7	4
AVERAGE HOURLY WAGE	$2.95	

PETROLEUM AND COAL PRODUCTS establishments in Alabama in 1967 were mostly involved in petroleum refining and the production of paving and roofing materials, and asphalt. Of the 27 total establishments, 12 employed over 20 people, and four of these were located in Tuscaloosa County.

Water transportation is almost essential to firms which require large bulk shipments of petroleum and coal. All of the counties which contained the larger companies were served by major waterways, such as the Black Warrior and Tennessee rivers.

		Percent of State Total
TOTAL ESTABLISHMENTS	27	1
WITH 20 OR MORE EMPLOYEES	12	1
VALUE ADDED BY		
MANUFACTURE (millions)	$18.4	1
EMPLOYEES (thousands)	9	.3
PAYROLL (millions)	$ 5.8	.4
PRODUCTION WORKERS (thousands)	.7	.3
WAGES (millions)	$ 4.2	.4
AVERAGE HOURLY WAGE	$3.00	
AVERAGE HOURLY WAGE OF ALL		
STATE INDUSTRIES	$2.49	

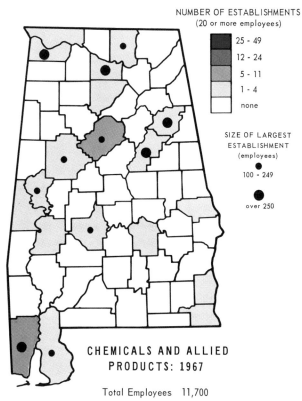

NUMBER OF ESTABLISHMENTS
(20 or more employees)

- 25 - 49
- 12 - 24
- 5 - 11
- 1 - 4
- none

SIZE OF LARGEST
ESTABLISHMENT
(employees)

- 100 - 249
- over 250

CHEMICALS AND ALLIED
PRODUCTS: 1967

Total Employees   11,700

Source: Census of Manufactures

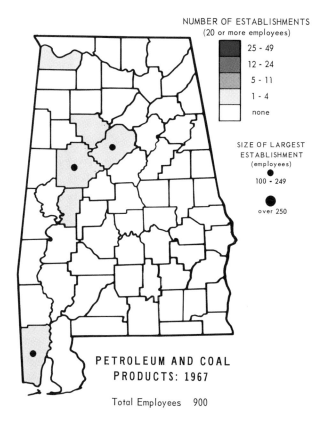

NUMBER OF ESTABLISHMENTS
(20 or more employees)

- 25 - 49
- 12 - 24
- 5 - 11
- 1 - 4
- none

SIZE OF LARGEST
ESTABLISHMENT
(employees)

- 100 - 249
- over 250

PETROLEUM AND COAL
PRODUCTS: 1967

Total Employees   900

Source: Census of Manufactures

RUBBER AND PLASTIC PRODUCTS establishments with 20 or more employees were located in 14 of Alabama's 67 counties in 1967.

Many miscellaneous plastic products were produced in the State; however, rubber tires (manufactured at Tuscaloosa, Gadsden, Opelika, and Huntsville) accounted for most of the value added by manufacture in this category.

		Percent of State Total
TOTAL ESTABLISHMENTS	40	1
WITH 20 OR MORE EMPLOYEES	21	2
VALUE ADDED BY		
MANUFACTURE (millions)	$190.5	5
EMPLOYEES (thousands)	7.8	3
PAYROLL (millions)	$ 56.3	4
PRODUCTION WORKERS (thousands)	6.6	3
WAGES (millions)	$ 45.6	4
AVERAGE HOURLY WAGE	$ 3.43	
AVERAGE HOURLY WAGE OF ALL		
STATE INDUSTRIES	$ 2.49	

LEATHER AND LEATHER PRODUCTS industries numbered only two establishments employing 20 or more persons in Alabama in 1967. Madison County, along the Tennessee River, and Barbour County, in the southeastern portion of the State, each possessed one firm employing more than 249 persons. However, because of the possibility of divulging specific information about individual companies no additional data were available in the 1967 *Census of Manufactures*.

		Percent of State Total
TOTAL ESTABLISHMENTS	7	.1
WITH 20 OR MORE EMPLOYEES	2	.1
VALUE ADDED BY		
MANUFACTURE (millions)	...	
EMPLOYEES	500–999	
PAYROLL (millions)	...	
PRODUCTION WORKERS (thousands)	...	
WAGES (millions)	...	
AVERAGE HOURLY WAGE	...	
AVERAGE HOURLY WAGE OF ALL		
STATE INDUSTRIES	$2.49	

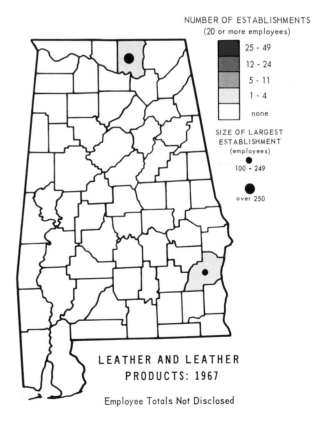

NUMBER OF ESTABLISHMENTS
(20 or more employees)

25 - 49
12 - 24
5 - 11
1 - 4
none

SIZE OF LARGEST ESTABLISHMENT
(employees)
100 - 249
over 250

RUBBER AND PLASTICS PRODUCTS: 1967

Total Employees 7,800

Source: Census of Manufactures

NUMBER OF ESTABLISHMENTS
(20 or more employees)

25 - 49
12 - 24
5 - 11
1 - 4
none

SIZE OF LARGEST ESTABLISHMENT
(employees)
100 - 249
over 250

LEATHER AND LEATHER PRODUCTS: 1967

Employee Totals Not Disclosed

Source: Census of Manufactures

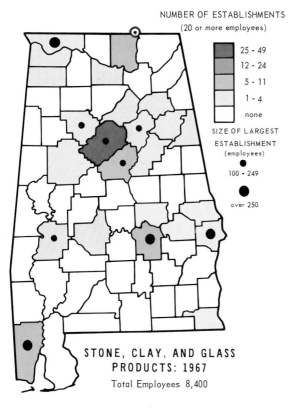

NUMBER OF ESTABLISHMENTS
(20 or more employees)

25 - 49
12 - 24
5 - 11
1 - 4
none

SIZE OF LARGEST
ESTABLISHMENT
(employees)

● 100 - 249

● over 250

STONE, CLAY, AND GLASS PRODUCTS: 1967
Total Employees 8,400

Source: Census of Manufactures

STONE, CLAY, AND GLASS PRODUCTS establishments numbered 275, of which 102 employed 20 or more employees in 1967 in Alabama. Half of these plants produced items derived from the processing of limestone into cement, mortar, or plaster of Paris. The variety of items produced by other companies included glassware, bricks, pottery, concrete blocks, and ready-mix concrete.

The location factors of this industry are mainly the availability of raw materials and a proximity to urban markets, due to the high transportation costs of moving the heavy, bulky materials.

		Percent of State Total
TOTAL ESTABLISHMENTS	275	6
WITH 20 OR MORE EMPLOYEES	102	7
VALUE ADDED BY		
MANUFACTURE (millions)	$113.7	3
EMPLOYEES (thousands)	8.4	3
PAYROLL (millions)	$ 46.9	3
PRODUCTION WORKERS (thousands)	6.8	3
WAGES (millions)	$ 34.9	3
AVERAGE HOURLY WAGE	$ 2.53	

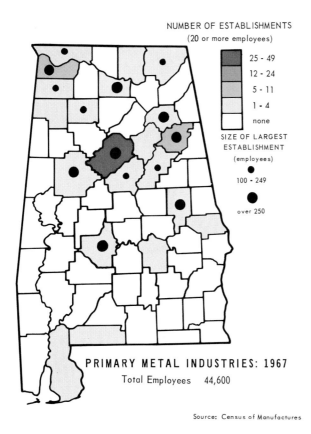

NUMBER OF ESTABLISHMENTS
(20 or more employees)

25 - 49
12 - 24
5 - 11
1 - 4
none

SIZE OF LARGEST
ESTABLISHMENT
(employees)

● 100 - 249

● over 250

PRIMARY METAL INDUSTRIES: 1967
Total Employees 44,600

Source: Census of Manufactures

THE PRIMARY METAL INDUSTRIES establishments were the largest individual manufacturing employers in Alabama in 1967, most being involved in the production of steel, iron, and aluminum products. Of the 112 industries, 92 employed 20 persons or more, and 40 of these were located in Birmingham, Fairfield, and Ensley in Jefferson County. Birmingham, the "Pittsburgh of the South," and its suburbs comprise the center of iron and steel production in the State.

Most plant locations in Alabama have been determined primarily by the availability of raw materials (locally derived or imported), as is the case with iron and steel, or by available hydroelectricity and water transportation in the case of aluminum.

		Percent of State Total
TOTAL ESTABLISHMENTS	112	2
WITH 20 OR MORE EMPLOYEES	92	6
VALUE ADDED BY		
MANUFACTURE (millions)	$638.6	18
EMPLOYEES (thousands)	44.6	15
PAYROLL (millions)	$329.7	21
PRODUCTION WORKERS (thousands)	37.6	16
WAGES (millions)	$255.3	22
AVERAGE HOURLY WAGE	$ 3.47	

THE FABRICATED METAL PRODUCTS establishments in Alabama in 1967 produced cutlery, bolts, rivets, pipe fittings, and other hardware. There were over 250 establishments, with approximately half employing 20 persons or more. Most of the companies were engaged in the production of structural metal products such as sheet metal work and door and sash trim.

Most of the companies were located in the northern half of the State, closely corresponding to the location of the primary metal industry and, therefore, the necessary raw materials.

		Percent of State Total
TOTAL ESTABLISHMENTS	255	5
WITH 20 OR MORE EMPLOYEES	115	8
VALUE ADDED BY		
MANUFACTURE (millions)	$216.5	6
EMPLOYEES (thousands)	16.1	6
PAYROLL (millions)	$ 95.5	6
PRODUCTION WORKERS (thousands)	13.4	6
WAGES (millions)	$ 70.4	6
AVERAGE HOURLY WAGE	$ 2.66	
AVERAGE HOURLY WAGE OF ALL		
STATE INDUSTRIES	$ 2.49	

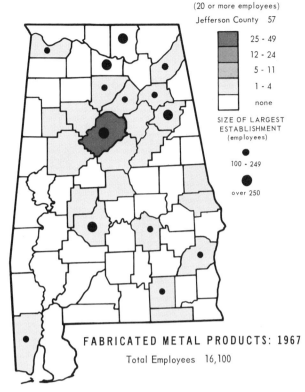

NUMBER OF ESTABLISHMENTS
(20 or more employees)
Jefferson County 57

25 - 49
12 - 24
5 - 11
1 - 4
none

SIZE OF LARGEST ESTABLISHMENT
(employees)

100 - 249

over 250

FABRICATED METAL PRODUCTS: 1967

Total Employees 16,100

Source: Census of Manufactures

MACHINERY, EXCEPT ELECTRICAL, produced in Alabama in 1967 included farm and construction machinery, industrial trucks, woodworking lathes, and turbines. There were over 270 establishments and, of the 60 companies with at least 20 employees, 21 were located in Jefferson County.

Access to iron and steel is a prime location factor for the machinery industry. Most machinery manufacturers in Alabama are located in the same areas as the primary metals industries.

		Percent of State Total
TOTAL ESTABLISHMENTS	271	5
WITH 20 OR MORE EMPLOYEES	60	4
VALUE ADDED BY		
MANUFACTURE (millions)	$100.4	3
EMPLOYEES (thousands)	8.6	3
PAYROLL (millions)	$ 49.2	3
PRODUCTION WORKERS (thousands)	6.6	3
WAGES (millions)	$ 33.4	3
AVERAGE HOURLY WAGE	$ 2.46	
AVERAGE HOURLY WAGE OF ALL		
STATE INDUSTRIES	$ 2.49	

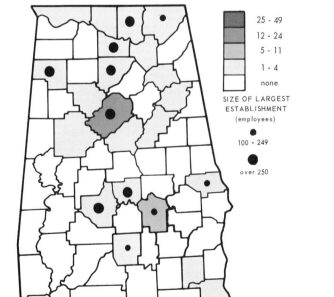

NUMBER OF ESTABLISHMENTS
(20 or more employees)

25 - 49
12 - 24
5 - 11
1 - 4
none

SIZE OF LARGEST ESTABLISHMENT
(employees)

100 - 249

over 250

MACHINERY, EXCEPT ELECTRICAL: 1967

Total Employees 8,600

Source: Census of Manufactures

ELECTRICAL EQUIPMENT AND SUPPLIES establishments numbered forty-seven in Alabama in 1967, half of which employ 20 persons or more. They produced such items as electrical lighting equipment, lamps, transformers, and communication equipment. The largest number of establishments were engaged in manufacturing electrical lighting and wiring equipment.

It appears that manufacturing plants in this category tend to be either close to markets or near good transportation access to markets.

		Percent of State Total
TOTAL ESTABLISHMENTS	47	1
WITH 20 OR MORE EMPLOYEES	21	1
VALUE ADDED BY		
MANUFACTURE (millions)	$70.3	2
EMPLOYEES (thousands)	5.5	2
PAYROLL (millions)	$34.5	2
PRODUCTION WORKERS (thousands)	4.6	2
WAGES (millions)	$25.9	2
AVERAGE HOURLY WAGE	$ 2.88	
AVERAGE HOURLY WAGE OF ALL		
STATE INDUSTRIES	$ 2.49	

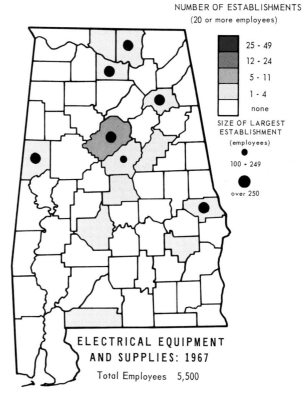

NUMBER OF ESTABLISHMENTS
(20 or more employees)

25 - 49
12 - 24
5 - 11
1 - 4
none

SIZE OF LARGEST ESTABLISHMENT
(employees)

100 - 249

over 250

ELECTRICAL EQUIPMENT AND SUPPLIES: 1967

Total Employees   5,500

Source: Census of Manufactures

TRANSPORTATION EQUIPMENT establishments with 20 or more employees were found in 22 counties in Alabama in 1967. They produced truck trailers, bodies for buses and trucks, aircraft engines, and railroad freight cars. Several companies built and repaired boats and ships; Bayou La Batre in Mobile county produced shrimp boats. Fifty of the 89 total establishments in the State employed at least twenty persons. Jefferson and Mobile counties each contained eight of these larger firms.

Transportation Equipment firms need access to both markets and fabricated steel and aluminum materials.

		Percent of State Total
TOTAL ESTABLISHMENTS	89	2
WITH 20 OR MORE EMPLOYEES	50	3
VALUE ADDED BY		
MANUFACTURE (millions)	$163.4	5
EMPLOYEES (thousands)	16.3	6
PAYROLL (millions)	$104.7	7
PRODUCTION WORKERS (thousands)	13.0	6
WAGES (millions)	$ 80.3	7
AVERAGE HOURLY WAGE	$ 3.08	
AVERAGE HOURLY WAGE OF ALL		
STATE INDUSTRIES	$ 2.49	

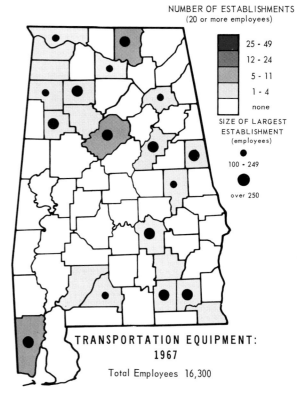

NUMBER OF ESTABLISHMENTS
(20 or more employees)

25 - 49
12 - 24
5 - 11
1 - 4
none

SIZE OF LARGEST ESTABLISHMENT
(employees)

100 - 249

over 250

TRANSPORTATION EQUIPMENT: 1967

Total Employees   16,300

Source: Census of Manufactures

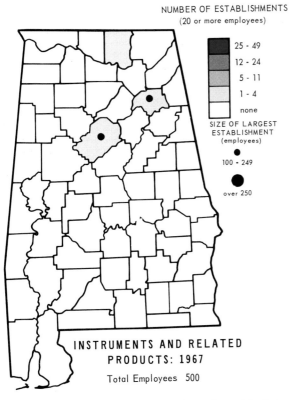

NUMBER OF ESTABLISHMENTS
(20 or more employees)

25 - 49
12 - 24
5 - 11
1 - 4
none

SIZE OF LARGEST
ESTABLISHMENT
(employees)

100 - 249

over 250

**INSTRUMENTS AND RELATED
PRODUCTS: 1967**

Total Employees 500

Source: Census of Manufactures

INSTRUMENTS AND RELATED PRODUCTS establishments numbered eighteen in Alabama in 1967, and they manufactured chiefly watches, clocks, and watch cases. Only four of these, however, employed twenty persons or more, and they were located in Madison (Huntsville), Etowah (Gadsden), and Jefferson (Birmingham) counties.

The assembly of watch movements and watch cases is a process that appears to be oriented partly toward market areas and partly toward the availability of labor that can be trained to perform this operation.

		Percent of State Total
TOTAL ESTABLISHMENTS	18	.3
WITH 20 OR MORE EMPLOYEES	4	.3
VALUE ADDED BY		
MANUFACTURE (millions)	$3.4	.1
EMPLOYEES (thousands)	.5	.2
PAYROLL (millions)	$1.9	.1
PRODUCTION WORKERS (thousands)	.4	.2
WAGES (millions)	$1.3	.1
AVERAGE HOURLY WAGE	$1.86	
AVERAGE HOURLY WAGE OF ALL		
STATE INDUSTRIES	$2.49	

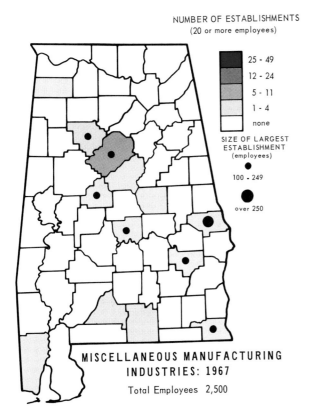

NUMBER OF ESTABLISHMENTS
(20 or more employees)

25 - 49
12 - 24
5 - 11
1 - 4
none

SIZE OF LARGEST
ESTABLISHMENT
(employees)

100 - 249

over 250

**MISCELLANEOUS MANUFACTURING
INDUSTRIES: 1967**

Total Employees 2,500

Source: Census of Manufactures

MISCELLANEOUS MANUFACTURING INDUSTRIES are those that cannot logically be included in any of the other 19 Standard Industrial Classification Groupings. In Alabama most of these miscellaneous concerns manufactured such items as toys, sporting goods, costume jewelry, brooms and brushes, signs and advertising displays, and morticians' goods.

Eighty-nine establishments in the State in 1967 were classified in this category, twenty-three of which employed twenty persons or more.

		Percent of State Total
TOTAL ESTABLISHMENTS	89	2
WITH 20 OR MORE EMPLOYEES	23	2
VALUE ADDED BY		
MANUFACTURE (millions)	$22.2	.6
EMPLOYEES (thousands)	2.5	1
PAYROLL (millions)	$10.3	1
PRODUCTION WORKERS (thousands)	2.2	1
WAGES (millions)	$ 7.4	1
AVERAGE HOURLY WAGES	$ 1.72	
AVERAGE HOURLY WAGE OF ALL		
STATE INDUSTRIES	$2.49	

Jo Ann Bonham
Neal G. Lineback

CONSTRUCTION

Construction includes the activities of all persons engaged in contract construction. These activities include both new work and additions, alterations, and repairs to existing structures. A description of construction in Alabama includes an analysis of the numbers and concentration of people working in contract construction and the value associated with their efforts. Construction activity for 1970, as measured by average monthly covered (by Unemployment Compensation Law) employment, involved 47,181 workers. These workers were engaged in activities which, when measured in terms of building contracts awarded, totaled $1.069 billion in value.[1]

The value of building contracts awarded reached an all-time high in Alabama during 1970. All three sectors of construction activity—residential, non-residential, and public works and utilities—are important when measured by value of contracts awarded. During the last decade, residential construction has been the most important segment of total construction activity, and the public works and utilities sector has been the least important. This construction activity, while occurring through-out the State, is concentrated in certain well-defined areas.

The average monthly covered construction employment varies between counties, with the eleven counties in the seven Standard Metropolitan Statistical Areas (SMSA's) employing over sixty-one percent of the State total. The only counties with over 1,000 persons employed in contract construction and not in SMSA's are Jackson and Houston Counties. As might be expected, the SMSA's also have the largest proportion of the State's residential and non-residential construction (fifty-seven percent). Additionally, construction activity is concentrated in the northern half of the State. Of the nine counties with 1,000 or more people employed in contract construction, six are in the northern portion. Since this concentration is very evident, an analysis of the activities within the SMSA's should produce an excellent idea of Alabama's construction industry.

Within each SMSA, the central county accounts for most of the construction activity. For example, Jefferson County in the Birmingham SMSA accounts for 90 percent (by value) of the SMSA's construction activity and 93

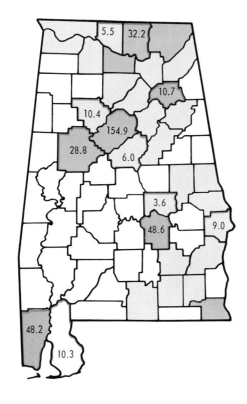

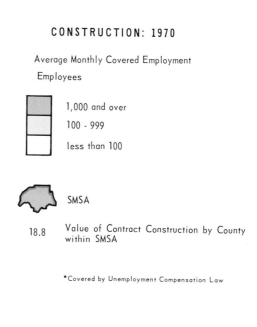

CONSTRUCTION: 1970

Average Monthly Covered Employment

Employees

1,000 and over

100 - 999

less than 100

SMSA

18.8   Value of Contract Construction by County within SMSA

*Covered by Unemployment Compensation Law

Sources: Alabama Department of Industrial Relations, Division of Employment Security, Statistical Bulletin; July, 1971.

F. W. Dodge Division, McGraw-Hill Information Systems Company, proprietary data provided by special permission.

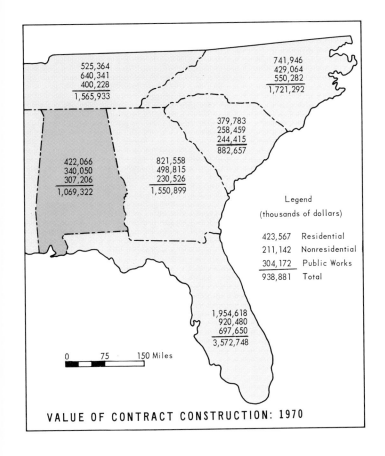

VALUE OF CONTRACT CONSTRUCTION: 1970

525,364
640,341
400,228
‾‾‾‾‾‾‾
1,565,933

741,946
429,064
550,282
‾‾‾‾‾‾‾
1,721,292

379,783
258,459
244,415
‾‾‾‾‾‾‾
882,657

422,066
340,050
307,206
‾‾‾‾‾‾‾
1,069,322

821,558
498,815
230,526
‾‾‾‾‾‾‾
1,550,899

Legend
(thousands of dollars)

423,567   Residential
211,142   Nonresidential
304,172   Public Works
‾‾‾‾‾‾‾
938,881   Total

1,954,618
920,480
697,650
‾‾‾‾‾‾‾
3,572,748

0   75   150 Miles

percent of the covered construction employment. The validity of comparisons between SMSA's would be somewhat affected by the 1970 construction strike in Jefferson County. Even so, Birmingham, Montgomery, and Mobile clearly account for more construction activity than any other areas within the State.

In summary, most of the construction activity is concentrated within small portions of the State. The State SMSA's account for a preponderance of this activity, and most of these SMSA's are located in the northern part of the State. Within these SMSA's, the core county dominates the other SMSA counties. For the State as a whole, residential construction is the most valuable sector, with public works and utilities, together, of less total importance. All three sectors must be considered major contributors to Alabama construction employment.

[1]F. W. Dodge Division, McGraw-Hill Information Systems Company, Proprietary Data Provided by Special Permission.

Reuel Huffman, III
Paul F. Schultz, Jr.

VALUE OF BUILDING CONTRACTS: 1970

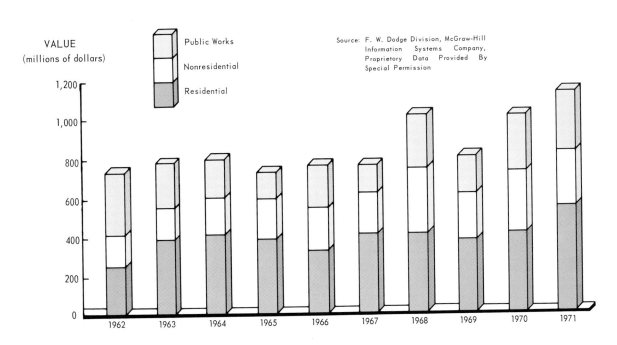

VALUE
(millions of dollars)

Public Works
Nonresidential
Residential

Source: F. W. Dodge Division, McGraw-Hill Information Systems Company, Proprietary Data Provided By Special Permission

Guntersville Lake

TRANSPORTATION, COMMUNICATION, AND PUBLIC UTILITIES

The Transportation, Communication, and Public Utility industries occupy an area of special interest and concern. They require considerable manpower and capital with which to operate. Their essential relationship to all other activities, or "public interests," has long been identified.

The accompanying graph indicates that direct employment in these industries in Alabama was approximately 80,000 persons in 1970. This constitutes more than six percent of the State's labor force, and considerably more persons are employed in secondary or supporting industries. No precise data are available for this purpose, but it can safely be assumed that total employment in these industries would be in excess of ten percent of the labor force. It should also be noted that direct employment in these industries is increasing faster than employment in general, the former having more than doubled in the past thirty years while the latter increased

by approximately one-third. The only area in which employment has declined is in the Railroad industry. Passengers have increasingly traveled by automobile and air transportation during this period.

The Utilities category has led the other four categories in numbers of employees since employment in Railroad and Railway Express Service began its decline during the 1950's. In fact, Utilities are growing at an increasing rate. Mainly responsible for the growth is the higher use of household and industrial mechanisms which utilize greater and greater amounts of power and gas. Higher standards of living place a larger demand upon the Utilities than any other of the above categories.

Most of these industries require tremendous capital investment with which to operate. Furthermore, it is widely believed that firms within the industries need to be large to operate efficiently. These attributes and the essential nature of the services to the public have

EMPLOYMENT IN TRANSPORTATION, COMMUNICATION AND PUBLIC UTILITIES: 1940-1970

NUMBER OF EMPLOYEES

1940 ☐ 1950 ☐ 1960 ☐ 1970 ☐

25,000

20,000

15,000

10,000

5,000

0

Railroad and Railway Express Service · Trucking Service and Warehousing · Other Transportation · Communication · Utilities

Source: U.S. Census of Population, 1970

been factors in the development of a number of governmental regulatory agencies. Federal regulatory agencies whose responsibilities embrace regulation of various aspects of these industries include the Interstate Commerce Commission (established in 1887), Civil Aeronautics Board (1938), Federal Power Commission (1930), Federal Communications Commission (1933). The state agency with similar concern is the Alabama Public Service Commission which was originally established in 1881 but whose present structure dates from 1915. All these agencies attempt to prevent certain undesirable aspects of competition and insure that rates and services are fair and reasonable.

In the following sections the Transportation, Communication, and Public Utilities industries are discussed individually and in greater detail.

Richard E. Olson

Holt Lock and Dam

LARRY WALKER

99

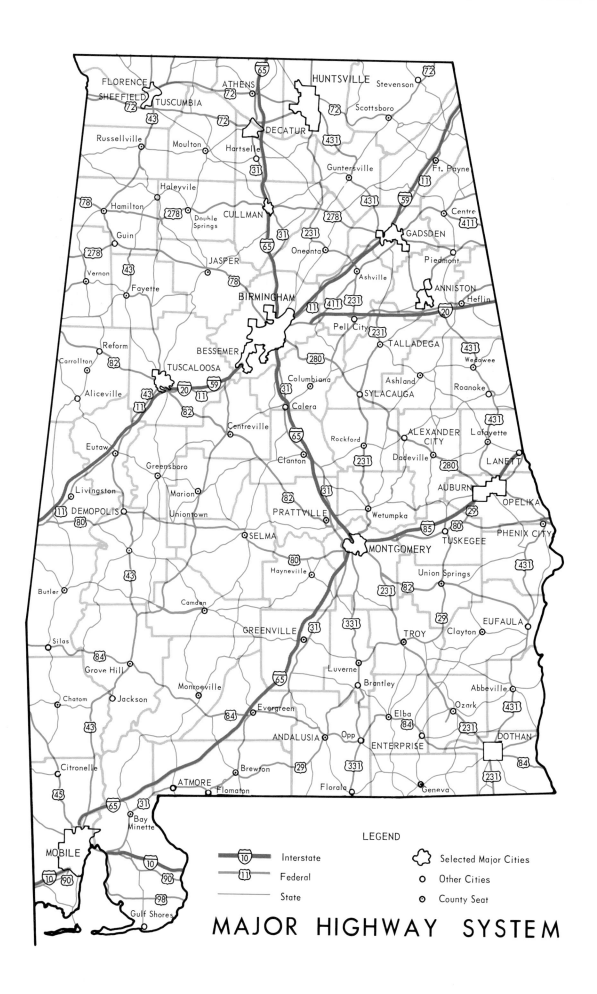

MAJOR HIGHWAY SYSTEM

LEGEND

Interstate
Federal
State

Selected Major Cities
Other Cities
County Seat

MAJOR STATE AND FEDERAL HIGHWAYS

In 1970 the total mileage of roads and streets in Alabama was 78,597, representing 2.1 percent of such mileage in the United States. By way of contrast, in 1969 Alabama contained 1.7 percent of the population and 1.6 percent of the licensed drivers of the United States. Approximately 85 percent of the total Alabama mileage is rural. Most (60 percent) of the rural mileage is controlled by the counties, with the State being largely responsible for the remainder.

More than 87 percent of the total mileage in Alabama is surfaced compared to less than 79 percent for the nation as a whole. In terms of rural mileage, slightly more than 75 percent of the mileage in both Alabama and the nation is surfaced. Likewise, approximately 95 percent of the municipal mileage in Alabama and the nation is surfaced.

State highway mileage in Alabama has increased rapidly in recent years. In 1950 state highway mileage totaled 7,722 compared to slightly less than 4,000 miles in 1925. By 1970, the total had increased to 20,669 miles. In 1969, the total state primary highway system (officially designated as such by the State, and comprising the principal inter-county and inter-city roads) included 10,072 miles, all of which was surfaced. The State secondary system totaled 10,589 miles, of which 9,627 were paved. In strictly rural areas average daily traffic does not exceed 20,000 vehicles on any part of the State primary system, but it increases to a maximum average daily volume of 30,000-39,999 vehicles on the State Primary System–Municipal Extensions and much of this is accounted for by commuters.

In 1970, the federal-aid highway system totaled 21,530 miles in Alabama. Of this, 15,296 miles were part of the federal-state secondary system, and almost entirely rural. Federal-aid primary mileage totaled 6,234

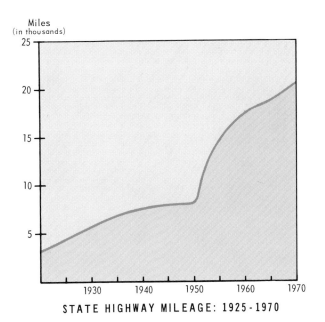

STATE HIGHWAY MILEAGE: 1925-1970

in 1970, again with most of this located in rural areas. The newest major addition to the State's highway system is the Federal-Aid Interstate System, by which the State is well served. The mileage by Interstate route in Alabama is as follows: I-10, 66; I-20, 85; I-59, 242; I-65, 366; I-85, 80; I-359, 2; I-459, 33; I-565, 20; and I-759, 5. The identification codes provided for the System are based on direction. The north-south routes are odd numbered, for example, I-65; the east-west routes are even numbered, for example, I-20. The interstate spur routes are symbolized by three-digit numbers, e.g., I-359, with an odd-numbered first digit. The loop or beltline roads around cities are identified by three-digit numbers, e.g. I-459, with an even-numbered first digit.

J. Barry Mason

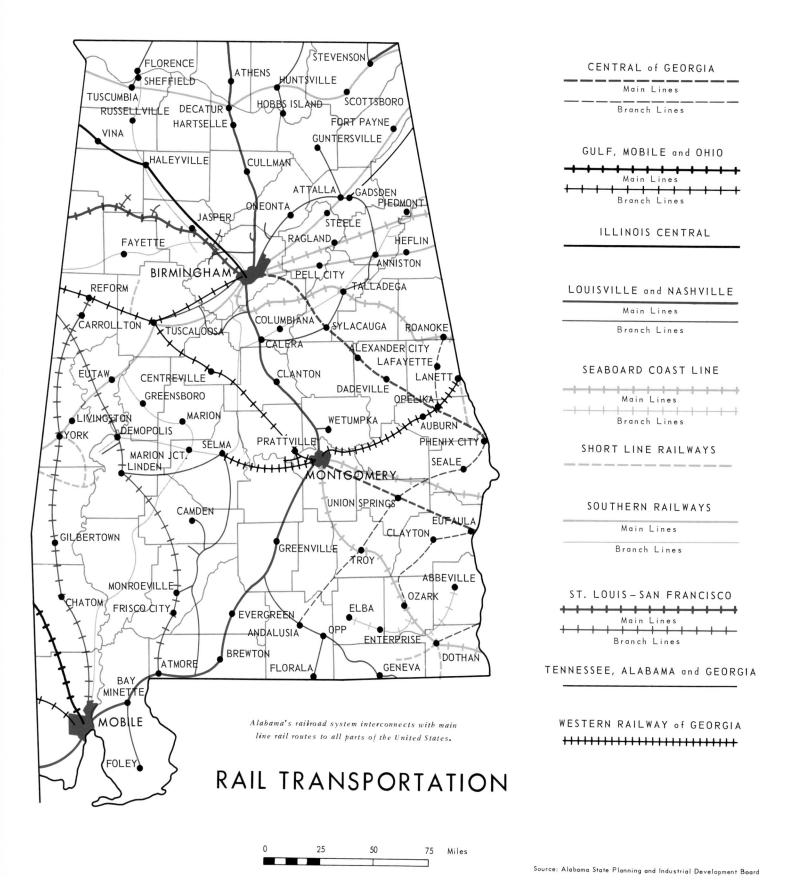

CENTRAL of GEORGIA
Main Lines
Branch Lines

GULF, MOBILE and OHIO
Main Lines
Branch Lines

ILLINOIS CENTRAL

LOUISVILLE and NASHVILLE
Main Lines
Branch Lines

SEABOARD COAST LINE
Main Lines
Branch Lines

SHORT LINE RAILWAYS

SOUTHERN RAILWAYS
Main Lines
Branch Lines

ST. LOUIS – SAN FRANCISCO
Main Lines
Branch Lines

TENNESSEE, ALABAMA and GEORGIA

WESTERN RAILWAY of GEORGIA

Alabama's railroad system interconnects with main line rail routes to all parts of the United States.

RAIL TRANSPORTATION

0   25   50   75   Miles

Source: Alabama State Planning and Industrial Development Board

RAILWAYS AND RAILWAY TRAFFIC

Muscle Shoals on the Tennessee River gave birth in 1830 to Alabama's first railroad—a 2½-mile road from the Tennessee River to Tuscumbia, which was later linked to a line known as the Tuscumbia, Courtland and Decatur Railroad. The Tennessee River was navigable from Chattanooga to Decatur, but the shoals from there to Tuscumbia prevented movement by water of the great amounts of cotton and other products produced in this fertile valley. The first railroad in Alabama thus served as part of the by-pass which permitted further downstream shipment from Tuscumbia via the Tennessee River to the Ohio River, and thence to the Mississippi River and New Orleans.

In the 1830's railroads were becoming popular and many roads were chartered, some soundly planned, others not. Twenty companies were chartered before 1840. Construction proceeded slowly and was, of course, interrupted by the War between the States. When Jefferson Davis was inaugurated President of the Confederacy in Montgomery, he went from his Mississippi home by coach to Memphis, thence by rail to Chattanooga. He then went via Atlanta to Montgomery on the new Atlanta and West Point and the Montgomery and West Point Railroads.

Geography influenced the location of railroads, and the existence of railroads influenced the establishment and growth of cities. As track mileage increased, so did the growth of cities and the tonnage of freight moved.

After 1865, during Reconstruction, dozens of railroads were promoted, chartered by the Legislature, and financed with state-guaranteed bonds. These were known as "Carpetbagger" bonds. Most of these roads were either never built or later absorbed into other lines.

Today only eight Class I railroads operate in the State. There are the Alabama Great Southern, Central of Georgia, Gulf Mobile and Ohio, Illinois Central, Louisville and Nashville (now part of the Seaboard Coastline system), Seaboard Coastline, St. Louis and San Francisco, and Southern Railway.

The railway industry is vitally important to the economy of the State. There are 9,300 railroad employees whose annual incomes total nearly $86,000,000 a year. A total of 4,567 miles of railroad exist in Alabama, serving even the more remote areas of the State.

As a means of personal transportation, the importance of railroads today is at an all-time low. With the advent of the automobile and the airplane, passenger traffic has dwindled to the point of unprofitability for the railroads, and the number of passenger trains in service has steadily declined since the end of the Second World War.

In addition to Class I railroads, there are a few privately-owned and/or special purpose lines in the State. Among these is the Alabama Terminal Railroad at the State Docks, owned by the State of Alabama. The Atlanta & St. Andrews Bay Railroad Company, known as the Bay Line, connects Dothan with Panama City, Florida. The Chattahoochee Valley Railroad is privately owned and serves the textile complex in east Alabama. There are also the Hartford & Slocomb Railroad Company in Geneva County and the Sumter & Choctaw Railway in west Alabama.

The ability of railroads to move freight rapidly and efficiently ensures their continuing importance to the economy of the State. The day of the "Iron Horse" is far from over.

C. C. (Jack) Owen

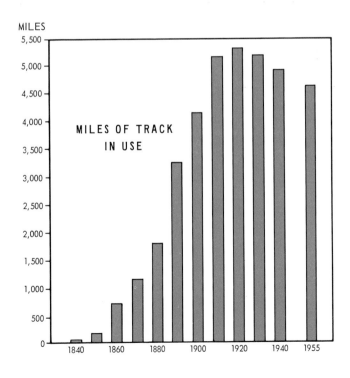

Source: Alabama Public Service Commission

COMMERCIAL WATER ROUTES

——— Lock and Dam

——— Navigable Waterway

- - - Proposed Waterway

0   25   50   75 Miles

Source: U.S. Army Corps of Engineer

COMMERCIAL WATER TRAFFIC

Water transportation has been of importance in Alabama since before the State's founding. Early use of streams involved passenger and freight movement, but most of the commercial water traffic in the State today is comprised of freight carriers on waterways developed by the U.S. Army Corps of Engineers. Federal funds have been appropriated for water resource improvement since early in the nineteenth century. The major inland water-

ways all have been maintained at a standard depth of nine feet or greater. For classification purposes it is convenient to group these projects into harbors, channels, and navigation systems.

The port of Mobile is one of the busiest in the United States. It was established on its present site by the French in 1711. The original Federal project for improving the channels in Mobile Bay was in 1826, with an initial appropriation of $10,000. Since then over $34,000,000 has been spent on improvement in the harbor, in addition to investments in terminals, docks, and the surrounding industrial area. Metallic ores and concentrates (39 percent) and crude oil and petroleum products (25 percent) constitute a majority of the tonnages handled at Mobile.

The major channel in Alabama is the 60-mile portion of the Gulf Intracoastal Waterway. In its entirety, the Gulf Intracoastal provides a water route from Carrabelle, Florida, to the Mexican border for light draft vessels not suited to navigating long stretches of the open Gulf of Mexico. There are no locks on the portion of the Intracoastal within Alabama. Within the State the Intracoastal traverses, from west to east, the Mississippi Sound, lower Mobile Bay, Bon Secour Bay, a land cut near the coast in Baldwin County (authorized in 1930), and Perdido Bay. Important tonnages of crude oil and petroleum products (53 percent) and coal (23 percent) move eastward from Mobile. Westward from Mobile the largest tonnages moved are petroleum products (46 percent) and chemicals (11 percent).

A number of smaller channels are also located in the southwestern part of the State. They are at Bayou La Batre, Bayou Coden, Dauphin Island, Fly Creek (Fairhope), and Perdido Pass. Many of these are less than nine feet in depth. Tonnages involved are relatively small; the largest reported is that of Bayou La Batre, which has averaged less than 40,000 tons annually.

The navigable portions of two waterways are completely within the State at the present time. These are the 463-mile Black Warrior-Tombigbee Rivers (including the Mobile River) from Mobile almost to Birmingham and 295 miles of the Alabama River from Mobile to Montgomery. A two-hundred-mile-long portion of the Tennessee River is within Alabama, and 136 miles of the Chattahoochee-Apalachicola-Flint River system is navigable as far north as Phenix City. Major authorized projects are extensions of the Alabama-Coosa River navigation from Montgomery to Rome, Georgia (282 miles, of which 30 are in Georgia), and the 253-mile Tennessee-Tombigbee Waterway. Of the latter, 107 miles (from Demopolis northwest to the state line) would be in Alabama. The proposed system would then continue northward in eastern Mississippi to the Tennessee River.

Black Warrior-Tombigbee. The present navigation system on the Black Warrior–Tombigbee Waterway dates from a series of Congressional Acts beginning in 1884. The original system consisted of seventeen dams and eighteen locks. Modernization of the system was begun in 1937. Much of this work has been completed and, when finished, will total six locks and dams. The locks' dimensions will be of a uniform 110 by 600 feet. Traffic has grown steadily on this waterway and is dominated by coal (39 percent) and metallic ores (17 percent).

Alabama-Coosa Rivers. Channel improvement and a series of three dams and locks completed in 1971 have made possible navigation by modern barge vessels from Mobile to Montgomery. Traffic is expected to develop rapidly as the system becomes fully operational. Even while under construction, this waterway handled 1,222,560 tons of traffic in 1970. At present, most of the reported tonnage is sand and gravel (88 percent).

Tennessee River. A 200-mile portion of the Tennessee River lies in an east-west direction across northern Alabama. The total navigable portion of this river is from Knoxville, Tennessee, to the Ohio River, which in turn flows into the Mississippi. Improved navigation is a part of the overall development plan of the Tennessee Valley Authority. There are three locks and dams within the State, and the dimensions of all locks are a uniform 110 by 600 feet. For the entire river system, leading tonnages are comprised of crude petroleum and products (50 percent) and non-metallic minerals including sand and gravel (23 percent). Data are not separately available for the portion of the waterway within Alabama.

Chattahoochee-Apalachicola. The Chattahoochee River forms the southern half of the boundary between Alabama and Georgia. Though work on the streams dates back to the early nineteenth century, the modern facilities were completed between 1957 and 1963. The Chattahoochee (and the Flint River in Georgia) terminates at Lake Seminole, which was formed by construction of the Jim Woodruff Lock and Dam in northern Florida. From this point navigation continues southward to Apalachicola, Florida. As was true for the Tennessee River, data are not separately available for Alabama. For the system, sand and gravel (39 percent) and petroleum products (23 percent) constitute the largest tonnages.

Richard E. Olson

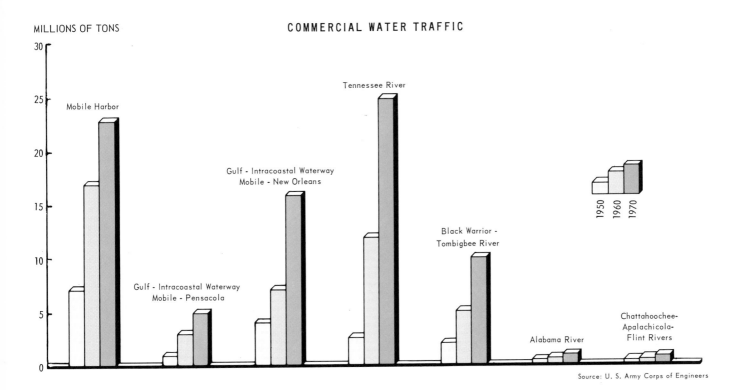

COMMERCIAL WATER TRAFFIC

MILLIONS OF TONS

Mobile Harbor

Gulf - Intracoastal Waterway
Mobile - Pensacola

Gulf - Intracoastal Waterway
Mobile - New Orleans

Tennessee River

Black Warrior -
Tombigbee River

Alabama River

Chattahoochee-
Apalachicola-
Flint Rivers

Source: U. S. Army Corps of Engineers

COMMERCIAL FLIGHT ROUTES

TRUNKLINE CARRIERS

D.A.L.	Delta Air Lines, Inc.
E.A.L.	Eastern Air Lines, Inc.
N.A.L.	National Airlines, Inc.
U.A.L.	United Air Lines, Inc.

LOCAL CARRIERS

All local routes are scheduled by Southern Airways, Inc.

Alabama's air transportation system interconnects with scheduled flights to all parts of the United States.

Source: Civil Aeronautics Board

AIRPORTS AND AIR TRAFFIC

Alabama has possibly the finest system of general aviation airport facilities in the United States. These airports have been developed with a state aviation fuel tax, and at no cost to the State General Fund. In 1971, there were 167 airports, both public and private, with 118 of them licensed and available for public use. Eighty-nine of the airports had paved runways, most of which were long enough for use by business jets. All but three of the sixty-seven counties in the State had airports suitable for general aviation use.

Nine cities in Alabama have commercially scheduled air carriers in operation. For the year 1970 the total passenger emplanements from these airports was approximately 1,190,000 and the total freight and express loaded was 6,830 tons.

Birmingham had the largest number of passengers boarding (495,352), followed by Huntsville/Decatur (218,056), and Mobile (206,673). The airlines serving Alabama and number of passengers boarded were Eastern, 387,534; Delta, 322,724; Southern, 269,706; United, 171,108; and National, serving only Mobile, 39,532.

Only Birmingham, Montgomery, Huntsville/Decatur and Mobile have trunkline carrier service with direct connections to distant points. Southern Airways, Inc., a local carrier, serves certain cities within Alabama with connections to Atlanta, Memphis, New Orleans, and points in Florida, as well as with some flights to much more distant places, such as Washington, D.C. There is also some third-level air service, such as commuter flights which operate mainly between Birmingham and Huntsville.

H. Don Hays

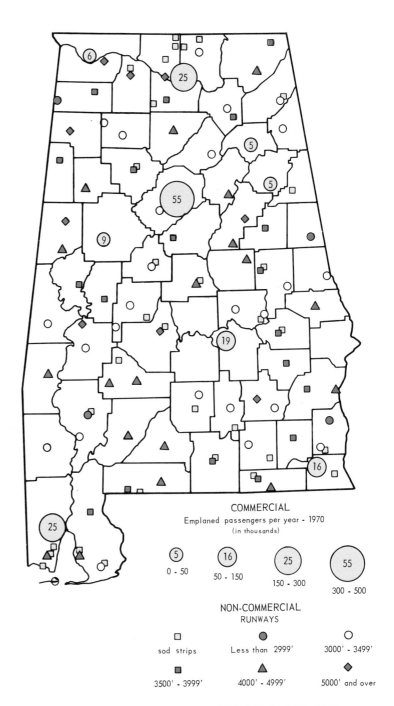

COMMERCIAL
Emplaned passengers per year - 1970
(in thousands)

| 5 | 16 | 25 | 55 |
| 0 - 50 | 50 - 150 | 150 - 300 | 300 - 500 |

NON-COMMERCIAL
RUNWAYS

□ sod strips   ● Less than 2999'   ○ 3000' - 3499'

■ 3500' - 3999'   ▲ 4000' - 4999'   ◆ 5000' and over

ALABAMA AIRFIELDS: 1971

*Numbers within circles indicate average number of daily departures.
Source: Federal Aviation Administration

TELEPHONES

The first complete telephone message was transmitted by Alexander Graham Bell on March 10, 1876. Two and one half years later, on November 15, 1879, the first telephone exchange in Alabama was established in Mobile.

A charter for Southern Bell Telephone and Telegraph Company was issued in the State of New York on December 20, 1879, at which time there were eleven southern cities under Southern Bell with company headquarters located temporarily in New York City.

Exchanges were subsequently established in Alabama in the following cities: Selma (1880), Montgomery (1880), Birmingham (1882), Gadsden (1883), Huntsville (1883), Tuscaloosa (1883), and Anniston (1884). Long distance lines were gradually constructed until all of these exchanges were connected with the rapidly-developing Bell System. With division headquarters established in Atlanta, new exchanges were built, and independently-owned exchanges were acquired as the system expanded.

In January, 1923, the Alabama Division was created, with Birmingham serving as division headquarters. At this time there were 59,652 subscribers in the State. Rapid growth was experienced until April, 1930, when there were 78 exchanges with 106,683 company-owned stations. At that time the effects of the depression were felt and the number of stations decreased to 78,019. The setback lasted until 1933.

The first dial service became available in 1926, when several dial central offices were installed in Birmingham. Additional conversions were made during 1927 and 1928, and the last manual office in Birmingham converted to dial in 1940.

The Tuscaloosa exchange converted to dial service in 1940, as did Montgomery in 1941 and Mobile in 1942. During the same period, a dial system was developed for smaller exchanges; and Childersburg, Gardendale, Mt. Pinson, Siluria, and Waverly were among the first to receive this automated service.

By the end of World War II, Southern Bell had 187,680 telephones in Alabama, and a period of expansion began. During the years immediately following the

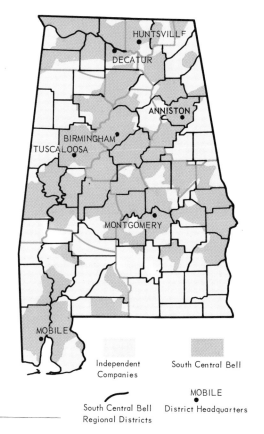

TELEPHONE DISTRICTS

Source: South Central Bell Telephone Company

Listed below are the percentages of homes with telephone service in each South Central Bell district as defined on the map. These percentages do not include independent company territory.

	Percent
ANNISTON	82.6
BIRMINGHAM	84.4
DECATUR	77.8
HUNTSVILLE	83.1
MOBILE	80.2
MONTGOMERY	79.4
TUSCALOOSA	71.4

Source: South Central Bell Telephone Company

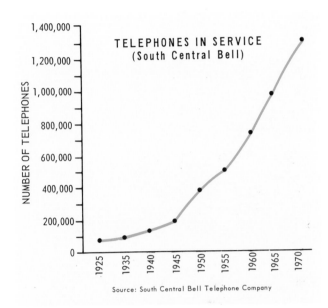

TELEPHONES IN SERVICE
(South Central Bell)

Source: South Central Bell Telephone Company

war, construction crews set 1.7 million poles to carry over two billion feet of wire from subscribers to central offices, and placed underground facilities for another 2.5 billion feet. In 1947 construction expenditures for the entire Southern Bell Company surpassed $100 million for the first time.

By 1952 exchanges in Bessemer, Dora, Eutaw, Flomaton, Gadsden, Jackson, Jasper, Linden, Sylacauga, and Thomasville were converted to dial service; and new community dial centers had been established in Maplesville, Marion Junction, McIntosh, Mt. Vernon, and Vincent. By January 1, 1953, Southern Bell had 428,831 telephones in service in Alabama.

Innovations in telephone service were becoming available to customers. A new crossbar switching system was put into service in Atlanta on April 17, 1955. In August, 1958, Decatur became the first exchange in Alabama to get Direct Distance Dialing, and Decatur and Sheffield were the first cities served by Southern Bell to have Touch Tone service—March 15, 1964. Less than four years later, on June 16, 1968, the last manual exchange—in York, Alabama—converted to dial service.

On July 1, 1968, the South Central Bell Telephone Company was formed, splitting the nine-state organization of Southern Bell. South Central Bell, headquartered in Birmingham, includes Alabama, Kentucky, Louisiana, Mississippi, and Tennessee. At the time it was formed, the company operated some five and one-half million telephones. In October, 1968, construction began on the new 30-story headquarters building in Birmingham.

By mid-1971 there were more than 1,600,000 telephones in Alabama, including those operated by 39 independent telephone companies in the State. In 1971, South Central Bell employed 9,363 people in Alabama with an average annual payroll of $78 million. On an average business day, more than nine million local and 240,000 long distance calls are made in the State. A proposed budget of more than $250 million has been allocated for new and improved telephone service for South Central Bell customers in the years 1972 and 1973.

South Central Bell Telephone Company

GSA

RADIO STATIONS: 1972

○ AM

■ FM

△ AM·FM

0   25   50   75 Miles

Source: Federal Communication Commission

RADIO AND TELEVISION

As in the rest of the nation, Alabama radio broadcasting began with point-to-point communication. Radio-telegraphy, or wireless-telegraphy, as it was often called, enabled ships at sea to communicate with the shore and other ships at sea. The port of Mobile, located on the Gulf of Mexico, was a natural site for a radio-telegraphy station. Alabama radio broadcasting thus had its beginning in the Mobile area shortly after the turn of the century.

Early radio-telegraphy amateurs in Alabama helped to stimulate interest in radio. Newspapers publicized their activities, and they contributed significantly to the new technology which established the basis for state-wide broadcasting. This early amateur activity also centered around Mobile. Later, this activity came to center on Birmingham, and was well-developed there by 1922, the year the first Alabama commercial voice radio stations were established. Some of the Alabama amateurs became voice radio station operators and broadcasters.

Interest in broadcasting developed in Alabama when newspapers began to publicize the medium, and the selling of radios became a profitable business in the State. The first commercial stations in Alabama made radio reception possible for the average citizen who lacked the more expensive sets necessary to receive distant stations. With the increase in the number of household receiving sets came the incentive to build additional broadcasting stations. Thus, the stage was set for the birth of the commercial broadcasting industry in the State.

According to records available, the first commercial radio broadcasting license in Alabama was granted to the Montgomery Light and Power Company early in 1922. This company's station, WGH, however, discontinued operation between March and December, 1922. Of the five radio stations existing in the State in 1922, one each was the property of the Alabama Power Company in Birmingham (WSY) and the Montgomery Light and Power Company (WGH), one was operated by John M. Wilder (WOAY), one was operated by the Mobile Radio Company (WEAP), and the other by Auburn Polytechnic Institute (WMAV). By 1934, the year of the enactment of the Communications Act to regulate ten remained on the air. Seven of these stations continue in operation today: WAPI, WBRC, and WSGN, Birmingham; WUNI, Mobile; WHHY, Montgomery; WLAY Muscle Shoals; and WAGF, Troy. Only WBRC in Birmingham both remained in the city where it was first licensed and retained the same call letters.

At the end of World War II in 1945, there were nineteen AM commercial radio stations on the air in Alabama. A dramatic growth of AM stations occurred between 1946 and 1948 when 32 more stations began operating. Today there are 137 AM radio stations broadcasting in Alabama. Frequency Modulation (FM) radio stations commenced operating when three Alabama stations went on the air in 1947. Today there are 57 such stations. In 1959 there were two television stations in operation; 17 are in operation today.

The accompanying maps indicate that the people of the State have access to a number of radio and television stations for entertainment, information, and news. Almost all homes in Alabama can receive two or more television stations and have a large selection of radio stations. Twenty-six Community Antenna Television (CATV) systems supply 9 percent of Alabama households with a service usually including clearer reception, reception of additional television stations, and special programming.

The Alabama Educational Television Commission (AETC) was organized in August, 1953, and became the first educational television network in the United States. From two non-commercial television stations in 1955, the system has grown to nine stations today, as indicated by the accompanying map, and provides service to nearly the entire State. A State-owned and -operated microwave system of relay channels links the nine stations and the three translator-transmitters for simulcasting state-wide educational and public television.

The AETC contracts with several major universities, city boards of education, the State Board of Education, and the Public Broadcasting Service for the network's programming. The state law establishing the AETC directed that it be composed of five Commissioners, appointed by the Governor and approved by the State Senate. The Program Board is composed of the AETC-appointed General Manager and the heads of the sponsoring agencies.

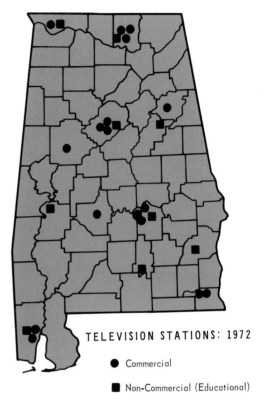

TELEVISION STATIONS: 1972

● Commercial

■ Non-Commercial (Educational)

Source: Federal Communication Commission

In 1970, Alabama ranked 12th nationally in the total number of AM and FM radio stations and 4th in the Southeast. The State ranked 9th nationally in the total number of television stations and second in the Southeast after Georgia. Ninety-eight percent of Alabama households have one or more radio sets, which is generally true of the rest of the United States, and ninety-three percent of Alabama households have at least one television set.

W. Knox Hagood

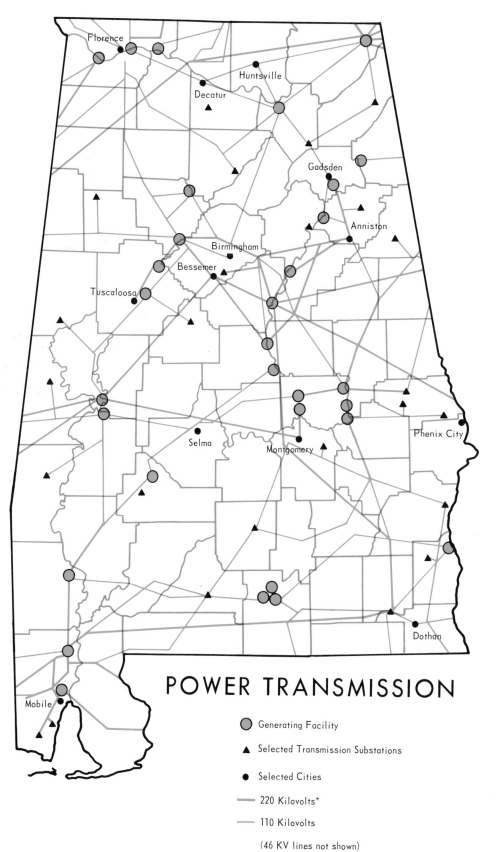

POWER TRANSMISSION

Florence
Huntsville
Decatur
Gadsden
Anniston
Birmingham
Bessemer
Tuscaloosa
Selma
Montgomery
Phenix City
Dothan
Mobile

○ Generating Facility

▲ Selected Transmission Substations

● Selected Cities

— 220 Kilovolts*

— 110 Kilovolts

(46 KV lines not shown)

*Also includes multiple lines of lesser voltage.

Source: Alabama Power Company
Tennessee Valley Authority

ELECTRIC POWER
PRODUCTION AND TRANSMISSION

The rivers of Alabama were harnessed in the early part of this century to provide the beginning of the present statewide electrical generating and transmission system now serving over 1.25 million customers throughout the State. Power from the hydroelectric projects supplied the bulk of the electrical requirements of Alabama until the early 1950's when the electricity demand began to surpass the power supplied by the hydro projects. This generating resource was supplemented by steam-driven generators using coal from the abundant resources available in the State. Today hydro-powered generators supply less than 25 percent of the State's generating capability, with fuel-powered generators supplying over 75 percent. The rivers play two important roles for the fuel-powered generators. First, they provide sources of water for making steam and for cooling purposes; and second, they provide low-cost transportation for barging coal from the mines to the plants.

There are four major suppliers of electric power in Alabama. These are: Alabama Power, an investor-owned system supplying the greater part of the State; the Tennessee Valley Authority, an entity of the U.S. Government serving the northern part of the State; Alabama Electric Cooperative, Inc., a generating and transmission cooperative serving the south-central portion of the State; and Southeastern Electric Power Administration, the marketing agency of the Department of Interior supplying power to electric cooperatives and municipalities through the transmission facilities of Alabama Power Company and Alabama Electric Cooperative. Some industries and larger commercial establishments also own generating facilities, but these account for only a very small part of the State's total capability.

As the economy of the State has continued to develop and more people have sought higher standards of living for their families, the use of increased amounts of electricity in the home has become more prevalent. From 1940 to 1969, the annual average use per residential customer increased from less than 1,200 kilowatt-hours to over 9,000 kilowatt-hours—more than 7-1/2 times as much. This is the principal reason that the total use of electricity increased from slightly over two billion kilowatt-hours in 1940 to over 33 billion kilowatt-hours in 1969, an increase of over 16 times in a span of 29 years.

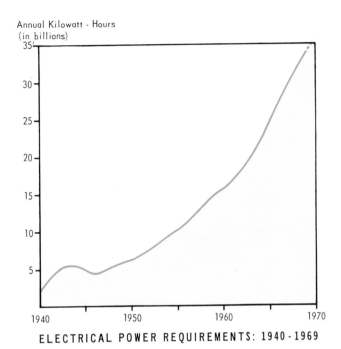

Annual Kilowatt - Hours
(in billions)

ELECTRICAL POWER REQUIREMENTS: 1940-1969

Source: Alabama Power Company

The sizes of electrical power loads vary considerably with the local demand. In the residential areas, both rural and urban, the size of load per house will vary from the requirements of a few light bulbs for illumination up to the total requirements of an all-electric customer having a large central heating and cooling system. In the commercial areas, the electrical loads vary from the requirements of a small store or cafe up to those of very large all-electric department stores or shopping centers. In like manner the size of the industrial customer load may vary from that of the small industry having limited power requirements up to the larger steel-producing customer using electric furnaces, rolling mills, and other large machinery in its processing.

The generating facilities now in service to meet the electric requirements in Alabama thus vary in size from less than one megawatt (1,000 kilowatts or 1,000,000 watts) to over 700 megawatts. Also, the transmission lines required to move this electricity from the generating plants to the load centers vary in voltage size from 46,000 volts up to 500,000 volts. The bulk of transmission is accomplished at voltages of 115,000 volts and 161,000 volts, supplemented by substantial amounts at 230,000 volts. Voltages of 46,000 and below are used for sub-

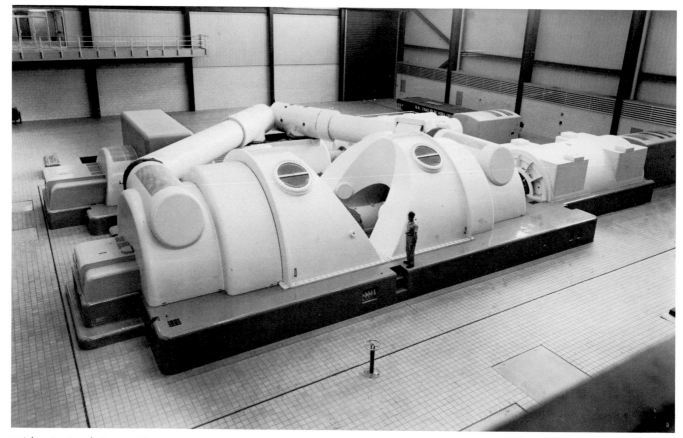

Widow's Creek Steam Plant

transmission and distribution circuits to move the power from the transmission system to the customer.

Because of the large amount of hydro development in Alabama and the availability of low-cost fuel for use by the steam plants, the rates for electric power in Alabama are among the lowest anywhere.

For many years, rates were kept low by advances in technology. In recent years, however, the rising costs of materials, labor, and fuel have necessitated increases in consumer rates.

The demand for more and more electrical power has placed a demand upon fossil-fuel resources which cannot be met economically in the foreseeable future. This has caused the electric industry to turn to nuclear-powered generators in its expansion program. Two such plants are now under construction in Alabama. TVA's Brown's Ferry Plant, on the Tennessee River northwest of Decatur, is expected to have its first nuclear unit in service in the Fall of 1972, to be followed by a second such unit in 1973. Alabama Power Company's Joseph M. Farley Plant, on the Chattahoochee River east of Dothan, is expected to have its first nuclear unit in service in the Spring of 1975, to be followed by a second similar unit in the Spring of 1977. These, no doubt, will be supplemented in time by additional nuclear plants. It is also expected that additional 500,000 volt transmission lines will be constructed as required.

The accompanying graphics concerning generating plants and units show location, size, and type of energy for units in service in mid-1971. The effect of the rising economy following World War II upon the comsumption of energy in the State can be seen in the growth of electrical power requirements between 1940 and 1969. Since about 1950 the power requirements have followed a rather steady pattern of growth.

Grady L. Smith

GENERATING PLANT	NO.	SYSTEM*	TYPE	KW
BANKHEAD DAM	1	APC	Hydro	45,125
BARRY	5	APC	Thermal	1,525,000
BOULDIN DAM	3	APC	Hydro	225,000
CHICKASAW	3	APC	Thermal	120,000
COLBERT	5	TVA	Thermal	1,396,500
DEMOPOLIS	2	APC	Turbine	48,860
GASTON	5	SEGCO	Thermal	1,019,680
GADSDEN	2	APC	Thermal	120,000
GANTT	3	AEC	Hydro	2,640
GEORGE DAM	4	CE	Hydro	130,000
GORGAS	6	APC	Thermal	1,641,250
GREENE COUNTY	2	APC	Thermal	500,000
GUNTERSVILLE	4	TVA	Hydro	97,200
HENRY DAM	3	APC	Hydro	79,900
HOLT DAM	1	APC	Hydro	40,000
JORDAN DAM	4	APC	Hydro	100,000
LAY DAM	6	APC	Hydro	177,000
LEWIS SMITH DAM	2	APC	Hydro	157,500
LOGAN MARTIN DAM	3	APC	Hydro	128,250
MARTIN DAM	4	APC	Hydro	154,000
McWILLIAMS	3	AEC	Thermal	40,000
MILLER'S FERRY	3	CE	Hydro	75,000
MITCHELL DAM	4	APC	Hydro	72,500
POINT A	3	AEC	Hydro	5,200
THURLOW DAM	3	APC	Hydro	58,000
TOMBIGBEE	1	AEC	Thermal	75,000
WEISS DAM	3	APC	Hydro	87,750
WHEELER	8	TVA	Hydro	259,200
WIDOW'S CREEK	8	TVA	Thermal	1,977,985
WILSON	18	TVA	Hydro	436,000
YATES DAM	2	APC	Hydro	32,000

TOTAL NUMBER OF GENERATORS - <u>124</u>
TOTAL NUMBER OF KILOWATTS - <u>9,826,540</u>

*APC - Alabama Power Corporation
TVA - Tennessee Valley Authority
SEGCO - Southern Electric Generating Company
CE - Corps of Engineers
AEC - Alabama Electric Cooperation

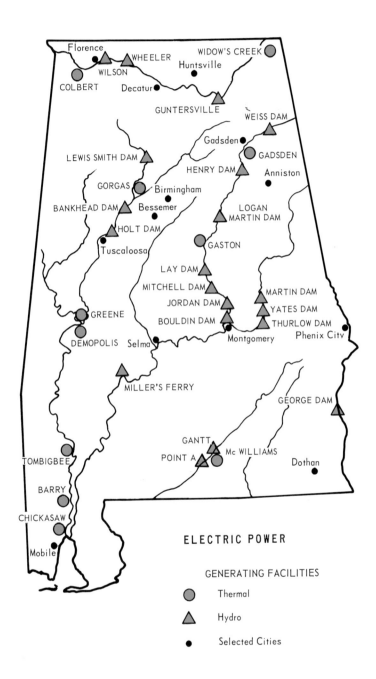

ELECTRIC POWER

GENERATING FACILITIES

◯   Thermal

▲   Hydro

●   Selected Cities

Source: Alabama Power Company

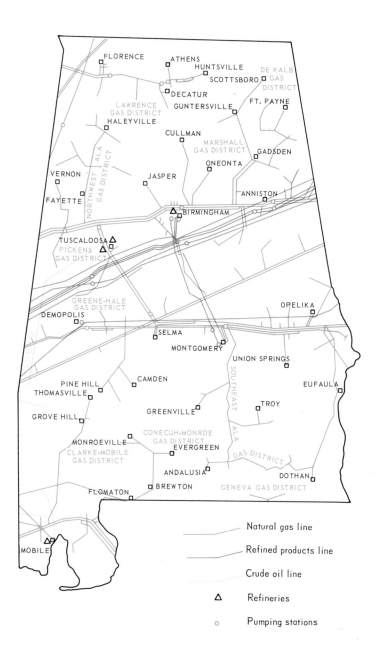

PETROLEUM AND NATURAL GAS PIPELINES

0   25   50   75 Miles

Source: Geological Survey of Alabama

PETROLEUM AND NATURAL GAS LINES

The arteries of the nation—petroleum and natural gas lines—supply energy vital for homes, industry, and transportation. The ever-expanding network of pipelines becomes more complex as the population and the demand for energy increase.

During the period 1960 to 1970, the pipelines transporting crude oil and refined products in Alabama increased from 615 to 1167 miles in length. Construction of two new refined-products pipelines to the Birmingham area began in 1971. The new lines will increase the total miles of crude oil and products pipeline in Alabama to 1482. In 1971, a new crude oil pipeline 125 miles long, from Choctaw County to Tuscaloosa, was in the planning stage.

Crude oil lines carry oil from producing fields directly to refineries, or to loading terminals for shipment by rail, barge, or tanker to refineries in other areas. In 1970, there were five refineries in Alabama which produced jet fuel, diesel, asphalt, solvents, and other products. All the refineries received their crude oil by water or rail transportation, but many products from the refineries were shipped by pipeline.

Product pipelines carry gasoline, kerosene, diesel fuel, and heating oil. Different products are shipped through the same pipeline in "batches." In 1969, 1.5 billion gallons of gasoline and 352 million gallons of diesel fuel were purchased in Alabama. In 1971 the consumption was 1.6 billion gallons of gasoline and 424 million gallons of diesel fuel.

The number of miles of natural gas pipelines in Alabama increased from 11,380 to 15,570 miles between 1960 and 1970. In 1970, Alabama had about 5000 miles of major transmission pipeline, and an additional 10,550 miles of pipeline for distribution of natural gas within the State. In 1965 Alabama used 243 billion cubic feet of gas. In 1971, it was estimated that 343 billion cubic feet were required, an increase in demand of 100 billion cubic feet per year in 6 years.

The petroleum industry, with its vast network of pipelines to transport petroleum products and natural gas, has demonstrated a capability to meet the growing demand for more petroleum products.

Thomas J. Joiner

116

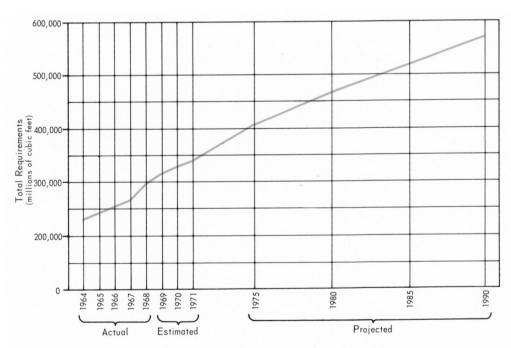

U.S. FUTURE NATURAL GAS REQUIREMENTS

Source: Future Requirements Agency
Denver Research Institute,
1969.

SELECTED SERVICES AND
RETAIL TRADE : 1967

RETAIL SALES AND SELECTED
SERVICES RECEIPTS
(millions of dollars)

NUMBER OF EMPLOYEES

100 and over

50 - 99

25 - 49

0 - 24

● over 5,000

· 1,000 - 5,000

Jefferson County   1,110

Source: U. S. Department of Commerce

BUSINESS AND COMMERCE

Neither cotton nor agriculture is "King" now that Alabama has completed the economic transition of the 1950's and 1960's. In these twenty years, farm income has declined from 12 percent to 3.5 percent of total State personal income. During the same period, approximately 470,000 people in the work-eligible population left their farm residences, a decline of 74 percent in the work-eligible farm-resident population. Farm-resident employment dropped at a faster rate as more than 229,400 jobs were eliminated. This number represented 75 percent of the total 1950 farm-resident employment. As a result of these changes, the proportion of Alabama's rural farm residents declined from 31.3 to 6.5 percent of the total population between 1950 and 1970.

Alabama also became a predominately urban state during this same period; more urban, in fact, than one-third of the other states. The proportion of population living in urban areas changed from 43.8 percent to 58.4 percent. In this more urban Alabama society, manufacturing is the most important single source of employment, accounting for more than one in four employed workers. The textile, apparel, and primary metals industries form the core of the employment base of the State's manufacturing economy. This base is that of an advanced economy. Less than 5 percent of personal income comes from agrarian and extractive sources, while 95 percent comes from pursuits developed later in the course of economic history. The advanced economy is stronger and richer than an extractive and agricultural economy. It is a bigger and more diverse market.

The new Alabama economy is moving to furnish enough money for the consumers of the State to buy almost any kind of service or product they desire. Estimated per capita income in Alabama more than doubled in the 1950's and increased by 92 percent in the 1960's to reach $2,853 for every man, woman, and child by 1970. Even so, per capita income in Alabama still trailed far behind that of the United States. A look at various categories of income for Alabama and the United States reveals that Alabama in 1970 accounted for a greater share of the national income from manufacturing, wholesale and retail trade, and total personal income than in 1950. Alabama's income from services actually

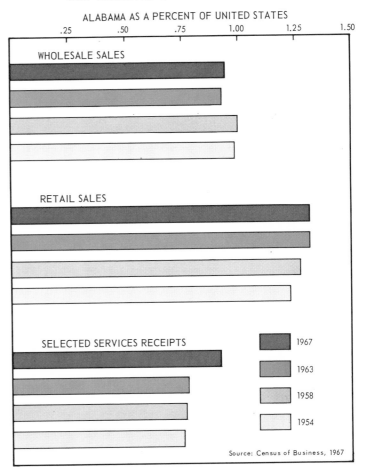

ALABAMA AS A PERCENT OF UNITED STATES

WHOLESALE SALES

RETAIL SALES

SELECTED SERVICES RECEIPTS

1967
1963
1958
1954

Source: Census of Business, 1967

declined as a percentage of the U.S. total, although Alabama's twenty-year increase of 392 percent closely approximated the national service income increase of 410 percent. Among the income categories in Alabama and the United States, service income showed the fastest twenty-year growth rate. The slowest income growth rate of these categories in Alabama was in wholesale and retail trade, while the slowest growing national income category was manufacturing.

The new Alabama economy has shown an employment growth pattern somewhat similar to its income growth pattern. Although agricultural employment declined sharply during the twenty-year period, annual average employment of nonagricultural full-time and part-time wage and salary workers rose by more than 63 percent to a 1970 total of 1,010,400. The nonagricultural category with the highest growth rate was services and miscellaneous, which rose by more than 112 percent to reach 131,800 by 1970. Annual average manufacturing, retail, and wholesale employment during this same period rose by 50, 58, and 59 percent, respectively.

Another key factor in the changing nature of Alabama business and commerce is the State's population. The more urban 1970 Alabama population is older, whiter, more female, and has an increasing percentage of females and a decreasing percentage of males participating in the labor force. In the twenty-year period, median age in Alabama rose from 25.5 to 27 years, the nonwhite population declined from 32 to 26 percent of the State's population, and the female percentage of the population rose from 51 to 52 percent. These twenty-year changes in the population occurred as a group of people exceeding the total 1970 population of Mobile and Montgomery Counties left the State. During this same period, the proportion of males aged 14 and older seeking work or working declined from 78 to 69 percent and the proportion of females in this same category rose from 27 to 36 percent. Thus, Alabama's 1970 labor force now has a much greater proportion of women than the 1950 labor force.

Other sections of the atlas deal in more detail with each facet of the business and commerce picture in Alabama. This short sketch has attempted to portray the vitality and changing nature of Alabama's economy dur-

ing one of the most interesting and remarkable transitions in economic history. The transition is not yet fully accomplished; but, as it proceeds, Alabama will move further toward establishing its rightful position in the national economy.

Data Sources: U.S. Department of Commerce, Bureau of the Census, General Social and Economic Characteristics, Alabama, 1950, 1960, 1970.

U.S. Department of Commerce, Office of Business Economics, Survey of Current Business, August 1961 and 1971, and Personal Income Supplements, 1956. Research and Statistics Division, Alabama Department of Industrial Relations, Alabama Employment Review, 1950 through 1970.

Reuel L. Huffman, III
Paul F. Schultz, Jr.

WHOLESALE TRADE

An investigation of the status of wholesaling in the State of Alabama demands an analysis of: (1) the number of wholesale establishments in Alabama, (2) the value of wholesale trade (sales) in dollars within the State, and (3) employment in Alabama within the wholesale sector of the economy.[1] In addition, this text also highlights relevant changes in these components of wholesaling between the years 1940 and 1967 (1970, where data are available).

In 1967, the State recorded a total of $4.4 million dollars in wholesale sales. The Standard Metropolitan Statistical Areas (SMSA's) within the State accounted for more than 76 percent of the State's total wholesale trade. The Birmingham SMSA alone accounted for almost 50 percent of the total. These data indicate the concentrated nature of wholesaling within Alabama; 18 percent of the counties accounted for more than three-fourths of all wholesale sales within the State. Wholesaling has traditionally been highly concentrated within urban areas, and Alabama is no exception in this regard.

The map showing employment in wholesaling in Alabama during 1970 indicates a concentration comparable to that of sales. Over 73 percent of total wholesale employment in Alabama was accounted for within the seven SMSA's, with Birmingham alone being responsible

for over 39 percent. Stated in another way, 18 percent of Alabama counties accounted for over 73 percent of wholesale employment.

The increase in wholesale trade during the period 1940 to 1967 is graphically presented by the accompanying bar chart. The most dramatic increase is evidenced in the sales component [2] of wholesale trade—a 325 percent increase in about 30 years. The number of establishments increased by 119 percent, while employment increased by 210 percent during the same period. The apparent conclusion to be reached from these figures is that the average size of Alabama wholesale establishments increased substantially during the period, in terms of both sales volume and employment. The dramatic increase in wholesale trade over the past thirty years is a phenomenon to be expected in light of the change from primarily a rural, agricultural state to an industrialized, urban state. Wholesaling is essentially an urbanized activity and reflects the degree of urbanization of an area. As the urban centers of the State grew, wholesaling could be expected to grow along with them.

Although not included graphically here, percentage changes in sales, establishments, and employment were calculated for each county for the period 1940–1967. Several conclusions were drawn. Most rural counties

showed substantial percentage increases in each of the components; however, in many cases the original base was so very small that a small net increase was equivalent to a large percentage increase. Thus, the analysis yielded little in the rural counties; far more meaningful was the SMSA performance. A comparison of SMSA's indicates that the Huntsville SMSA, and specifically Madison County, had the most dramatic growth in the State. Following were the Columbus, Georgia—Phenix City, Alabama, SMSA (Russell County); the Mobile SMSA; the Tuscaloosa SMSA; and the Birmingham SMSA. These data reflect growth and not absolute numbers. Birmingham still is the wholesaling center of the State, employing nearly three times as many wholesale workers and doing over five times as much business as its next closest competitor, Mobile.

[1] The Bureau of the Census enumerates business data on the basis of establishments, and an establishment is classified as "wholesale" if over 50 percent of its business (sales) is at wholesale. With this classification scheme in existence, the actual amount of wholesale trade and employment therein is understated in that many firms perform wholesale functions in addition to other business activities (e.g. manufacturing and/or retailing), but the firms are classified on the basis of the majority of their dollar transactions.

[2] Wholesale trade sales figures were adjusted by inflating 1940 figures and deflating 1967 figures in respect to the base years (1957–59 = 100).

[3] Ben Blake and J. R. Jones, Graduate Assistants in the Department of Marketing at the University of Alabama, were responsible for the data collection used as the base for this analysis.

Morris L. Mayer

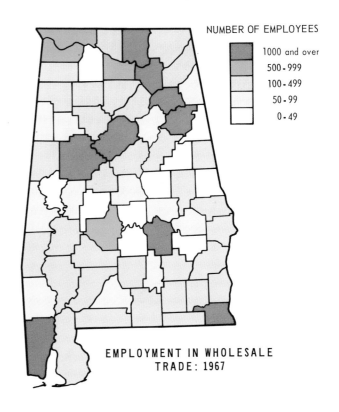

NUMBER OF EMPLOYEES

	1000 and over
	500 - 999
	100 - 499
	50 - 99
	0 - 49

EMPLOYMENT IN WHOLESALE TRADE: 1967

Source: 1970 County Business Patterns

WHOLESALE TRADE :1940- 1967

PERCENT INCREASE

	0	100	200	300	400
SALES					
ESTABLISHMENTS					
EMPLOYMENT					

Source: Census of Business

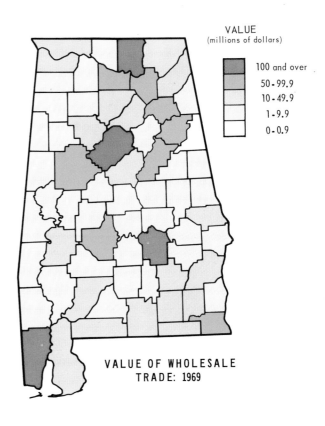

VALUE
(millions of dollars)

	100 and over
	50 - 99.9
	10 - 49.9
	1 - 9.9
	0 - 0.9

VALUE OF WHOLESALE TRADE: 1969

Source: U.S. Census of Business, 1967

121

RETAIL TRADE

Retail trade in Alabama includes the activities of all establishments primarily engaged in selling merchandise for personal or household use. Under the definition of the Alabama Sales Tax Law, sales of non-personal items such as business, scientific, and medical equipment, as well as certain personal services, are included in retail trade. Additionally, any direct sale to the consumer or his household made by a manufacturer or wholesaler falls within the definition of retail trade.

As might be expected, retail trade makes up an enormously important segment of Alabama business activity. From 1965 to 1969, during each year for which estimates of total personal income are available, statistics indicate that the people of the State spent more than 75 percent of their estimated incomes on goods and services at retail. Sales at retail in 1965 amounted to about 83 percent of that year's estimated personal income.

The largest portion of the retail dollars is spent in food stores. Since food stores carry so many nonfood items, the entire amount is not actually for food; however, the largest portion is undoubtedly for edibles. After food, the Alabama consumer allocates the second largest share of his retail expenditures for automotive repair, automobiles, auto accessories, motorcycles, and motorboats. General merchandise stores (such as department stores), retail stores not specifically classified, and gasoline service stations, respectively, receive most of the consumer's remaining retail dollars. The phrase, "retail stores not specifically classified," refers to a wide variety of specialty shops, and these claim a substantial share of retail sales.

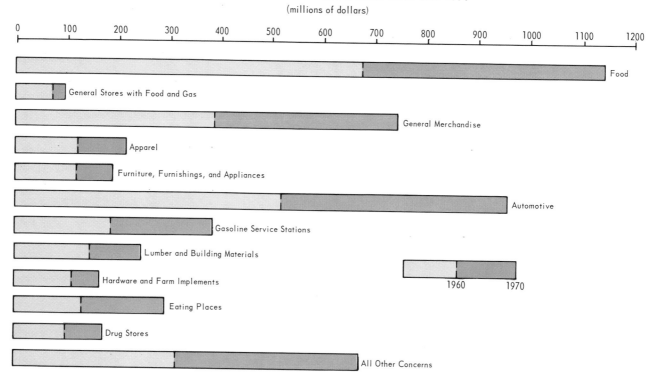

DISTRIBUTION OF RETAIL SALES: 1960 and 1970
(millions of dollars)

Source: Alabama Department of Revenue, Center for Business and Economic Research

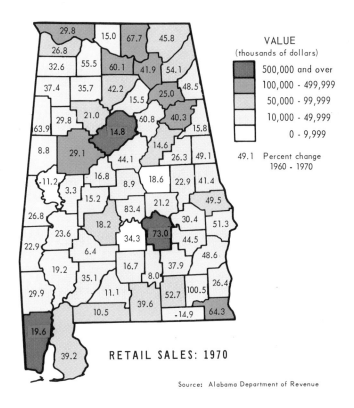

VALUE
(thousands of dollars)

500,000 and over
100,000 - 499,999
50,000 - 99,999
10,000 - 49,999
0 - 9,999

49.1 Percent change
1960 - 1970

RETAIL SALES: 1970

Source: Alabama Department of Revenue

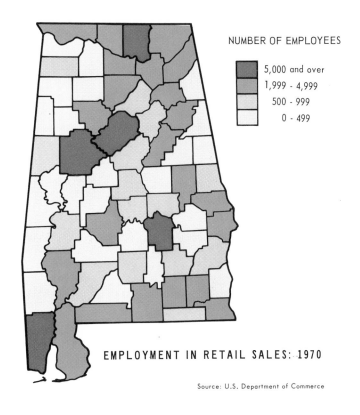

NUMBER OF EMPLOYEES

5,000 and over
1,999 - 4,999
500 - 999
0 - 499

EMPLOYMENT IN RETAIL SALES: 1970

Source: U.S. Department of Commerce

An examination of the accompanying figure shows the distribution of sales by kind of retail business. It reveals that Alabama consumers have not greatly changed their pattern of purchasing during the past decade. Only the *catch-all* category, "other retail concerns," has changed its share of total sales by more than 1 percent. The percentage changes from 1960 to 1970 for each business category after the sales data have been adjusted for price level changes.

A large proportion of retail trade is being conducted by firms that are not classified as retailers. Firms are classified for most statistical purposes into that category under which the bulk of their commercial activity falls. However, wholesalers and manufacturers have every right to sell at retail, and many often do. The proportion of retail sales made by nonretailers in Alabama is declining, but is still quite significant. Thus, the most accurate picture only emerges when these sales by nonretailers are taken into consideration as part of total sales.

The bulk of retail sales in Alabama is concentrated in the twelve counties making up the Standard Metropolitan Statistical Areas (Russell County is part of the Columbus, Georgia SMSA). The sales in these counties accounted for 54 percent of total sales at retail during 1970. Three counties (Jefferson, Montgomery, and Mobile) achieved retail sales levels in excess of $5 million during 1970. Jefferson County far surpassed all other counties in retail sales by accounting for just over 25 percent ($1.8 billion) of the entire State's retail sales. Madison, Tuscaloosa, Morgan, Houston, Calhoun, Etowah, Marshall, and Lauderdale Counties (ranked in order) each recorded sales in excess of $1 million during 1970.

Edward P. Rutledge

123

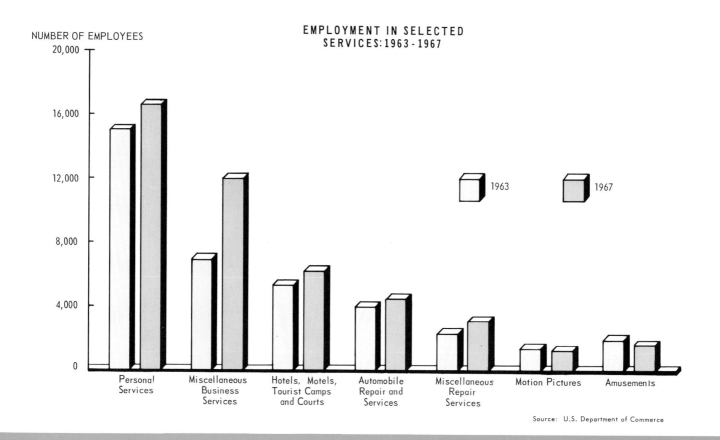

NUMBER OF EMPLOYEES

EMPLOYMENT IN SELECTED
SERVICES: 1963 - 1967

1963   1967

Personal Services · Miscellaneous Business Services · Hotels, Motels, Tourist Camps and Courts · Automobile Repair and Services · Miscellaneous Repair Services · Motion Pictures · Amusements

Source: U.S. Department of Commerce

SELECTED SERVICES

The service sector of the Alabama economy continues to be an important supplement to the increase in manufacturing employment. Included as Selected Services are (1) Personal Services, (2) Miscellaneous Business Services, (3) Hotel, Motel, Tourist Camps and Courts, (4) Auto Repair and Services, (5) Miscellaneous Repair Services, (6) Motion Pictures, and (7) Amusements. The relative importance of each of these seven categories varies, and each has experienced a different rate of growth or decline during the period 1963–1967. Of these, Personal Services was the most important, accounting for more than 35 percent of the paid employment in Selected Services.

The second most important is Miscellaneous Business Services. This category includes advertising, equipment rental, credit services, and building services considered essential to the efficient operation of most business concerns. Between 1963 and 1967, employment in this category increased by over 79 percent, the largest

percentage increase of any of the seven categories.

During the four-year period, two categories, Motion Pictures and Amusements, each showed a decline in number of people employed. As leisure time increases in America, the provision of services to satisfy leisure time demands will become increasingly important, and this trend may then be reversed.

The total receipts of all establishments in Selected Services showed an increase of over 58 percent between 1963 and 1967, reflecting the increase in demand for services in Alabama. The value of services by county is measured by the total receipts of Selected Services establishments. In 1967 the concentration of total receipts occurred in the more populous counties of the State, with a positive relationship between increases in value and increases in population. In counties where total receipts are low relative to the total population, it is quite possible that residents may be crossing county lines to obtain services not available locally.

Only nine counties showed absolute declines in value of receipts between 1963 and 1967. They were Clay, Conecuh, Coosa, Escambia, Fayette, Marion, Monroe, Pickens, and Washington. Together, these nine counties accounted for less than 2 percent of the total value of receipts of Selected Services in the State in 1967. Significant increases in value of receipts were posted by eighteen counties, which accounted for almost 98 percent of the increase for the entire State. Quite expectedly, the eighteen counties were the population centers of the State, and included Jefferson, Mobile, Madison, Montgomery, and Tuscaloosa. Residents of surrounding counties quite probably commuted to the nearest population center where a greater variety of services was generally available.

Because the Service Sector is assuming an increasing role in the economic expansion of the United States, it is important to note the trends in employment in this category. More specifically, if the size and quality of the Service Sector is related to manufacturing employment, it would follow that, over time, an increasing ratio of service employees to manufacturing employees would reflect a greater availability of services in the State. For the State as a whole, in 1963 there were 6.54 manufacturing jobs for every job in the selected services. By 1967, the ratio had fallen only slightly to 6.22, compared to a national average of 5.03 manufacturing jobs for each service job.

It is obviously not economically feasible for each county to provide the variety and range of services found within the State as a whole, and a comparison of ratios between counties may be somewhat misleading. Consequently, any local data should be cautiously interpreted as only a description of trends, and should not have any positive or negative implications with respect to local economic growth. Additional analysis, provided by reference to other parts of this atlas, would be required for meaningful conclusions about the relative importance of the Service Sector, and changes therein, to the economic progress of a particular county.

William D. Gunther

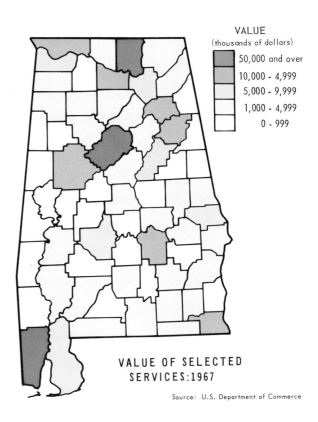

VALUE
(thousands of dollars)

	50,000 and over
	10,000 - 4,999
	5,000 - 9,999
	1,000 - 4,999
	0 - 999

VALUE OF SELECTED
SERVICES: 1967

Source: U.S. Department of Commerce

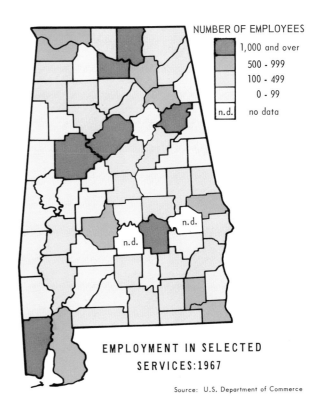

NUMBER OF EMPLOYEES

	1,000 and over
	500 - 999
	100 - 499
	0 - 99
n.d.	no data

EMPLOYMENT IN SELECTED
SERVICES: 1967

Source: U.S. Department of Commerce

SUMMARY OF BUSINESS AND COMMERCE

Business and commerce in Alabama comprise retail trade, wholesale trade, and selected services which can be analyzed by number of establishments and value of sales and receipts by county.

Establishments devoted to retail trade are predominately engaged in selling products of a personal- or household-use nature. Jefferson County, the State's largest metropolitan area, accounted for 4,603 retail establishments in 1967. Mobile County listed 2,241 establishments, and Montgomery and Madison Counties recorded 1,327 and 1,234 establishments, respectively. In the remaining counties, the number of establishments generally was in direct proportion to the size of the population. Value of retail sales for the entire State was $3.8 billion in 1967.

The pattern for wholesale trade establishments throughout the State was similar to that of retail trade. Jefferson County led with 1,141 establishments. Mobile County ranked second with 493 wholesale firms, Montgomery County, third (319), and Madison County, fourth (207). Alabama experienced a $1.1 billion increase in value of wholesale sales from 1963 to 1967.

Jefferson County also led in the number of selected services establishments (2921), and Mobile County ranked second (1,518). The value of receipts in selected services increased $199 million or 61 percent from 1963 to 1967. During this same period, value of sales in wholesale and retail trade increased 30.8 and 18 percent, respectively. These percentages indicate that selected services, over several years, have been the most rapidly expanding segment of the State's business and commercial enterprises.

Clay Paradiso Davis

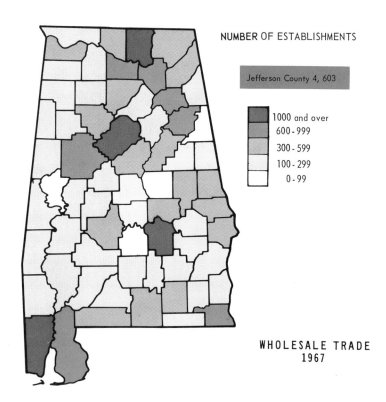

NUMBER OF ESTABLISHMENTS

Jefferson County 4, 603

1000 and over
600 - 999
300 - 599
100 - 299
0 - 99

WHOLESALE TRADE
1967

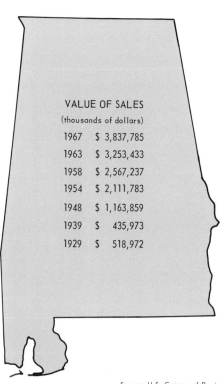

VALUE OF SALES
(thousands of dollars)

1967	$ 3,837,785
1963	$ 3,253,433
1958	$ 2,567,237
1954	$ 2,111,783
1948	$ 1,163,859
1939	$ 435,973
1929	$ 518,972

Source: U.S. Census of Business, 1967

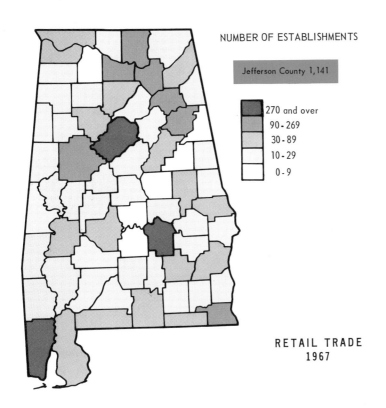

NUMBER OF ESTABLISHMENTS

Jefferson County 1,141

270 and over
90 - 269
30 - 89
10 - 29
0 - 9

RETAIL TRADE
1967

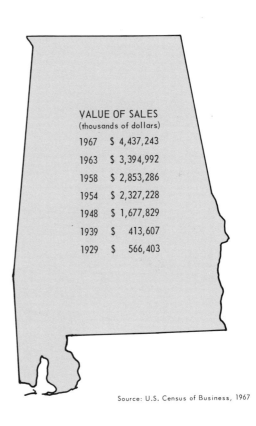

VALUE OF SALES
(thousands of dollars)

1967	$ 4,437,243
1963	$ 3,394,992
1958	$ 2,853,286
1954	$ 2,327,228
1948	$ 1,677,829
1939	$ 413,607
1929	$ 566,403

Source: U.S. Census of Business, 1967

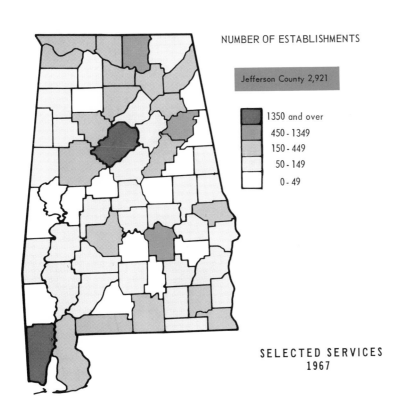

NUMBER OF ESTABLISHMENTS

Jefferson County 2,921

1350 and over
450 - 1349
150 - 449
50 - 149
0 - 49

SELECTED SERVICES
1967

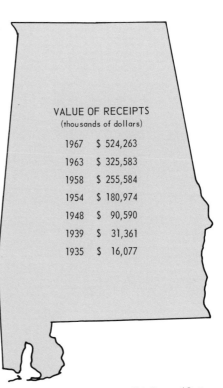

VALUE OF RECEIPTS
(thousands of dollars)

1967	$ 524,263
1963	$ 325,583
1958	$ 255,584
1954	$ 180,974
1948	$ 90,590
1939	$ 31,361
1935	$ 16,077

Source: U.S. Census of Business, 1967

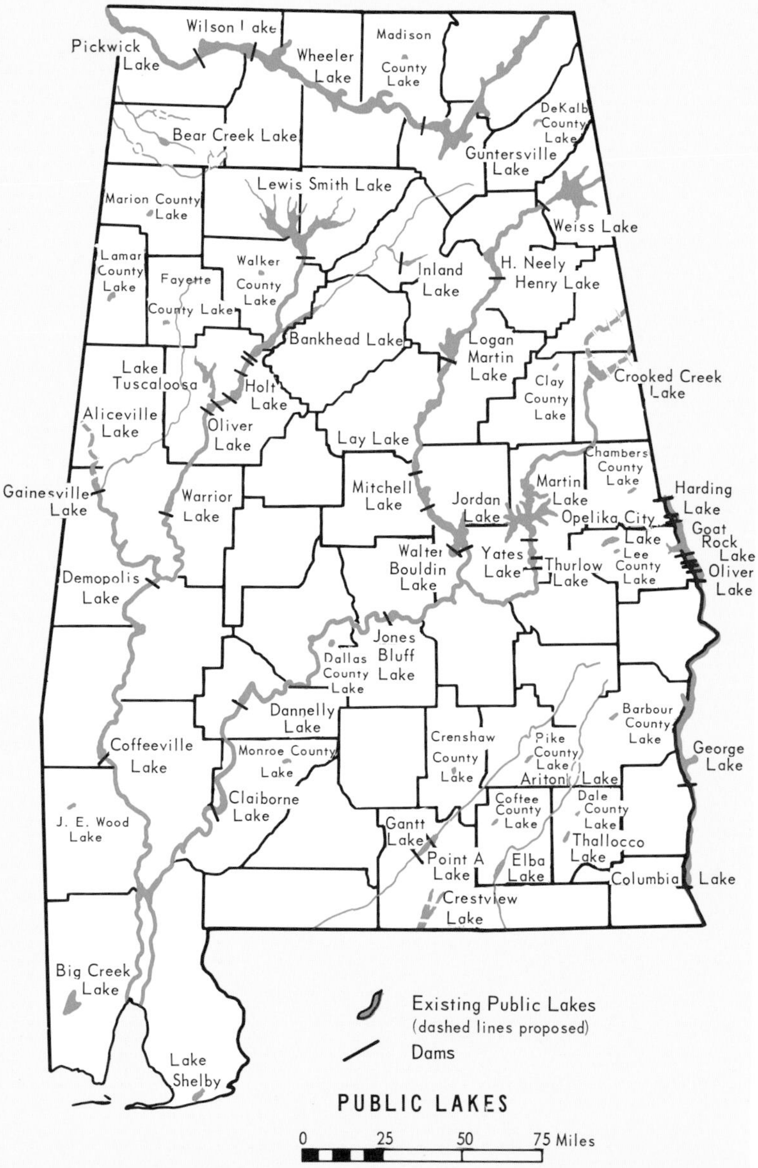

OUTDOOR RECREATION

Opportunities for outdoor recreation, on both land and water, abound in Alabama. They are found from the Appalachian Plateau and the TVA lakes of the north, through the lake area of mid-Alabama, to the 115 miles of beaches on the Gulf of Mexico.

State boundaries encompass 33,029,760 surface acres, of which 32,432,860 are land and 596,900 acres are water. Approximately two-thirds of the water acreage is in impoundments of 40 acres or more, and the remaining one-third is divided somewhat equally between creeks, rivers, ponds, and lakes.

About two-thirds of the land area of the State is classed as forest or woodland. These lands abound in wild plants (4,500 different species) and wildlife, including a variety of birds, with over 350 species having been identified within the State. Hunters find an abundant supply of deer, turkey, rabbit, squirrel, bob-white (quail), and dove in most of the counties of the State. Ownership

Existing Public Lakes
(dashed lines proposed)

Dams

PUBLIC LAKES

0   25   50   75 Miles

Source: Alabama Department of Conservation

LAKES AND RESERVOIRS OVER 10,000 ACRES

Pickwick	42,800
Wilson	15,930
Wheeler	67,100
Guntersville	69,100
Weiss	30,200
H. Neely Henry	11,200
Lewis Smith	21,200
Logan Martin	15,263
Crooked Creek (proposed)	11,000
Demopolis	10,000
William Danelley [1]	17,500
Jones Bluff	12,300
Lay	12,000
Martin	40,000
Crestview (proposed)	19,500 [2]
Walter F. George	46,000 [3]

[1] Formerly Miller's Ferry
[2] Alabama Portion
[3] Partially located in Georgia

128

of the 3 million acres of "recreation land" in Alabama varies. Most of it is in private ownership, with the Federal Government, and State and local governments (combined), in that order, owning lesser amounts.

State Parks. A recent $43-million State program has increased the size of the State park system to include 13 major parks and numerous minor parks. Major State parks vary in size from 103 acres (Blue Springs State Park) to 10,000 acres (Oak Mountain State Park), and appear to be receiving the most attention in the expansion program. Minor parks range in size from "a very few acres" to slightly more than 1,000 acres. Lakes are found within or immediately adjacent to many of the major parks. Oak Mountain State Park has two 85-acre lakes and an 18-acre lake within its bounds, while Wind Creek State Park borders on the 40,000-acre Lake Martin. Camden State Park is located adjacent to a 17,500-acre Corps of Engineers lake.

ACREAGE OF MAJOR STATE PARKS

Joe Wheeler	2,600
Monte Sano	2,140
DeSoto State Park	4,825
Lake Guntersville	5,670
Lake Lurleen	1,630
Oak Mountain	10,000
Cheaha State Park	2,719
Wind Creek State Park	1,354
Camden State Park	200
Chewacla State Park	577
Lakepoint Resort	1,000
Blue Springs State Park	103
Gulf State Park	5,687

Source: Alabama Department of Conservation

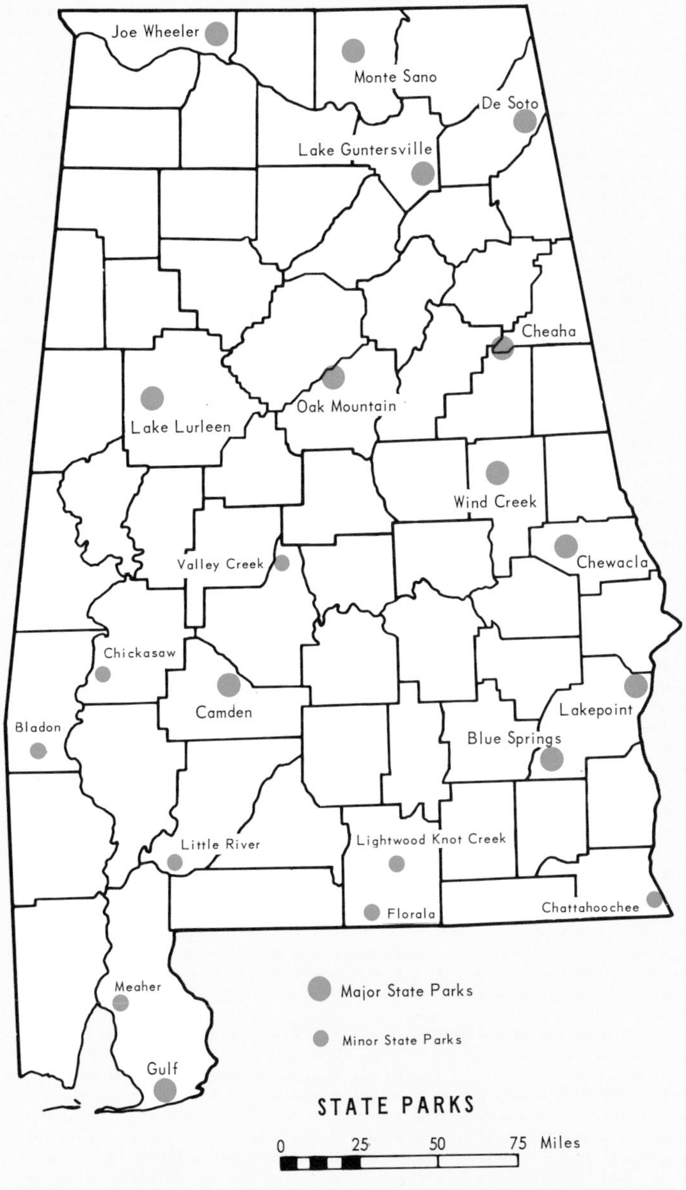

STATE PARKS

Source: Alabama Department of Conservation

National Parks. Although there are no formal national parks in Alabama, the National Park Service maintains 4,600 acres of land in the State—most of which is for recreation use. These areas are Natchez Trace Parkway, Russell Cave National Monument, and Horseshoe Bend National Military Park.

Forests. Alabama is proud of its eight State forests (total area over 14,000 acres), and both residents and non-residents make great recreational use of them.

The U.S. Forest Service recreation areas in Alabama consist of the 635,000 acres in its four National forests: Bankhead, Talladega, Tuskegee, and Conecuh. Included in these forests are 19 recreational areas that provide opportunity for camping, picnicking, hiking, swimming, boating, and fishing. Regulated hunting in season is permitted on all U.S. Forest land in Alabama.

Recreational Water. The major recreational water areas (with a total of about 597,000 acres) in Alabama consist of the following:

1. Four large Tennessee Valley Authority (TVA) reservoirs in the northern sector of the State contain 193,600 surface water acres and 2,602 miles of shoreline.

2. With the construction of eleven water impoundments, the U.S. Corps of Engineers provides approximately 150,000 acres of surface water and 3,547 miles of shoreline on four of Alabama's major rivers.

3. The Division of Fish and Game of the State Government administers 17 public fishing lakes. These lakes range in size from 12 acres to 250 acres. The Division also manages 29 public hunting areas that include approximately 650,000 acres—25,000 of which are state-owned.

4. Ten lakes, consisting of 145,087 water surface acres and 2,861 miles of shoreline, have been developed and maintained by the Alabama Power Company. Fishing, boating, skiing, and the other conventional outdoor recreation activities are permitted on or around all 10 lakes, and it is evident that additional recreation areas will be developed by the company on company-owned land adjacent to some of these lakes. The lakes range in size from 574 acres to 40,000 acres, and are reasonably well-located with respect to state population centers.

Recreation areas and facilities of counties (43 sites), cities and towns (1,292 sites), quasipublic bodies (139 sites), and private owners (1,237 sites) add considerably to the availability and diversity of outdoor recreation facilities in Alabama.

George H. Stopp

PROJECTED OUTDOOR RECREATION: 1980

Millions of Activity Occasions *

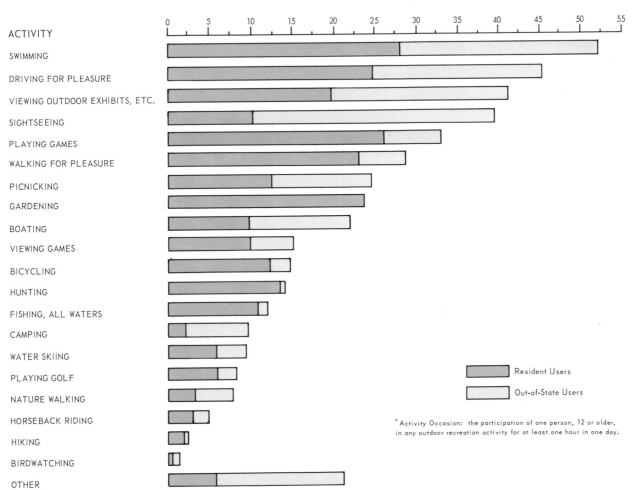

ACTIVITY	
SWIMMING	
DRIVING FOR PLEASURE	
VIEWING OUTDOOR EXHIBITS, ETC.	
SIGHTSEEING	
PLAYING GAMES	
WALKING FOR PLEASURE	
PICNICKING	
GARDENING	
BOATING	
VIEWING GAMES	
BICYCLING	
HUNTING	
FISHING, ALL WATERS	
CAMPING	
WATER SKIING	
PLAYING GOLF	
NATURE WALKING	
HORSEBACK RIDING	
HIKING	
BIRDWATCHING	
OTHER	

Resident Users

Out-of-State Users

* Activity Occasion: the participation of one person, 12 or older,
in any outdoor recreation activity for at least one hour in one day.

Source: Alabama Department of Conservation

131

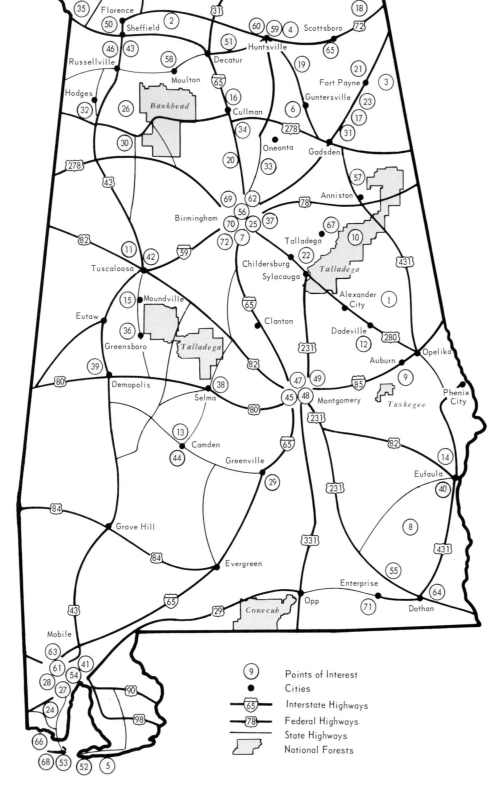

POINTS OF INTEREST

NATIONAL AND STATE PARKS

1. Horseshoe Bend National Military Park
2. Joe Wheeler State Park
3. De Soto State Park
4. Monto Sano State Park
5. Gulf State Park
6. Lake Guntersville State Park
7. Oak Mountain State Park
8. Blue Springs State Park
9. Chewacla State Park
10. Cheaha State Park
11. Lake Lurleen State Park
12. Wind Creek State Park
13. Camden State Park
14. Lake Point Resort
15. Mound State Monument

PRIVATE PARKS

16. Hurricane Creek Park
17. Canyon Land Park

CAVERNS AND CAVES

18. Russell Cave National Monument
19. Cathedral Caverns
20. Rickwood Caverns
21. Sequoyah Cave
22. Kymulga Onyx Cave
23. Manitou Cave

GARDENS AND SCENIC TRAILS

24. Bellingrath Gardens
25. Botanical Gardens
26. Dismals Wonder Garden
27. Long's Gardens
28. Azalea Trail
29. Greenville - "Camellia City"
30. Natural Bridge
31. Noccalula Falls
32. Rock Bridge Canyon
33. Horse Pens 40
34. Ave Maria Grotto
35. Natchez Trace National Parkway

HISTORIC SITES

36. Magnolia Grove Hobson Memorial
37. Arlington Ante-Bellum Home
38. Sturdivant Hall
39. Gaineswood
40. Shorter Mansion
41. Oakleigh
42. Gorgas Home
43. Helen Keller's Birthplace
44. The Starr Home
45. Teague House
46. The Oaks
47. State Capital
48. White House of The Confederacy
49. Governor's Mansion
50. Pope's Tavern
51. Mooresville Post Office
52. Fort Morgan
53. Fort Gaines
54. Battleship U.S.S. Alabama

MUSEUMS

55. National Army Aviation Museum
56. Museum of Art
57. Regar Museum of Natural History
58. Pioneer House Museum
59. Alabama Space and Rocket Center
60. Space Orientation Center

FESTIVALS AND PAGEANTS

61. Mardi Gras
62. Festival of Arts
63. America's Junior Miss Pageant
64. National Peanut Festival and Fair
65. First Monday (Market Day)
66. Blessing of the Fleet, Bayou La Batre

SPORTING EVENTS

67. Alabama International Motor Speedway
68. Fishing Rodeo

OTHER

69. Vulcan
70. Miss Liberty Tour
71. Boll Weevil Monument
72. Jimmy Morgan Zoo

TOURIST ATTRACTIONS

Source: Bureau of Publicity and Information

132

Alabama Space and Rocket Center

TOURISM

Goods and services purchased by travelers in Alabama amounted to an estimated $545 million in 1971. This sum represents spending both by out-of-state visitors and the away-from-home cost of living of Alabamians while traveling within the State. About 64 percent, or close to two-thirds of this amount, was spent by out-of-state tourists. The phrase "out-of-state tourist" refers to visitors who come for at least a day visit or overnight stay, while an "Alabama tourist" is a State resident involved in at least a day trip, overnight stay, or a "journey of 100 miles or more."

Out-of-state tourist travel comprises about a fifth of the passenger traffic on main interstate routes between Alabama cities. These travelers accounted for 30 percent of the passenger miles of travel generated by all tourists on Alabama's highways and common carriers.

In 1971 over 33 million out-of-state tourists came to Alabama. Many of these were transients, passing through the State on journeys between the Midwest and Florida, or between the east coast and Louisiana or Texas.

The business stimulated by tourists provides employment in service stations, eating places, lodging places, and places of amusement. Motels and hotels are, by definition, supported solely by tourists. The four above types of enterprises (excluding motion picture theatres as places of amusement) provided employment for about 69,000 people, with a total personal income of $237 million in 1971. These figures do not include employment and income generated by public transportation facilities.

The State benefits from tourism in other ways. First, travel services generate considerable revenue for both state and local governments through various taxes. About $37 million in State taxes can be traced to travelers from other states, and 11 cents of each dollar spent by travelers in Alabama is collected for some form of State revenue. Second, employment generated by tourism means industrial diversification which caters to a wider variety of employee skills. Third, the money spent by out-of-state tourists for services represents an export of those services and a net monetary gain for the State. The same is true for sales taxes on goods purchased by out-of-state tourists.

James J. Britton

133

PROSPECTS FOR THE FUTURE

The State of Alabama is frequently perceived by people from across the nation in exaggerated images created by historical circumstances and political rhetoric—sometimes good and sometimes bad. Magnolias, mint juleps, plantation homes, and easy living are some of the favorable perceptions; racial injustice, poverty, outmigration, and rural provincialism are among the bad. Opinions are based partly on prejudice and partly on reality; but whether true or false, these preconceptions exist. The basis for judging Alabama, however, is changing rapidly.

A new day is dawning in Alabama. No longer a rural state, Alabama is moving forward with new social and economic attitudes and renewed self-assurance. The new generation Alabamian thinks about human rights, industrial jobs, expanded educational opportunities, conservation of natural resources, and world politics. He is disturbed that old ideas and ideals are being forsaken in some instances where they still work best, and that innovations are sometimes not accepted when acceptance is warranted. In short, Alabama and Alabamians are in step with modern America.

But what of the times to come? Few who intimately know the State can fail to be excited about Alabama's future. With an abundance of untapped natural and human resources, declining outmigration, and a steady growth in the number of jobs, the State's outlook for the future is bright. Increasingly, industrialists and businessmen are selecting Alabama for new plant sites and retail and wholesale outlets. The future shows definite promise for higher incomes and greater availability of goods and services.

Yes, Alabama stands at the threshold of a new day. We hope that this book will help its readers to recognize the State's potential and to obtain a more realistic image of Alabama.

Neal G. Lineback

GLOSSARY

Acid Friable Horizon   A crumbly, acid layer within the soil.

Adherents   People who relate to a certain group or idea.

Alluvial Soils   Soils which have been transported and deposited by water or ice.

Amur Valley   A river valley of eastern Siberia dividing China and the Soviet Union.

Anticline   An upward bend or fold of rock layers, resembling an inverted "U".

Appalachian Plateau   An area of nearly horizontal sedimentary rocks which has been uplifted and then cut by numerous streams. The Appalachian Plateau extends from Tuscaloosa, Alabama, to the Mohawk Valley in New York State.

Appalachian Revolution   The episode, occurring between 250 to 320 million years ago, during which the earth's rocky crust was buckled up to form the Appalachian mountains.

Automated Data Systems   Commonly consisting of interconnected and very sophisticated computer facilities which store and manipulate data.

Azonal   Refers to soils composed of minerals little affected by present climate and drainage; includes immature "soils" such as alluvium.

Beryl   A hard mineral, valuable mainly for the beryllium metal it contains.

Black Belt   A region of black soils extending in an arc from northeast Mississippi through west central Alabama.

Black Population   People of the Negroid or dark-skinned race.

Board Feet   A method used in the measurement of sawn lumber; i.e., one board foot equals 12 inches x 12 inches x 1 inch thick.

Cambrian   The period of the Earth's history from 500 to 600 million years ago. Atmosphere finally clears, sunshine reaches the earth and first marine fauna preserved as fossils.

Canebrake   A dense growth of tall reedy plants, such as the giant cane.

Carbonates   A sedimentary rock containing carbon and oxygen in the form of the carbonate ion ($CO_3 =$); i.e., limestone, calcium carbonate ($CaCO_3$).

Cartographer   A person skilled at designing and drawing maps.

Cedar Glades   A grove or stand of cedars, usually in a low or marshy area.

Cenozoic   The Era comprising the last 70 million years of the Earth's history. All main groups of mammals existed; widespread dispersion of plants prevailed.

Chalk   A sedimentary carbonate rock composed of disintegrated skeletons of marine animals.

Chert   A hard sedimentary rock formed of silica.

Citronelle Field   Alabama's largest oil field, located in north Mobile County.

Class I Railroads   Railroads that operate to serve the public rather than to serve a private company or group of individuals.

Clastic   Particles that were produced by the disintegration of rocks through weathering.

Clear-Cut Method   A method used in cutting timber where all the trees are removed and the area is then reseeded or replanted. Versus selective cutting.

Coal Measures   Rock strata or beds containing coal.

Coastal Plain   A plain bordering a coast; most often formed of sedimentary rocks. In Alabama the Coastal Plain extends southward from Tuscaloosa and Montgomery.

Coke   A coal derivative obtained by baking coal and used in smelting iron ore.

Concrete Aggregate   Rock or gravel used in the mixing of concrete.

Conglomerate   A sedimentary rock made up of rounded grains of gravel cemented together.

Consumer Price Index   Expresses a percentage change in consumer prices from a given base year (1967).

Cord   A stack of wood 4x4x8 feet or 128 cubic feet.

County of Occurrence   The county in which something takes place.

County of Residence   The county in which a person lives.

Cretaceous   The period of the Earth's history from 70 to 135 million years ago. Widespread deposition of chalk in shallow seas and rich land flora.

Croakers   Edible saltwater fish, the name of which derives from its grunting noise.

Crossbar Switching   Automatic switching mechanism which helps to speed up the process of telephoning.

Crystalline Rocks   Igneous or metamorphic rocks, found mainly in the Piedmont in Alabama.

Cuesta   A linear ridge, usually formed of sandstone. Characteristic of plains underlain by incline of beds of sedimentary rock. The Ripley Cuesta is an example in Alabama.

Deciduous   The property of trees to shed their leaves due to seasonal changes in climate.

Demographic Shifts   The movement of populations from one place (or type of region) to another.

Density Map   A map showing the differences in amount between areas of equal size, such as people per square mile.

135

Devonian   The period of the Earth's history from 350 to 400 million years ago. Earliest conquest of land by plants and animals.

Dissected Landscape   A land area cut up by many stream valleys.

Ecology   The study of the interrelationships of organisms and their environment.

Electors   Persons who are elected by the people to cast a vote for a presidential candidate.

Emigration   The movement of people away from or out of a place—usually movement from one country to another.

Emplanement   People boarding an airplane at a certain place, such as Birmingham.

Federal-Aid Interstate System   Consisting of all official Interstate Highways.

Federal-Aid Primary Mileage   Consisting of all U.S. Highways, except Interstates.

Feldspar   The most common mineral in the crust of the earth, generally light in color. Used as an abrasive as well as in the manufacture of fine china.

Flomaton Field   An oil field in Escambia County, Alabama.

Floodplain   The area bordering a river and subject to periodic flooding; also called "bottom land."

Flotilla   A small group of ships.

Flux   Any material used as a cleansing agent in metallurgy; for example, dolomitic limestone is used as a flux in smelting iron ore to remove impurities.

Fossiliferous   Containing fossils, such as parts or imprints of animal or plant remains.

Fossil-Fuel Resources   Any combustible materials made up of fossil organic material; for example, coal, oil, natural gas.

Friable   Easily crumbled, pulverized, or reduced to powder.

Geography   The spatial study of interrelationships between physical, social, and economic characteristics on the earth's surface.

Geology   The study of the Earth, particularly earth history, processes, resources, and their relationships with man.

Geomorphology   A study of the land surface forms of the earth.

Gill Nets   Nets which capture fish by entangling in their gills.

Gneiss   A coarse-grained metamorphic rock in which light and dark minerals are separated into distinct bands; common in the Alabama Piedmont.

Granite   An igneous rock formed of feldspar and quartz; common in the Alabama Piedmont.

Gross Assessed Value   Percentage of actual market value for property tax purposes before any special exemption.

Ground Water   Water found beneath the land surface, and obtained from wells or springs.

Grumusol   A clay soil which swells when wet and develops cracks when dry.

Hardwood Forest   A broadleaf, usually deciduous forest of the mid-latitudes, such as oak, maple, elm, etc.

Horticultural Crops   Vegetables, flowers, and tree fruits and nuts, such as peaches and pecans.

Humic Gley   A poorly-drained lowland soil, subject to being waterlogged.

Hydrogen Sulfide   A gas, H_2S, with the odor of rotten eggs.

Igneous Rock   Rock which forms when melted rock material solidifies. In Alabama the most common example is granite.

Intensive-Care Units   Rooms in hospitals where patients can get very technical treatment.

Invertebrate   Term referring to an animal lacking a backbone, such as a snail, oyster, or an insect.

Irish Potato Famines   The failures of the potato crop in Ireland in the 1840's which caused mass emigration of the Irish to other countries.

Iron Works   A small foundry or factory in which iron products are made.

Junior Colleges   Schools beyond high school which offer chiefly the courses needed for the first two years of college.

Jurassic Sediments   Sedimentary rocks formed during the Jurassic period, 135 to 180 million years ago. Dinosaurs, lizards, first mammals, and abundant conifers and ferns.

Kilowatt-Hour   A unit of energy equal to using up 1000 watts or 1.34 HP per hour.

Laterization   A soil-forming process most characteristic of a hot, humid climate and which produces an infertile, slightly acid soil.

Latitude   A measurement of distance in degrees north or south of the Equator.

Limestone   A sedimentary rock composed mostly of carbonate minerals of inorganic origin; widespread in Alabama.

Lithosol   Thin soil over bedrock. Characteristic of mountain areas.

Loams   A soil mixture containing about 40 percent sand, 40 percent silt, and 20 percent clay particles.

Locks and Dams   A system of dams on a river to develop pools of water with enough depth for boat traffic. Locks allow the boats to pass through the dams.

Logistics   The military science of planning, handling, and movement of personnel, material, and facilities.

Longitude   A measurement of distance in degrees east or west of the Principal Meridian.

Mardi Gras   The French term for Shrove Tuesday, the day before Ash Wednesday, the beginning of the Lenten period.

Median Age   The age of a person in a group

who separates equally the persons older and younger than himself.

Meridians   A line representing a great circle on the surface of the earth passing through the poles.

Mesophytic Forest   A forest that grows under conditions of moderate moisture.

Metallurgical Processes   The processes of separating metals from their ores and refining them for use.

Metamorphic Rock   Rock within the earth's crust which has been changed because of heat and pressure. In Alabama, marble has been formed from limestone in this manner.

Mississippian   The period of the Earth's history from 310 to 350 million years ago. Earliest land vertebrates formed.

Monadnocks   Knobby hills, often low, found on an eroded surface such as that of the Piedmont.

Natural Population Increase   The rise in populations due to a greater number of births than deaths.

Nitre Works   A factory which makes gunpowder using potassium nitrate or other nitrous substances.

Obstetrics   The medical science that deals with birth.

Ordnance   A general term including all types of military weapons.

Ordovician   The period of the Earth's history from 440 to 500 million years ago. Prevalence of true corals, clams, and other invertebrates in the seas.

Out-Patient Departments   Parts of hospitals that treat patients who do not spend the night in the hospital.

Otter Trawl Fishery   A fishing activity utilizing a bag-shaped net dragged by boat along the bottom.

Orogeny   An episode of mountain-building, such as the Appalachian Revolution.

Paleozoic   The Era of the Earth's history ranging from 225 to 600 million years ago. Age of first vertebrates, enormous mountain-building, and rich swamp flora.

Pecker Wood Sawmills   Small semi-portable sawmills which can be transported from place to place and operated by a small crew of men.

Pedogenic   Relating to the processes of soil formation.

Peneplain   An erosion surface of considerable area and slight relief.

Pennsylvanian   The period of the Earth's history from 270 to 310 million years ago. Rich swamp flora, parent material for coal, was abundant.

Per Capita Income   The total money earned by the people of a group or place divided by the number of people in the group or place.

Personal Income   The money earned by individuals from their jobs, investments, and all other sources.

Piedmont   In the eastern United States, an area underlain by old, granitic types of rock. It includes a sizeable area in eastern Alabama and extends northward into eastern Pennsylvania.

Pincer Movement   A military maneuver in which two columns of an army advance on two sides of the enemy to eventually surround them.

Podzolization   A soil-forming process most characteristic of a cool, humid climate and which produces an infertile, acid soil.

Precambrian   The portion of the Earth's history before 600 million years ago. First evidence of life on earth and several mountain-building cycles.

Privation   A lack of something needed for comfort or existence; hardship.

Radiotelegraphy   Radio or wireless transmission of messages using Morse Code.

Reconstruction Era   The historical period between 1868 and 1875 when the South was rebuilt following the Civil War.

Red and Yellow Podzolic Soil   An acid soil of limited fertility. The subsoil is rich in clay, the color of which determines the name—red podzolic or yellow podzolic.

Reddish-Brown Lateritic Soil   Reddish, somewhat acid clay soil; may be derived from limestone or basic igneous rocks.

Regosols   Soils formed on loose or soft rock material. Regosols have few, if any, distinct soil characteristics.

Rendzina   An alkaline clay soil formed from soft limestone in a humid climate; common in the Black Belt, namely the Sumter clay.

Ridge and Fence Rows   Areas along fences that are allowed to grow up in weeds, hedge, or trees.

Rolling Stock   The equipment used by railroads such as engines, freight cars, pullman cars, etc.

Rural Exodus   The continued and regular movement of people from farming regions to the cities and towns.

Rural Population   People living in the country and in small farming towns.

Sand Mountain   The southwestern margins of the Appalachian Plateau in Alabama, bordering on the Valley and Ridge.

Sandy Loams   A soil mixture containing 65 percent sand-size particles, 15 percent clay particles and 20 percent silt particles—usually an excellent agricultural soil.

Schist   A metamorphic rock with a layered structure, generally containing micas, quartz, feldspar, and other minerals; found in the Piedmont of Alabama.

Sedimentary Rock   A rock made of sediments which have been cemented, i.e., limestone, sandstone, shale, conglomerate, etc.

Seed Oysters   Very young oysters which are spread from a boat into areas for commercial production.

Senior Colleges   Schools which offer four years of advanced work leading to a bachelor's (or college) degree.

Service Sector   That portion of the economy in which people do things for each other, such as dentistry, dry cleaning, barber, TV repair, etc.

Shale   A sedimentary rock formed of clay-sized particles, generally dark in color.

Siege   A military blockage or the surrounding of a city or fort to compel surrender.

Silurian   The period of the Earth's history from 400 to 440 million years ago. Enormous mountain-building; first land plants.

Silica   Silicon dioxide SiO_2. May occur as sandy quartz grains, or be combined with other elements to form clay.

Skirmishes   Roving fights between small military units separate from a major battle.

Smackover   An oil producing formation of Jurassic age in southern Alabama.

Sols Bruns Acides   Acid forest soils.

Sovereignty   The condition of supreme political power, subject to no higher authority.

Squatter   One who lives on land to which he has no right to title.

Standard Metropolitan Statistical Areas (SMSA'S). Areas with at least 50,000 people in a central city and designated by the Bureau of the Census for special study.

State Primary System—Municipal Extensions Those U.S. Highways other than Interstates.

Solution Channels   Cavities found in carbonate rocks (such as limestone) which were formed when ground water dissolved the rock. Limestone caverns are an example.

State Secondary Road System   State highways as distinguished from county and U.S. Highways.

State General Fund   Monies which have not been allocated for any specific purpose.

Submarginal Farm   A farm which is too small or whose land is of such quality that a farmer cannot support his family from farming operations.

Technical Institutes   Schools beyond high schools for practical training in the applications of science and technology.

Tenant-Operated Farms   Farms operated by persons who do not own the land, and usually receive a share or percentage of the farm income.

Tennessee-Tombigbee Waterway   A proposed system of canals and locks to connect the Tennessee and Tombigbee Rivers for use by large traffic.

Tennessee Valley Authority (TVA)   A Federal Authority authorized by Congress in 1933 to develop the region drained by the Tennessee River and its tributaries.

Tenure Provisions   Agreements in employment where persons cannot be fired unless special actions are taken.

Tertiary   The period of the Earth's history from 3 to 70 million years ago.

Tidewater   Coastal land adjacent to streams affected by the ebb and flow of ocean tides.

Tilled Land   Land which is being cultivated for crops.

Township   An area 6 miles square containing 36 square miles or 36 sections of one square mile each.

Trade Schools   Schools which prepare students for practical careers in crafts and services such as plumbing, barbering, auto mechanics, etc.

Trammel Net   A fine meshed fishing net.

Trunkline Carrier Service   Interstate public transportation passenger service between major metropolitan areas.

Ultisol   A soil order which includes many of the red and yellow soils of limited fertility in Alabama.

Urbanization   The settlement of people in large numbers in small space to create cities and towns.

Urban Population   People living in cities and towns with at least 2,500 persons.

Valley and Ridge   An area of folded sedimentary and lightly-metamorphosed rocks which extends from Tuscaloosa, Alabama, northeastward through Eastern Pennsylvania. The ridges and valleys trend northeast-southwest.

Value Added By Manufacture   The value added during manufacture to a product over and above the cost of raw materials.

Waldseemuller, Martin   Alsatian cartographer. In 1507 he made a world map which was the first to use the name "America."

Warrior Coal Field   A large coal-producing sedimentary basin located in northwest Alabama; includes parts of Tuscaloosa, Walker, Fayette, Marion, Blount, Jefferson, and some other counties in north Alabama.

Wiregrass Area   The southeastern one-quarter of Alabama, given its name by the natural, narrow-bladed grass used for grazing which grows there.